FUNDAMENTALS OF
COMPUTER ORGANIZATION AND
ARCHITECTURE

FUNDAMENTALS OF COMPUTER ORGANIZATION AND ARCHITECTURE

Mostafa Abd-El-Barr
King Fahd University of Petroleum & Minerals (KFUPM)

Hesham El-Rewini
Southern Methodist University

WILEY-INTERSCIENCE

A JOHN WILEY & SONS, INC PUBLICATION

Library of Congress Cataloging-in-Publication Data:

Abd-El-Barr, Mostafa.
   Fundamentals of computer organization and architecture / Mostafa Abd-El-Barr, Hesham El-Rewini
      p. cm. — (Wiley series on parallel and distributed computing)
   Includes bibliographical references and index.
   ISBN 0-471-46741-3 (cloth volume 1) — ISBN 0-471-46740-5 (cloth volume 2)
   1. Computer architecture. 2. Parallel processing (Electronic computers) I. Abd-El-Barr, Mostafa, 1950–
II. Title. III. Series.
   QA76.9.A73E47 2004
   004.2′2—dc22
                                                                                        2004014372

To my family members (Ebtesam, Muhammad, Abd-El-Rahman, Ibrahim, and Mai)
for their support and love
—Mostafa Abd-El-Barr

To my students, for a better tomorrow
—Hesham El-Rewini

■■■■ CONTENTS

◼◼◼ PREFACE

This book is intended for students in computer engineering, computer science, and electrical engineering. The material covered in the book is suitable for a one-semester course on "Computer Organization & Assembly Language" and a one-semester course on "Computer Architecture." The book assumes that students studying computer organization and/or computer architecture must have had exposure to a basic course on digital logic design and an introductory course on high-level computer language.

This book reflects the authors' experience in teaching courses on computer organization and computer architecture for more than fifteen years. Most of the material used in the book has been used in our undergraduate classes. The coverage in the book takes basically two viewpoints of computers. The first is the programmer's viewpoint and the second is the overall structure and function of a computer. The first viewpoint covers what is normally taught in a junior level course on Computer Organization and Assembly Language while the second viewpoint covers what is normally taught in a senior level course on Computer Architecture. In what follows, we provide a chapter-by-chapter review of the material covered in the book. In doing so, we aim at providing course instructors, students, and practicing engineers/scientists with enough information that can help them select the appropriate chapter or sequences of chapters to cover/review.

Chapter 1 sets the stage for the material presented in the remaining chapters. Our coverage in this chapter starts with a brief historical review of the development of computer systems. The objective is to understand the factors affecting computing as we know it today and hopefully to forecast the future of computation. We also introduce the general issues related to *general-purpose* and *special-purpose* machines. Computer systems can be defined through their interfaces at a number of levels of abstraction, each providing functional support to its predecessor. The interface between the application programs and high-level language is referred to as *Language Architecture*. The *Instruction Set Architecture* defines the interface between the basic machine instruction set and the *Runtime* and *I/O Control*. A different definition of computer architecture is built on four basic viewpoints. These are the structure, the organization, the implementation, and the performance. The structure defines the interconnection of various hardware components, the organization defines the dynamic interplay and management of the various components, the implementation defines the detailed design of hardware components, and the performance specifies the behavior of the computer system. Architectural development and styles are covered in Chapter 1. We devote the last part of our coverage in this chapter to a discussion on the different CPU performance measures used.

The sequence consisting of Chapters 2 and 3 introduces the basic issues related to instruction set architecture and assembly language programming. Chapter 2 covers the basic principles involved in instruction set architecture and design. We start by addressing the issue of storing and retrieving information into and from memory, followed by a discussion on a number of different addressing modes. We also explain instruction execution and sequencing in some detail. We show the application of the presented addressing modes and instruction characteristics in writing sample segment codes for performing a number of simple programming tasks. Building on the material presented in Chapter 2, Chapter 3 considers the issues related to assembly language programming. We introduce a programmer's view of a hypothetical machine. The mnemonics and syntax used in representing the different instructions for the machine model are then introduced. We follow that with a discussion on the execution of assembly programs and an assembly language example of the *X86 Intel CISC family*.

The sequence of chapters 4 and 5 covers the design and analysis of arithmetic circuits and the design of the Central Processing Unit (CPU). Chapter 4 introduces the reader to the fundamental issues related to the arithmetic operations and circuits used to support computation in computers. We first introduce issues such as number representations, base conversion, and integer arithmetic. In particular, we introduce a number of algorithms together with hardware schemes that are used in performing integer addition, subtraction, multiplication, and division. As far as floating-point arithmetic, we introduce issues such as floating-point representation, floating-point operations, and floating-point hardware schemes. Chapter 5 covers the main issues related to the organization and design of the CPU. The primary function of the CPU is to execute a set of instructions stored in the computer's memory. A simple CPU consists of a set of registers, Arithmetic Logic Unit (ALU), and Control Unit (CU). The basic principles needed for the understanding of the instruction fetch-execution cycle, and CPU register set design are first introduced. The use of these basic principles in the design of real machines such as the 80×86 and the MIPS are shown. A detailed discussion on a typical CPU data path and control unit design is also provided.

Chapters 6 and 7 combined are dedicated to Memory System Design. A typical memory hierarchy starts with a small, expensive, and relatively fast unit, called the *cache*. The cache is followed in the hierarchy by a larger, less expensive, and relatively slow *main memory* unit. Cache and main memory are built using solid-state semiconductor material. They are followed in the hierarchy by a far larger, less expensive, and much slower magnetic memories that consist typically of the (hard) disk and the tape. We start our discussion in Chapter 6 by analyzing the factors influencing the success of a memory hierarchy of a computer. The remaining part of Chapter 6 is devoted to the design and analysis of cache memories. The issues related to the design and analysis of the main and the virtual memory are covered in Chapter 7. A brief coverage of the different read-only memory (ROM) implementations is also provided in Chapter 7.

I/O plays a crucial role in any modern computer system. A clear understanding and appreciation of the fundamentals of I/O operations, devices, and interfaces are of great importance. The focus of Chapter 8 is a study on input–output (I/O) design and organization. We cover the basic issues related to programmed and Interrupt-driven I/O. The interrupt architecture in real machines such as 80×86 and MC9328MX1/MXL AITC are explained. This is followed by a detailed discussion on Direct Memory Access (DMA), busses (synchronous and asynchronous), and arbitration schemes. Our coverage in Chapter 8 concludes with a discussion on I/O interfaces.

There exists two basic techniques to increase the instruction execution rate of a processor. These are: to increase the clock rate, thus decreasing the instruction execution time, or alternatively to increase the number of instructions that can be executed simultaneously. Pipelining and instruction-level parallelism are examples of the latter technique. Pipelining is the focus of the discussion provided in Chapter 9. The idea is to have more than one instruction being processed by the processor at the same time. This can be achieved by dividing the execution of an instruction among a number of sub-units (stages), each performing part of the required operations, i.e., instruction fetch, instruction decode, operand fetch, instruction execution, and store of results. Performance measures of a pipeline processor are introduced. The main issues contributing to instruction pipeline hazards are discussed and some possible solutions are introduced. In addition, we present the concept of arithmetic pipelining together with the problems involved in designing such pipeline. Our coverage concludes with a review of two pipeline processors, i.e., the ARM 1026EJ-S and the UltraSPARC-III.

Chapter 10 is dedicated to a study of Reduced Instruction Set Computers (RISCs). These machines represent a noticeable shift in computer architecture paradigm. The RISC paradigm emphasizes the enhancement of computer architectures with the resources needed to make the execution of the most frequent and the most time-consuming operations most efficient. RISC-based machines are characterized by a number of common features, such as, simple and reduced instruction set, fixed instruction format, one instruction per machine cycle, pipeline instruction fetch/execute units, ample number of general purpose registers (or alternatively optimized compiler code generation), Load/Store memory operations, and hardwired control unit design. Our coverage in this chapter starts with a discussion on the evolution of RISC architectures and the studies that led to their introduction. Overlapped Register Windows, an essential concept in the RISC development, is also discussed. We show the application of the basic RISC principles in machines such as the Berkeley RISC, the Stanford MIPS, the Compaq Alpha, and the SUN UltraSparc.

Having covered the essential issues in the design and analysis of uniprocessors and pointing out the main limitations of a single stream machine, we provide an introduction to the basic concepts related to multiprocessors in Chapter 11. Here a number of processors (two or more) are connected in a manner that allows them to share the simultaneous execution of a single task. The main advantage for using multiprocessors is the creation of powerful computers by connecting many existing smaller ones. In addition, a multiprocessor consisting of a number of single uniprocessors is expected to be more cost effective than building a high-performance single processor. We present a number of different topologies used for interconnecting multiple processors, different classification schemes, and a topology-based taxonomy for interconnection networks. Two memory-organization schemes for MIMD (multiple instruction multiple data) multiprocessors, i.e., Shared Memory and Message Passing, are also introduced. Our coverage in this chapter ends with a touch on the analysis and performance metrics for multiprocessors. Interested readers are referred to more elaborate discussions on multiprocessors in our book entitled *Advanced Computer Architectures and Parallel Processing*, John Wiley and Sons, Inc., 2005.

From the above chapter-by-chapter review of the topics covered in the book, it should be clear that the chapters of the book are, to a great extent, self-contained and inclusive. We believe that such an approach should help course instructors to selectively choose the set of chapters suitable for the targeted curriculum. However, our experience indicates that the group of chapters consisting of Chapters 1 to 5 and 8 is typically suitable for a junior level course on Computer Organization and Assembly Language for Computer Science, Computer Engineering, and Electrical Engineering students. The group of chapters consisting of Chapters 1, 6, 7, 9–11 is typically suitable for a senior level course on Computer Architecture. Practicing engineers and scientists will find it feasible to selectively consult the material covered in individual chapters and/or groups of chapters as indicated in the chapter-by-chapter review. For example, to find more about memory system design, interested readers may consult the sequence consisting of Chapters 6 and 7.

ACKNOWLEDGMENTS

We would like to express our thanks and appreciation to a number of people who have helped in the preparation of this book. Students in our Computer Organization and Computer Architecture courses at the University of Saskatchewan (UofS), SMU, KFUPM, and Kuwait University have used drafts of different chapters and provided us with useful feedback and comments that led to the improvement of the presentation of the material in the book; to them we are thankful. Our colleagues Donald Evan, Fatih Kocan, Peter Seidel, Mitch Thornton, A. Naseer, Habib Ammari, and Hakki Cankaya offered constructive comments and excellent suggestions that led to noticeable improvement in the style and presentation of the book material. We are indebted to the anonymous reviewers arranged by John Wiley for their suggestions and corrections. Special thanks to Albert Y. Zomaya, the series editor and to Val Moliere, Kirsten Rohstedt, and Christine Punzo of John Wiley for their help in making this book a reality. Of course, responsibility for errors and inconsistencies rests with us. Finally, and most of all, we want to thank our families for their patience and support during the writing of this book.

MOSTAFA ABD-EL-BARR
HESHAM EL-REWINI

CHAPTER 1

Introduction to Computer Systems

The technological advances witnessed in the computer industry are the result of a long chain of immense and successful efforts made by two major forces. These are the academia, represented by university research centers, and the industry, represented by computer companies. It is, however, fair to say that the current technological advances in the computer industry owe their inception to university research centers. In order to appreciate the current technological advances in the computer industry, one has to trace back through the history of computers and their development. The objective of such historical review is to understand the factors affecting computing as we know it today and hopefully to forecast the future of computation. A great majority of the computers of our daily use are known as *general purpose* machines. These are machines that are built with no specific application in mind, but rather are capable of performing computation needed by a diversity of applications. These machines are to be distinguished from those built to serve (tailored to) specific applications. The latter are known as *special purpose* machines. A brief historical background is given in Section 1.1.

Computer systems have conventionally been defined through their interfaces at a number of layered abstraction levels, each providing functional support to its predecessor. Included among the levels are the application programs, the high-level languages, and the set of machine instructions. Based on the interface between different levels of the system, a number of computer architectures can be defined. The interface between the application programs and a high-level language is referred to as a *language architecture*. The *instruction set architecture* defines the interface between the basic machine instruction set and the *runtime* and *I/O control*. A different definition of computer architecture is built on four basic viewpoints. These are the structure, the organization, the implementation, and the performance. In this definition, the structure defines the interconnection of various hardware components, the organization defines the dynamic interplay and management of the various components, the implementation defines the detailed design of hardware components, and the performance specifies the behavior of the computer system. Architectural development and styles are covered in Section 1.2.

Fundamentals of Computer Organization and Architecture, by M. Abd-El-Barr and H. El-Rewini
ISBN 0-471-46741-3   Copyright © 2005 John Wiley & Sons, Inc.

A number of technological developments are presented in Section 1.3. Our discussion in this chapter concludes with a detailed coverage of CPU performance measures.

1.1. HISTORICAL BACKGROUND

In this section, we would like to provide a historical background on the evolution of cornerstone ideas in the computing industry. We should emphasize at the outset that the effort to build computers has not originated at one single place. There is every reason for us to believe that attempts to build the first computer existed in different geographically distributed places. We also firmly believe that building a computer requires teamwork. Therefore, when some people attribute a machine to the name of a single researcher, what they actually mean is that such researcher may have led the team who introduced the machine. We, therefore, see it more appropriate to mention the machine and the place it was first introduced without linking that to a specific name. We believe that such an approach is fair and should eliminate any controversy about researchers and their names.

It is probably fair to say that the first program-controlled (mechanical) computer ever build was the Z1 (1938). This was followed in 1939 by the Z2 as the first operational program-controlled computer with fixed-point arithmetic. However, the first recorded university-based attempt to build a computer originated on Iowa State University campus in the early 1940s. Researchers on that campus were able to build a small-scale special-purpose electronic computer. However, that computer was never completely operational. Just about the same time a complete design of a fully functional programmable special-purpose machine, the Z3, was reported in Germany in 1941. It appears that the lack of funding prevented such design from being implemented. History recorded that while these two attempts were in progress, researchers from different parts of the world had opportunities to gain first-hand experience through their visits to the laboratories and institutes carrying out the work. It is assumed that such first-hand visits and interchange of ideas enabled the visitors to embark on similar projects in their own laboratories back home.

As far as general-purpose machines are concerned, the University of Pennsylvania is recorded to have hosted the building of the Electronic Numerical Integrator and Calculator (ENIAC) machine in 1944. It was the first operational general-purpose machine built using vacuum tubes. The machine was primarily built to help compute artillery firing tables during World War II. It was programmable through manual setting of switches and plugging of cables. The machine was slow by today's standard, with a limited amount of storage and primitive programmability. An improved version of the ENIAC was proposed on the same campus. The improved version of the ENIAC, called the Electronic Discrete Variable Automatic Computer (EDVAC), was an attempt to improve the way programs are entered and explore the concept of stored programs. It was not until 1952 that the EDVAC project was completed. Inspired by the ideas implemented in the ENIAC, researchers at the Institute for Advanced Study (IAS) at Princeton built (in 1946) the IAS machine, which was about 10 times faster than the ENIAC.

In 1946 and while the EDVAC project was in progress, a similar project was initiated at Cambridge University. The project was to build a stored-program computer, known as the Electronic Delay Storage Automatic Calculator (EDSAC). It was in 1949 that the EDSAC became the world's first full-scale, stored-program, fully operational computer. A spin-off of the EDSAC resulted in a series of machines introduced at Harvard. The series consisted of MARK I, II, III, and IV. The latter two machines introduced the concept of separate memories for instructions and data. The term *Harvard Architecture* was given to such machines to indicate the use of separate memories. It should be noted that the term Harvard Architecture is used today to describe machines with separate cache for instructions and data.

The first general-purpose commercial computer, the UNIVersal Automatic Computer (UNIVAC I), was on the market by the middle of 1951. It represented an improvement over the BINAC, which was built in 1949. IBM announced its first computer, the IBM701, in 1952. The early 1950s witnessed a slowdown in the computer industry. In 1964 IBM announced a line of products under the name IBM 360 series. The series included a number of models that varied in price and performance. This led Digital Equipment Corporation (DEC) to introduce the first *minicomputer*, the PDP-8. It was considered a remarkably low-cost machine. Intel introduced the first *microprocessor*, the Intel 4004, in 1971. The world witnessed the birth of the first *personal computer* (PC) in 1977 when Apple computer series were first introduced. In 1977 the world also witnessed the introduction of the VAX-11/780 by DEC. Intel followed suit by introducing the first of the most popular microprocessor, the 80 × 86 series.

Personal computers, which were introduced in 1977 by Altair, Processor Technology, North Star, Tandy, Commodore, Apple, and many others, enhanced the productivity of end-users in numerous departments. Personal computers from Compaq, Apple, IBM, Dell, and many others, soon became pervasive, and changed the face of computing.

In parallel with small-scale machines, supercomputers were coming into play. The first such supercomputer, the CDC 6600, was introduced in 1961 by Control Data Corporation. Cray Research Corporation introduced the best cost/performance supercomputer, the Cray-1, in 1976.

The 1980s and 1990s witnessed the introduction of many commercial parallel computers with multiple processors. They can generally be classified into two main categories: (1) shared memory and (2) distributed memory systems. The number of processors in a single machine ranged from several in a shared memory computer to hundreds of thousands in a massively parallel system. Examples of parallel computers during this era include Sequent Symmetry, Intel iPSC, nCUBE, Intel Paragon, Thinking Machines (CM-2, CM-5), MsPar (MP), Fujitsu (VPP500), and others.

One of the clear trends in computing is the substitution of centralized servers by networks of computers. These networks connect inexpensive, powerful desktop machines to form unequaled computing power. Local area networks (LAN) of powerful personal computers and workstations began to replace mainframes and minis by 1990. These individual desktop computers were soon to be connected into larger complexes of computing by wide area networks (WAN).

TABLE 1.1   Four Decades of Computing

Feature	Batch	Time-sharing	Desktop	Network
Decade	1960s	1970s	1980s	1990s
Location	Computer room	Terminal room	Desktop	Mobile
Users	Experts	Specialists	Individuals	Groups
Data	Alphanumeric	Text, numbers	Fonts, graphs	Multimedia
Objective	Calculate	Access	Present	Communicate
Interface	Punched card	Keyboard & CRT	See & point	Ask & tell
Operation	Process	Edit	Layout	Orchestrate
Connectivity	None	Peripheral cable	LAN	Internet
Owners	Corporate computer centers	Divisional IS shops	Departmental end-users	Everyone

CRT, cathode ray tube; LAN, local area network.

The pervasiveness of the Internet created interest in network computing and more recently in grid computing. Grids are geographically distributed platforms of computation. They should provide dependable, consistent, pervasive, and inexpensive access to high-end computational facilities.

Table 1.1 is modified from a table proposed by Lawrence Tesler (1995). In this table, major characteristics of the different computing paradigms are associated with each decade of computing, starting from 1960.

1.2. ARCHITECTURAL DEVELOPMENT AND STYLES

Computer architects have always been striving to increase the performance of their architectures. This has taken a number of forms. Among these is the philosophy that by doing more in a single instruction, one can use a smaller number of instructions to perform the same job. The immediate consequence of this is the need for fewer memory read/write operations and an eventual speedup of operations. It was also argued that increasing the complexity of instructions and the number of addressing modes has the theoretical advantage of reducing the "semantic gap" between the instructions in a high-level language and those in the low-level (machine) language. A single (machine) instruction to convert several binary coded decimal (BCD) numbers to binary is an example for how complex some instructions were intended to be. The huge number of addressing modes considered (more than 20 in the VAX machine) further adds to the complexity of instructions. Machines following this philosophy have been referred to as *complex instructions set computers* (CISCs). Examples of CISC machines include the Intel Pentium[TM], the Motorola MC68000[TM], and the IBM & Macintosh PowerPC[TM].

It should be noted that as more capabilities were added to their processors, manufacturers realized that it was increasingly difficult to support higher clock rates that would have been possible otherwise. This is because of the increased complexity of computations within a single clock period. A number of studies from the mid-1970s and early-1980s also identified that in typical programs more than 80% of the instructions executed are those using assignment statements, conditional branching and procedure calls. It was also surprising to find out that simple assignment statements constitute almost 50% of those operations. These findings caused a different philosophy to emerge. This philosophy promotes the optimization of architectures by speeding up those operations that are most frequently used while reducing the instruction complexities and the number of addressing modes. Machines following this philosophy have been referred to as *reduced instructions set computers* (RISCs). Examples of RISCs include the Sun SPARC^{TM} and MIPS^{TM} machines.

The above two philosophies in architecture design have led to the unresolved controversy as to which architecture style is "best." It should, however, be mentioned that studies have indicated that RISC architectures would indeed lead to faster execution of programs. The majority of contemporary microprocessor chips seems to follow the RISC paradigm. In this book we will present the salient features and examples for both CISC and RISC machines.

1.3. TECHNOLOGICAL DEVELOPMENT

Computer technology has shown an unprecedented rate of improvement. This includes the development of processors and memories. Indeed, it is the advances in technology that have fueled the computer industry. The integration of numbers of transistors (a transistor is a controlled on/off switch) into a single chip has increased from a few hundred to millions. This impressive increase has been made possible by the advances in the fabrication technology of transistors.

The scale of integration has grown from small-scale (SSI) to medium-scale (MSI) to large-scale (LSI) to very large-scale integration (VLSI), and currently to wafer-scale integration (WSI). Table 1.2 shows the typical numbers of devices per chip in each of these technologies.

It should be mentioned that the continuous decrease in the minimum devices feature size has led to a continuous increase in the number of devices per chip,

TABLE 1.2   Numbers of Devices per Chip

Integration	Technology	Typical number of devices	Typical functions
SSI	Bipolar	10–20	Gates and flip-flops
MSI	Bipolar & MOS	50–100	Adders & counters
LSI	Bipolar & MOS	100–10,000	ROM & RAM
VLSI	CMOS (mostly)	10,000–5,000,000	Processors
WSI	CMOS	>5,000,000	DSP & special purposes

SSI, small-scale integration; MSI, medium-scale integration; LSI, large-scale integration; VLSI, very large-scale integration; WSI, wafer-scale integration.

which in turn has led to a number of developments. Among these is the increase in the number of devices in RAM memories, which in turn helps designers to trade off memory size for speed. The improvement in the feature size provides golden opportunities for introducing improved design styles.

1.4. PERFORMANCE MEASURES

In this section, we consider the important issue of assessing the performance of a computer. In particular, we focus our discussion on a number of performance measures that are used to assess computers. Let us admit at the outset that there are various facets to the performance of a computer. For example, a user of a computer measures its performance based on the time taken to execute a given job (program). On the other hand, a laboratory engineer measures the performance of his system by the total amount of work done in a given time. While the user considers the program execution time a measure for performance, the laboratory engineer considers the throughput a more important measure for performance. A metric for assessing the performance of a computer helps comparing alternative designs.

Performance analysis should help answering questions such as how fast can a program be executed using a given computer? In order to answer such a question, we need to determine the time taken by a computer to execute a given job. We define the clock cycle time as the time between two consecutive rising (trailing) edges of a periodic clock signal (Fig. 1.1). Clock cycles allow counting unit computations, because the storage of computation results is synchronized with rising (trailing) clock edges. The time required to execute a job by a computer is often expressed in terms of clock cycles.

We denote the number of CPU clock cycles for executing a job to be the cycle count (CC), the cycle time by CT, and the clock frequency by $f = 1/CT$. The time taken by the CPU to execute a job can be expressed as

$$CPU\ time = CC \times CT = CC/f$$

It may be easier to count the number of instructions executed in a given program as compared to counting the number of CPU clock cycles needed for executing that

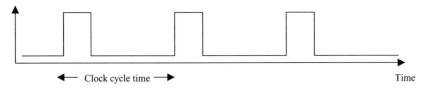

Clock cycle time   Time

Figure 1.1 Clock signal

program. Therefore, the average number of clock cycles per instruction (CPI) has been used as an alternate performance measure. The following equation shows how to compute the CPI.

$$CPI = \frac{CPU\ clock\ cycles\ for\ the\ program}{Instruction\ count}$$

$$CPU\ time = Instruction\ count \times CPI \times Clock\ cycle\ time$$

$$= \frac{Instruction\ count \times CPI}{Clock\ rate}$$

It is known that the instruction set of a given machine consists of a number of instruction categories: *ALU* (simple assignment and arithmetic and logic instructions), *load*, *store*, *branch*, and so on. In the case that the CPI for each instruction category is known, the overall CPI can be computed as

$$CPI = \frac{\sum_{i=1}^{n} CPI_i \times I_i}{Instruction\ count}$$

where I_i is the number of times an instruction of type i is executed in the program and CPI_i is the average number of clock cycles needed to execute such instruction.

Example   Consider computing the overall CPI for a machine A for which the following performance measures were recorded when executing a set of benchmark programs. Assume that the clock rate of the CPU is 200 MHz.

Instruction category	Percentage of occurrence	No. of cycles per instruction
ALU	38	1
Load & store	15	3
Branch	42	4
Others	5	5

Assuming the execution of 100 instructions, the overall CPI can be computed as

$$CPI_a = \frac{\sum_{i=1}^{n} CPI_i \times I_i}{Instruction\ count} = \frac{38 \times 1 + 15 \times 3 + 42 \times 4 + 5 \times 5}{100} = 2.76$$

It should be noted that the CPI reflects the organization and the instruction set architecture of the processor while the instruction count reflects the instruction set architecture and compiler technology used. This shows the degree of interdependence between the two performance parameters. Therefore, it is imperative that both the

CPI and the instruction count are considered in assessing the merits of a given computer or equivalently in comparing the performance of two machines.

A different performance measure that has been given a lot of attention in recent years is *MIPS* (million instructions-per-second (the rate of instruction execution per unit time)), which is defined as

$$MIPS = \frac{Instruction\ count}{Execution\ time \times 10^6} = \frac{Clock\ rate}{CPI \times 10^6}$$

Example   Suppose that the same set of benchmark programs considered above were executed on another machine, call it machine B, for which the following measures were recorded.

Instruction category	Percentage of occurrence	No. of cycles per instruction
ALU	35	1
Load & store	30	2
Branch	15	3
Others	20	5

What is the *MIPS* rating for the machine considered in the previous example (machine A) and machine B assuming a clock rate of 200 MHz?

$$CPI_a = \frac{\sum_{i=1}^{n} CPI_i \times I_i}{Instruction\ count} = \frac{38 \times 1 + 15 \times 3 + 42 \times 4 + 5 \times 5}{100} = 2.76$$

$$MIPS_a = \frac{Clock\ rate}{CPI_a \times 10^6} = \frac{200 \times 10^6}{2.76 \times 10^6} = 70.24$$

$$CPI_b = \frac{\sum_{i=1}^{n} CPI_i \times I_i}{Instruction\ count} = \frac{35 \times 1 + 30 \times 2 + 20 \times 5 + 15 \times 3}{100} = 2.4$$

$$MIPS_b = \frac{Clock\ rate}{CPI_a \times 10^6} = \frac{200 \times 10^6}{2.4 \times 10^6} = 83.67$$

Thus $MIPS_b > MIPS_a$.

It is interesting to note here that although *MIPS* has been used as a performance measure for machines, one has to be careful in using it to compare machines having different instruction sets. This is because *MIPS* does not track execution time. Consider, for example, the following measurement made on two different machines running a given set of benchmark programs.

Instruction category	No. of instructions (in millions)	No. of cycles per instruction
Machine (A)		
ALU	8	1
Load & store	4	3
Branch	2	4
Others	4	3
Machine (B)		
ALU	10	1
Load & store	8	2
Branch	2	4
Others	4	3

$$CPI_a = \frac{\sum_{i=1}^{n} CPI_i \times I_i}{Instruction\ count} = \frac{(8 \times 1 + 4 \times 3 + 4 \times 3 + 2 \times 4) \times 10^6}{(8 + 4 + 4 + 2) \times 10^6} \cong 2.2$$

$$MIPS_a = \frac{Clock\ rate}{CPI_a \times 10^6} = \frac{200 \times 10^6}{2.2 \times 10^6} \cong 90.9$$

$$CPU_a = \frac{Instruction\ count \times CPI_a}{Clock\ rate} = \frac{18 \times 10^6 \times 2.2}{200 \times 10^6} = 0.198\ s$$

$$CPI_b = \frac{\sum_{i=1}^{n} CPI_i \times I_i}{Instruction\ count} = \frac{(10 \times 1 + 8 \times 2 + 4 \times 4 + 2 \times 4) \times 10^6}{(10 + 8 + 4 + 2) \times 10^6} = 2.1$$

$$MIPS_b = \frac{Clock\ rate}{CPI_a \times 10^6} = \frac{200 \times 10^6}{2.1 \times 10^6} = 95.2$$

$$CPU_b = \frac{Instruction\ count \times CPI_a}{Clock\ rate} = \frac{20 \times 10^6 \times 2.1}{200 \times 10^6} = 0.21\ s$$

$$MIPS_b > MIPS_a \qquad and \qquad CPU_b > CPU_a$$

The example shows that although machine B has a higher *MIPS* compared to machine A, it requires longer CPU time to execute the same set of benchmark programs.

Million floating-point instructions per second, MFLOP (rate of floating-point instruction execution per unit time) has also been used as a measure for machines' performance. It is defined as

$$MFLOPS = \frac{Number\ of\ floating\text{-}point\ operations\ in\ a\ program}{Execution\ time \times 10^6}$$

While MIPS measures the rate of average instructions, MFLOPS is only defined for the subset of floating-point instructions. An argument against MFLOPS is the fact that the set of floating-point operations may not be consistent across machines and therefore the actual floating-point operations will vary from machine to machine. Yet another argument is the fact that the performance of a machine for a given program as measured by MFLOPS cannot be generalized to provide a single performance metric for that machine.

The performance of a machine regarding one particular program might not be interesting to a broad audience. The use of arithmetic and geometric means are the most popular ways to summarize performance regarding larger sets of programs (e.g., benchmark suites). These are defined below.

$$Arithmetic\ mean = \frac{1}{n}\sum_{i=1}^{n} Execution\ time_i$$

$$Geometric\ mean = \sqrt[n]{\prod_{i=1}^{n} Execution\ time_i}$$

where *execution time_i* is the execution time for the *i*th program and *n* is the total number of programs in the set of benchmarks.

The following table shows an example for computing these metrics.

Item	CPU time on computer A (s)	CPU time on computer B (s)
Program 1	50	10
Program 2	500	100
Program 3	5000	1000
Arithmetic mean	1835	370
Geometric mean	500	100

We conclude our coverage in this section with a discussion on what is known as the Amdahl's law for speedup (SU_o) due to enhancement. In this case, we consider speedup as a measure of how a machine performs after some enhancement relative to its original performance. The following relationship formulates Amdahl's law.

$$SU_o = \frac{Performance\ after\ enhancement}{Performance\ before\ enhancement}$$

$$Speedup = \frac{Execution\ time\ before\ enhancement}{Execution\ time\ after\ enhancement}$$

Consider, for example, a possible enhancement to a machine that will reduce the execution time for some benchmarks from 25 s to 15 s. We say that the speedup resulting from such reduction is $SU_o = 25/15 = 1.67$.

In its given form, Amdahl's law accounts for cases whereby improvement can be applied to the instruction execution time. However, sometimes it may be possible to achieve performance enhancement for only a fraction of time, Δ. In this case a new formula has to be developed in order to relate the speedup, SU_Δ due to an enhancement for a fraction of time Δ to the speedup due to an overall enhancement, SU_0. This relationship can be expressed as

$$SU_0 = \frac{1}{(1 - \Delta) + (\Delta/SU_\Delta)}$$

It should be noted that when $\Delta = 1$, that is, when enhancement is possible at all times, then $SU_0 = SU_\Delta$, as expected.

Consider, for example, a machine for which a speedup of 30 is possible after applying an enhancement. If under certain conditions the enhancement was only possible for 30% of the time, what is the speedup due to this partial application of the enhancement?

$$SU_0 = \frac{1}{(1 - \Delta) + (\Delta/SU_\Delta)} = \frac{1}{(1 - 0.3) + \dfrac{0.3}{30}} = \frac{1}{0.7 + 0.01} = 1.4$$

It is interesting to note that the above formula can be generalized as shown below to account for the case whereby a number of different independent enhancements can be applied separately and for different fractions of the time, $\Delta_1, \Delta_2, \ldots, \Delta_n$, thus leading respectively to the speedup enhancements $SU_{\Delta_1}, SU_{\Delta_2}, \ldots, SU_{\Delta_n}$.

$$SU_0 = \frac{1}{[1 - (\Delta_1 + \Delta_2 + \cdots + \Delta_n)] + \dfrac{(\Delta_1 + \Delta_2 + \cdots + \Delta_n)}{(SU_{\Delta_1} + SU_{\Delta_2} + \cdots + SU_{\Delta_n})}}$$

1.5. SUMMARY

In this chapter, we provided a brief historical background for the development of computer systems, starting from the first recorded attempt to build a computer, the Z1, in 1938, passing through the CDC 6600 and the Cray supercomputers, and ending up with today's modern high-performance machines. We then provided a discussion on the RISC versus CISC architectural styles and their impact on machine performance. This was followed by a brief discussion on the technological development and its impact on computing performance. Our coverage in this chapter was concluded with a detailed treatment of the issues involved in assessing the performance of computers. In particular, we have introduced a number of performance measures such as CPI, MIPS, MFLOPS, and Arithmetic/Geometric performance means, none of them defining the performance of a machine consistently. Possible ways of evaluating the speedup for given partial or general improvement measurements of a machine were discussed at the end of this Chapter.

EXERCISES

1. What has been the trend in computing from the following points of view?
   (a) Cost of hardware
   (b) Size of memory
   (c) Speed of hardware
   (d) Number of processing elements
   (e) Geographical locations of system components

2. Given the trend in computing in the last 20 years, what are your predictions for the future of computing?

3. Find the meaning of the following:
   (a) Cluster computing
   (b) Grid computing
   (c) Quantum computing
   (d) Nanotechnology

4. Assume that a switching component such as a transistor can switch in zero time. We propose to construct a disk-shaped computer chip with such a component. The only limitation is the time it takes to send electronic signals from one edge of the chip to the other. Make the simplifying assumption that electronic signals can travel at 300,000 kilometers per second. What is the limitation on the diameter of a round chip so that any computation result can by used anywhere on the chip at a clock rate of 1 GHz? What are the diameter restrictions if the whole chip should operate at 1 THz = 10^{12} Hz? Is such a chip feasible?

5. Compare uniprocessor systems with multiprocessor systems in the following aspects:
   (a) Ease of programming
   (b) The need for synchronization
   (c) Performance evaluation
   (d) Run time system

6. Consider having a program that runs in 50 s on computer A, which has a 500 MHz clock. We would like to run the same program on another machine, B, in 20 s. If machine B requires 2.5 times as many clock cycles as machine A for the same program, what clock rate must machine B have in MHz?

7. Suppose that we have two implementations of the same instruction set architecture. Machine A has a clock cycle time of 50 ns and a CPI of 4.0 for some program, and machine B has a clock cycle of 65 ns and a CPI of 2.5 for the same program. Which machine is faster and by how much?

8. A compiler designer is trying to decide between two code sequences for a particular machine. The hardware designers have supplied the following facts:

Instruction class	CPI of the instruction class
A	1
B	3
C	4

For a particular high-level language, the compiler writer is considering two sequences that require the following instruction counts:

Code sequence	Instruction counts (in millions)		
	A	B	C
1	2	1	2
2	4	3	1

What is the CPI for each sequence? Which code sequence is faster? By how much?

9. Consider a machine with three instruction classes and CPI measurements as follows:

Instruction class	CPI of the instruction class
A	2
B	5
C	7

Suppose that we measured the code for a given program in two different compilers and obtained the following data:

Code sequence	Instruction counts (in millions)		
	A	B	C
Compiler 1	15	5	3
Compiler 2	25	2	2

Assume that the machine's clock rate is 500 MHz. Which code sequence will execute faster according to MIPS? And according to execution time?

10. Three enhancements with the following speedups are proposed for a new machine: Speedup(a) = 30, Speedup(b) = 20, and Speedup(c) = 15. Assume that for some set of programs, the fraction of use is 25% for enhancement (a), 30% for enhancement (b), and 45% for enhancement (c). If only one enhancement can be implemented, which should be chosen to maximize the speedup? If two enhancements can be implemented, which should be chosen, to maximize the speedup?

REFERENCES AND FURTHER READING

J.-L. Baer, Computer architecture, *IEEE Comput.*, 17(10), 77–87, (1984).

S. Dasgupta, *Computer Architecture: A Modern Synthesis*, John Wiley, New York, 1989.

M. Flynn, *Some computer organization and their effectiveness*, *IEEE Trans Comput.*, C-21, 948–960 (1972).

D. Gajski, V. Milutinovic, H. Siegel, and B. Furht, *Computer Architecture: A Tutorial*, Computer Society Press, Los Alamitos, Calif, 1987.

W. Giloi, Towards a taxonomy of computer architecture based on the machine data type view, Proceedings of the 10th International Symposium on Computer Architecture, 6–15, (1983).

W. Handler, The impact of classification schemes on computer architecture, Proceedings of the 1977 International Conference on Parallel Processing, 7–15, (1977).

J. Hennessy and D. Patterson, *Computer Architecture: A Quantitative Approach*, 2nd ed., Morgan Kaufmann, San Francisco, 1996.

K. Hwang and F. Briggs, *Computer Architecture and Parallel Processing*, 2nd ed., McGraw-Hill, New York, 1996.

D. J. Kuck, *The Structure of Computers and Computations*, John Wiley, New York, 1978.

G. J. Myers, *Advances in Computer Architecture*, John Wiley, New York, 1982.

L. Tesler, Networked computing in the 1990s, reprinted from the Sept. 1991 Scientific American, The Computer in the 21st Century, 10–21, (1995).

P. Treleaven, Control-driven data-driven and demand-driven computer architecture (abstract), *Parallel Comput.*, 2, (1985).

P. Treleaven, D. Brownbridge, and R. Hopkins, Data drive and demand driven computer architecture, *ACM Comput. Surv.*, 14(1), 95–143, (1982).

Websites

http://www.gigaflop.demon.co.uk/~wasel

CHAPTER 2

Instruction Set Architecture and Design

In this chapter, we consider the basic principles involved in instruction set architecture and design. Our discussion starts with a consideration of memory locations and addresses. We present an abstract model of the main memory in which it is considered as a sequence of cells each capable of storing n bits. We then address the issue of storing and retrieving information into and from the memory. The information stored and/or retrieved from the memory needs to be addressed. A discussion on a number of different ways to address memory locations (addressing modes) is the next topic to be discussed in the chapter. A program consists of a number of instructions that have to be accessed in a certain order. That motivates us to explain the issue of instruction execution and sequencing in some detail. We then show the application of the presented addressing modes and instruction characteristics in writing sample segment codes for performing a number of simple programming tasks.

A unique characteristic of computer memory is that it should be organized in a hierarchy. In such hierarchy, larger and slower memories are used to supplement smaller and faster ones. A typical memory hierarchy starts with a small, expensive, and relatively fast module, called the *cache*. The cache is followed in the hierarchy by a larger, less expensive, and relatively slow *main memory* part. Cache and main memory are built using semiconductor material. They are followed in the hierarchy by larger, less expensive, and far slower magnetic memories that consist of the (hard) disk and the tape. The characteristics and factors influencing the success of the memory hierarchy of a computer are discussed in detail in Chapters 6 and 7. Our concentration in this chapter is on the (main) memory from the programmer's point of view. In particular, we focus on the way information is stored in and retrieved out of the memory.

2.1. MEMORY LOCATIONS AND OPERATIONS

The (main) memory can be modeled as an array of millions of adjacent cells, each capable of storing a binary *digit* (*bit*), having value of 1 or 0. These cells are

Fundamentals of Computer Organization and Architecture, by M. Abd-El-Barr and H. El-Rewini
ISBN 0-471-46741-3   Copyright © 2005 John Wiley & Sons, Inc.

organized in the form of groups of fixed number, say n, of cells that can be dealt with as an atomic entity. An entity consisting of 8 bits is called a *byte*. In many systems, the entity consisting of n bits that can be stored and retrieved in and out of the memory using one basic memory operation is called a *word* (the smallest addressable entity). Typical size of a word ranges from 16 to 64 bits. It is, however, customary to express the size of the memory in terms of bytes. For example, the size of a typical memory of a personal computer is 256 Mbytes, that is, $256 \times 2^{20} = 2^{28}$ bytes.

In order to be able to move a word in and out of the memory, a distinct address has to be assigned to each word. This address will be used to determine the location in the memory in which a given word is to be stored. This is called a memory *write* operation. Similarly, the address will be used to determine the memory location from which a word is to be retrieved from the memory. This is called a memory *read* operation.

The number of bits, l, needed to distinctly address M words in a memory is given by $l = \log_2 M$. For example, if the size of the memory is $64\,M$ (read as 64 mega-words), then the number of bits in the address is $\log_2 (64 \times 2^{20}) = \log_2 (2^{26}) = 26$ bits. Alternatively, if the number of bits in the address is l, then the maximum memory size (in terms of the number of words that can be addressed using these l bits) is $M = 2^l$. Figure 2.1 illustrates the concept of memory words and word address as explained above.

As mentioned above, there are two basic memory operations. These are the memory *write* and memory *read* operations. During a memory write operation a word is stored into a memory location whose address is specified. During a memory read operation a word is read from a memory location whose address is specified. Typically, memory read and memory write operations are performed by the *central processing unit* (CPU).

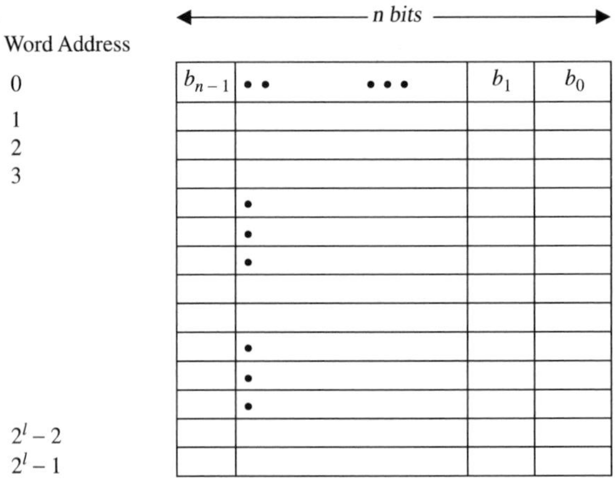

Figure 2.1 Illustration of the main memory addressing

Three basic steps are needed in order for the CPU to perform a write operation into a specified memory location:

1. The word to be stored into the memory location is first loaded by the CPU into a specified register, called the *memory data register* (*MDR*).
2. The address of the location into which the word is to be stored is loaded by the CPU into a specified register, called the *memory address register* (*MAR*).
3. A signal, called *write*, is issued by the CPU indicating that the word stored in the MDR is to be stored in the memory location whose address in loaded in the MAR.

Figure 2.2 illustrates the operation of writing the word given by 7E (in hex) into the memory location whose address is 2005. Part *a* of the figure shows the status of the registers and memory locations involved in the write operation before the execution of the operation. Part *b* of the figure shows the status after the execution of the operation.

It is worth mentioning that the *MDR* and the *MAR* are registers used exclusively by the CPU and are not accessible to the programmer.

Similar to the write operation, three basic steps are needed in order to perform a memory read operation:

1. The address of the location from which the word is to be read is loaded into the MAR.
2. A signal, called *read*, is issued by the CPU indicating that the word whose address is in the MAR is to be read into the MDR.
3. After some time, corresponding to the memory delay in reading the specified word, the required word will be loaded by the memory into the MDR ready for use by the CPU.

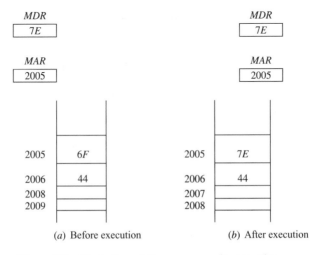

(*a*) Before execution   (*b*) After execution

Figure 2.2   Illustration of the memory write operation

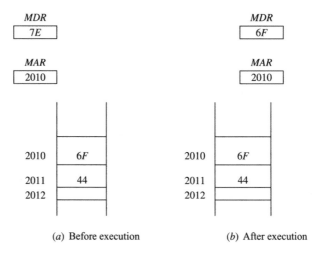

(a) Before execution   (b) After execution

Figure 2.3   Illustration of the memory read operation

Figure 2.3 illustrates the operation of reading the word stored in the memory location whose address is 2010. Part *a* of the figure shows the status of the registers and memory locations involved in the read operation before the execution of the operation. Part *b* of the figure shows the status after the read operation.

2.2. ADDRESSING MODES

Information involved in any operation performed by the CPU needs to be addressed. In computer terminology, such information is called the *operand*. Therefore, any instruction issued by the processor must carry at least two types of information. These are the operation to be performed, encoded in what is called the *op-code* field, and the address information of the operand on which the operation is to be performed, encoded in what is called the *address* field.

Instructions can be classified based on the number of operands as: *three-address*, *two-address*, *one-and-half-address*, *one-address*, and *zero-address*. We explain these classes together with simple examples in the following paragraphs. It should be noted that in presenting these examples, we would use the convention *operation, source, destination* to express any instruction. In that convention, operation represents the operation to be performed, for example, *add*, *subtract*, *write*, or *read*. The source field represents the source operand(s). The source operand can be a constant, a value stored in a register, or a value stored in the memory. The destination field represents the place where the result of the operation is to be stored, for example, a register or a memory location.

A three-address instruction takes the form *operation add-1, add-2, add-3*. In this form, each of *add-1*, *add-2*, and *add-3* refers to a register or to a memory location. Consider, for example, the instruction *ADD* R_1, R_2, R_3. This instruction indicates that the operation to be performed is *addition*. It also indicates that the values to be added are those stored in registers R_1 and R_2 that the results should be stored in register R_3. An example of a three-address instruction that refers to memory locations may take the form *ADD A,B,C*. The instruction adds the contents of memory location A to the contents of memory location B and stores the result in memory location C.

A two-address instruction takes the form *operation add-1, add-2*. In this form, each of *add-1* and *add-2* refers to a register or to a memory location. Consider, for example, the instruction *ADD R_1,R_2*. This instruction adds the contents of register R_1 to the contents of register R_2 and stores the results in register R_2. The original contents of register R_2 are lost due to this operation while the original contents of register R_1 remain intact. This instruction is equivalent to a three-address instruction of the form *ADD R_1,R_2,R_2*. A similar instruction that uses memory locations instead of registers can take the form *ADD A,B*. In this case, the contents of memory location A are added to the contents of memory location B and the result is used to override the original contents of memory location B.

The operation performed by the three-address instruction *ADD A,B,C* can be performed by the two two-address instructions *MOVE B,C* and *ADD A,C*. This is because the first instruction moves the contents of location B into location C and the second instruction adds the contents of location A to those of location C (the contents of location B) and stores the result in location C.

A one-address instruction takes the form *ADD R_1*. In this case the instruction implicitly refers to a register, called the *Accumulator R_{acc}*, such that the contents of the accumulator is added to the contents of the register R_1 and the results are stored back into the accumulator R_{acc}. If a memory location is used instead of a register then an instruction of the form *ADD B* is used. In this case, the instruction adds the content of the accumulator R_{acc} to the content of memory location B and stores the result back into the accumulator R_{acc}. The instruction *ADD R_1* is equivalent to the three-address instruction *ADD R_1,R_{acc},R_{acc}* or to the two-address instruction *ADD R_1,R_{acc}*.

Between the two- and the one-address instruction, there can be a one-and-half address instruction. Consider, for example, the instruction *ADD B,R_1*. In this case, the instruction adds the contents of register R_1 to the contents of memory location B and stores the result in register R_1. Owing to the fact that the instruction uses two types of addressing, that is, a register and a memory location, it is called a one-and-half-address instruction. This is because register addressing needs a smaller number of bits than those needed by memory addressing.

It is interesting to indicate that there exist zero-address instructions. These are the instructions that use *stack operation*. A stack is a data organization mechanism in which the last data item stored is the first data item retrieved. Two specific operations can be performed on a stack. These are the *push* and the *pop* operations. Figure 2.4 illustrates these two operations.

As can be seen, a specific register, called the *stack pointer* (SP), is used to indicate the stack location that can be addressed. In the stack push operation, the SP value is used to indicate the location (called the top of the stack) in which the value (5A) is to be stored (in this case it is location 1023). After storing (pushing) this value the SP is

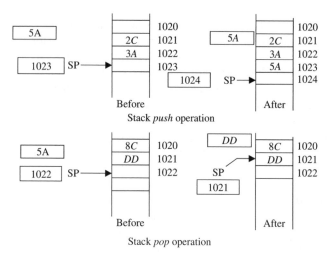

Figure 2.4 The stack push and pop operations

incremented to indicate to location 1024. In the stack pop operation, the SP is first decremented to become 1021. The value stored at this location (DD in this case) is retrieved (popped out) and stored in the shown register.

Different operations can be performed using the stack structure. Consider, for example, an instruction such as *ADD (SP)+, (SP)*. The instruction adds the contents of the stack location pointed to by the SP to those pointed to by the SP + 1 and stores the result on the stack in the location pointed to by the current value of the SP. Figure 2.5 illustrates such an addition operation. Table 2.1 summarizes the instruction classification discussed above.

The different ways in which operands can be addressed are called the *addressing modes*. Addressing modes differ in the way the address information of operands is specified. The simplest addressing mode is to include the operand itself in the instruction, that is, no address information is needed. This is called *immediate addressing*. A more involved addressing mode is to compute the address of the operand by adding a constant value to the content of a register. This is called *indexed addressing*. Between these two addressing modes there exist a number of other addressing modes including absolute addressing, direct addressing, and indirect addressing. A number of different addressing modes are explained below.

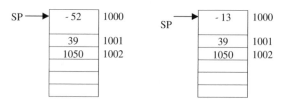

Figure 2.5 Addition using the stack

TABLE 2.1 Instruction Classification

Instruction class	Example
Three-address	$ADD\ R_1,R_2,R_3$
	$ADD\ A,B,C$
Two-address	$ADD\ R_1,R_2$
	$ADD\ A,B$
One-and-half-address	$ADD\ B,R_1$
One-address	$ADD\ R_1$
Zero-address	$ADD\ (SP)+,(SP)$

2.2.1. Immediate Mode

According to this addressing mode, the value of the operand is (immediately) available in the instruction itself. Consider, for example, the case of loading the decimal value 1000 into a register R_i. This operation can be performed using an instruction such as the following: $LOAD\ \#1000,\ R_i$. In this instruction, the operation to be performed is to load a value into a register. The source operand is (immediately) given as 1000, and the destination is the register R_i. It should be noted that in order to indicate that the value 1000 mentioned in the instruction is the operand itself and not its address (immediate mode), it is customary to prefix the operand by the special character (#). As can be seen the use of the immediate addressing mode is simple. The use of immediate addressing leads to poor programming practice. This is because a change in the value of an operand requires a change in every instruction that uses the immediate value of such an operand. A more flexible addressing mode is explained below.

2.2.2. Direct (Absolute) Mode

According to this addressing mode, the address of the memory location that holds the operand is included in the instruction. Consider, for example, the case of loading the value of the operand stored in memory location 1000 into register R_i. This operation can be performed using an instruction such as $LOAD\ 1000,\ R_i$. In this instruction, the source operand is the value stored in the memory location whose address is 1000, and the destination is the register R_i. Note that the value 1000 is not prefixed with any special characters, indicating that it is the (direct or absolute) address of the source operand. Figure 2.6 shows an illustration of the direct addressing mode. For

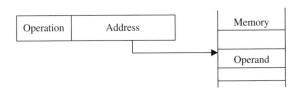

Figure 2.6 Illustration of the direct addressing mode

example, if the content of the memory location whose address is 1000 was (-345) at the time when the instruction *LOAD* 1000, R_i is executed, then the result of executing such instruction is to load the value (-345) into register R_i.

Direct (absolute) addressing mode provides more flexibility compared to the immediate mode. However, it requires the explicit inclusion of the operand address in the instruction. A more flexible addressing mechanism is provided through the use of the indirect addressing mode. This is explained below.

2.2.3. Indirect Mode

In the indirect mode, what is included in the instruction is not the address of the operand, but rather a name of a register or a memory location that holds the (effective) address of the operand. In order to indicate the use of indirection in the instruction, it is customary to include the name of the register or the memory location in parentheses. Consider, for example, the instruction *LOAD* (1000), R_i. This instruction has the memory location 1000 enclosed in parentheses, thus indicating indirection. The meaning of this instruction is to load register R_i with the contents of the memory location whose address is stored at memory address 1000. Because indirection can be made through either a register or a memory location, therefore, we can identify two types of indirect addressing. These are *register indirect addressing*, if a register is used to hold the address of the operand, and *memory indirect addressing*, if a memory location is used to hold the address of the operand. The two types are illustrated in Figure 2.7.

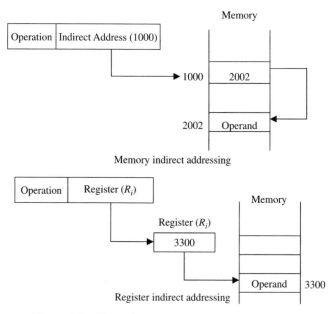

Figure 2.7   Illustration of the indirect addressing mode

2.2.4. Indexed Mode

In this addressing mode, the address of the operand is obtained by adding a constant to the content of a register, called the *index register*. Consider, for example, the instruction *LOAD* $X(R_{ind})$, R_i. This instruction loads register R_i with the contents of the memory location whose address is the sum of the contents of register R_{ind} and the value X. Index addressing is indicated in the instruction by including the name of the index register in parentheses and using the symbol X to indicate the constant to be added. Figure 2.8 illustrates indexed addressing. As can be seen, indexing requires an additional level of complexity over register indirect addressing.

2.2.5. Other Modes

The addressing modes presented above represent the most commonly used modes in most processors. They provide the programmer with sufficient means to handle most general programming tasks. However, a number of other addressing modes have been used in a number of processors to facilitate execution of specific programming tasks. These additional addressing modes are more involved as compared to those presented above. Among these addressing modes the *relative, autoincrement,* and the *autodecrement* modes represent the most well-known ones. These are explained below.

Relative Mode   Recall that in indexed addressing, an index register, R_{ind}, is used. Relative addressing is the same as indexed addressing except that the program counter (PC) replaces the index register. For example, the instruction *LOAD* $X(PC)$, R_i loads register R_i with the contents of the memory location whose address is the sum of the contents of the program counter (PC) and the value X. Figure 2.9 illustrates the relative addressing mode.

Autoincrement Mode   This addressing mode is similar to the register indirect addressing mode in the sense that the effective address of the operand is the content of a register, call it the *autoincrement register*, that is included in the instruction.

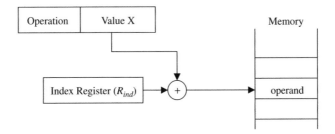

Figure 2.8   Illustration of the indexed addressing mode

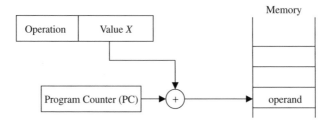

Figure 2.9 Illustration of relative addressing mode

However, with autoincrement, the content of the autoincrement register is automatically incremented after accessing the operand. As before, indirection is indicated by including the autoincrement register in parentheses. The automatic increment of the register's content after accessing the operand is indicated by including a (+) after the parentheses. Consider, for example, the instruction $LOAD (R_{auto})+, R_i$. This instruction loads register R_i with the operand whose address is the content of register R_{auto}. After loading the operand into register R_i, the content of register R_{auto} is incremented, pointing for example to the next item in a list of items. Figure 2.10 illustrates the autoincrement addressing mode.

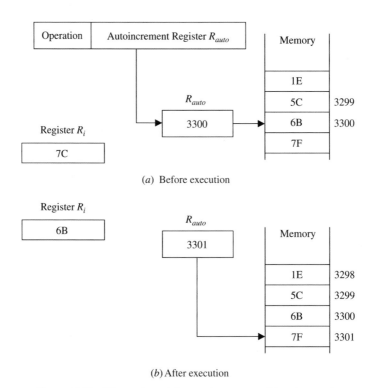

(a) Before execution

(b) After execution

Figure 2.10 Illustration of the autoincrement addressing mode

Autodecrement Mode   Similar to the autoincrement, the autodecrement mode uses a register to hold the address of the operand. However, in this case the content of the autodecrement register is first decremented and the new content is used as the effective address of the operand. In order to reflect the fact that the content of the autodecrement register is decremented before accessing the operand, a $(-)$ is included before the indirection parentheses. Consider, for example, the instruction $LOAD - (R_{auto}), R_i$. This instruction decrements the content of the register R_{auto} and then uses the new content as the effective address of the operand that is to be loaded into register R_i. Figure 2.11 illustrates the autodecrement addressing mode.

The seven addressing modes presented above are summarized in Table 2.2. In each case, the table shows the name of the addressing mode, its definition, and a generic example illustrating the use of such mode.

In presenting the different addressing modes we have used the *load* instruction for illustration. However, it should be understood that there are other types of instructions in a given machine. In the following section we elaborate on the different types of instructions that typically constitute the instruction set of a given machine.

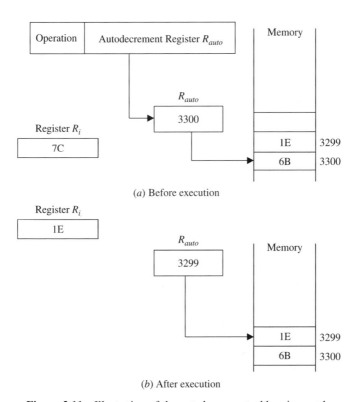

(*a*) Before execution

(*b*) After execution

Figure 2.11   Illustration of the autodecrement addressing mode

TABLE 2.2 Summary of Addressing Modes

Addressing mode	Definition	Example	Operation
Immediate	Value of operand is included in the instruction	*load* #1000, R_i	$R_i \leftarrow 1000$
Direct (Absolute)	Address of operand is included in the instruction	*load* 1000, R_i	$R_i \leftarrow M[1000]$
Register indirect	Operand is in a memory location whose address is in the register specified in the instruction	*load* (R_j), R_i	$R_i \leftarrow M[R_j]$
Memory indirect	Operand is in a memory location whose address is in the memory location specified in the instruction	*load* (1000), R_i	$R_i \leftarrow M[1000]$
Indexed	Address of operand is the sum of an index value and the contents of an index register	*load* $X(R_{ind})$, R_i	$R_i \leftarrow M[R_{ind} + X]$
Relative	Address of operand is the sum of an index value and the contents of the program counter	*load* $X(PC)$, R_i	$R_i \leftarrow M[PC + X]$
Autoincrement	Address of operand is in a register whose value is incremented after fetching the operand	*load* $(R_{auto})+$, R_i	$R_i \leftarrow M[R_{auto}]$ $R_{auto} \leftarrow R_{auto} + 1$
Autodecrement	Address of operand is in a register whose value is decremented before fetching the operand	*load* $- (R_{auto})$, R_i	$R_{auto} \leftarrow R_{auto} - 1$ $R_i \leftarrow M[R_{auto}]$

2.3. INSTRUCTION TYPES

The type of instructions forming the instruction set of a machine is an indication of the power of the underlying architecture of the machine. Instructions can in general be classified as in the following Subsections 2.3.1 to 2.3.4.

2.3.1. Data Movement Instructions

Data movement instructions are used to move data among the different units of the machine. Most notably among these are instructions that are used to move data among the different registers in the CPU. A simple register to register movement of data can be made through the instruction

$$MOVE\ R_i, R_j$$

TABLE 2.3 **Some Common Data Movement Operations**

Data movement operation	Meaning
MOVE	Move data (a word or a block) from a given source (a register or a memory) to a given destination
LOAD	Load data from memory to a register
STORE	Store data into memory from a register
PUSH	Store data from a register to stack
POP	Retrieve data from stack into a register

This instruction moves the content of register R_i to register R_j. The effect of the instruction is to override the contents of the (destination) register R_j without changing the contents of the (source) register R_i. Data movement instructions include those used to move data to (from) registers from (to) memory. These instructions are usually referred to as the *load* and *store* instructions, respectively. Examples of the two instructions are

$$LOAD\ 25838,\ R_j$$
$$STORE\ R_i,\ 1024$$

The first instruction loads the content of the memory location whose address is 25838 into the destination register R_j. The content of the memory location is unchanged by executing the *LOAD* instruction. The *STORE* instruction stores the content of the source register R_i into the memory location 1024. The content of the source register is unchanged by executing the *STORE* instruction. Table 2.3 shows some common data transfer operations and their meanings.

2.3.2. Arithmetic and Logical Instructions

Arithmetic and logical instructions are those used to perform arithmetic and logical manipulation of registers and memory contents. Examples of arithmetic instructions include the *ADD* and *SUBTRACT* instructions. These are

$$ADD\ R_1,R_2,R_0$$
$$SUBTRACT\ R_1,R_2,R_0$$

The first instruction adds the contents of source registers R_1 and R_2 and stores the result in destination register R_0. The second instruction subtracts the contents of the source registers R_1 and R_2 and stores the result in the destination register R_0. The contents of the source registers are unchanged by the *ADD* and the *SUBTRACT* instructions. In addition to the *ADD* and *SUBTRACT* instructions, some machines have *MULTIPLY* and *DIVIDE* instructions. These two instructions are expensive to implement and could be substituted by the use of repeated addition or repeated subtraction. Therefore, most modern architectures do not have *MULTIPLY* or

TABLE 2.4 Some Common Arithmetic Operations

Arithmetic operations	Meaning
ADD	Perform the arithmetic sum of two operands
SUBTRACT	Perform the arithmetic difference of two operands
MULTIPLY	Perform the product of two operands
DIVIDE	Perform the division of two operands
INCREMENT	Add one to the contents of a register
DECREMENT	Subtract one from the contents of a register

DIVIDE instructions on their instruction set. Table 2.4 shows some common arithmetic operations and their meanings.

Logical instructions are used to perform logical operations such as *AND, OR, SHIFT, COMPARE,* and *ROTATE.* As the names indicate, these instructions perform, respectively, and, or, shift, compare, and rotate operations on register or memory contents. Table 2.5 presents a number of logical operations.

2.3.3. Sequencing Instructions

Control (sequencing) instructions are used to change the sequence in which instructions are executed. They take the form of *CONDITIONAL BRANCHING (CONDITIONAL JUMP), UNCONDITIONAL BRANCHING (JUMP),* or *CALL* instructions. A common characteristic among these instructions is that their execution changes the program counter (*PC*) value. The change made in the *PC* value can be unconditional, for example, in the unconditional branching or the jump instructions. In this case, the earlier value of the *PC* is lost and execution of the program starts at a new value specified by the instruction. Consider, for example, the instruction *JUMP NEW-ADDRESS.* Execution of this instruction will cause the *PC* to be loaded with the memory location represented by NEW-ADDRESS whereby the instruction stored at this new address is executed. On the other hand,

TABLE 2.5 Some Common Logical Operations

Logical operation	Meaning
AND	Perform the logical ANDing of two operands
OR	Perform the logical ORing of two operands
EXOR	Perform the XORing of two operands
NOT	Perform the complement of an operand
COMPARE	Perform logical comparison of two operands and set flag accordingly
SHIFT	Perform logical shift (right or left) of the content of a register
ROTATE	Perform logical shift (right or left) with wraparound of the content of a register

TABLE 2.6   Examples of Condition Flags

Flag name	Meaning
Negative (N)	Set to 1 if the result of the most recent operation is negative, it is 0 otherwise
Zero (Z)	Set to 1 if the result of the most recent operation is 0, it is 0 otherwise
Overflow (V)	Set to 1 if the result of the most recent operation causes an overflow, it is 0 otherwise
Carry (C)	Set to 1 if the most recent operation results in a carry, it is 0 otherwise

the change made in the PC by the branching instruction can be conditional based on the value of a specific *flag*. Examples of these flags include the *Negative* (N), *Zero* (Z), *Overflow* (V), and *Carry* (C). These flags represent the individual bits of a specific register, called the *CONDITION CODE* (CC) *REGISTER*. The values of flags are set based on the results of executing different instructions. The meaning of each of these flags is shown in Table 2.6.

Consider, for example, the following group of instructions.

$$\begin{array}{lll} & LOAD & \#100, R_1 \\ Loop: & ADD & (R_2)+, R_0 \\ & DECREMENT & R_1 \\ & BRANCH\text{-}IF\text{-}GREATER\text{-}THAN\ Loop \end{array}$$

The fourth instruction is a conditional branch instruction, which indicates that if the result of decrementing the contents of register R_1 is greater than zero, that is, if the Z flag is not set, then the next instruction to be executed is that labeled by Loop. It should be noted that conditional branch instructions could be used to execute program loops (as shown above).

The *CALL* instructions are used to cause execution of the program to transfer to a subroutine. A *CALL* instruction has the same effect as that of the *JUMP* in terms of loading the PC with a new value from which the next instruction is to be executed. However, with the *CALL* instruction the incremented value of the PC (to point to the next instruction in sequence) is pushed onto the stack. Execution of a *RETURN* instruction in the subroutine will load the PC with the popped value from the stack. This has the effect of resuming program execution from the point where branching to the subroutine has occurred.

Figure 2.12 shows a program segment that uses the *CALL* instruction. This program segment sums up a number of values, N, and stores the result into memory location *SUM*. The values to be added are stored in N consecutive memory locations starting at *NUM*. The subroutine, called *ADDITION*, is used to perform the actual addition of values while the main program stores the results in *SUM*.

Table 2.7 presents some common transfer of control operations.

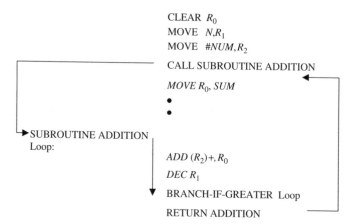

CLEAR R_0
MOVE N,R_1
MOVE $\#NUM,R_2$

CALL SUBROUTINE ADDITION

MOVE R_0, SUM

•

•

SUBROUTINE ADDITION
  Loop:

ADD $(R_2)+,R_0$

DEC R_1

BRANCH-IF-GREATER Loop

RETURN ADDITION

Figure 2.12 A program segment using a subroutine

2.3.4. Input/Output Instructions

Input and output instructions (I/O instructions) are used to transfer data between the computer and peripheral devices. The two basic I/O instructions used are the *INPUT* and *OUTPUT* instructions. The *INPUT* instruction is used to transfer data from an input device to the processor. Examples of input devices include a *keyboard* or a *mouse*. Input devices are interfaced with a computer through dedicated input *ports*. Computers can use dedicated addresses to address these ports. Suppose that the input port through which a keyboard is connected to a computer carries the unique address 1000. Therefore, execution of the instruction *INPUT 1000* will cause the data stored in a specific register in the interface between the keyboard and the computer, call it the *input data register*, to be moved into a specific register (called the accumulator) in the computer. Similarly, the execution of the instruction *OUTPUT 2000* causes the data stored in the accumulator to be moved to the *data output register* in the output device whose address is 2000. Alternatively, the computer can address these ports in the usual way of addressing memory locations. In this case, the computer can input data from an input device by executing an instruction such as *MOVE R_{in}, R_0*. This instruction moves the content of the register R_{in} into the register R_0. Similarly, the instruction *MOVE R_0, R_{in}* moves the contents of register R_0 into the register R_{in}, that is, performs an output operation. This

TABLE 2.7 Some Transfer of Control Operations

Transfer of control operation	Meaning
BRANCH-IF-CONDITION	Transfer of control to a new address if condition is true
JUMP	Unconditional transfer of control
CALL	Transfer of control to a subroutine
RETURN	Transfer of control to the caller routine

latter scheme is called *memory-mapped Input/Output*. Among the advantages of memory-mapped I/O is the ability to execute a number of memory-dedicated instructions on the registers in the I/O devices in addition to the elimination of the need for dedicated I/O instructions. Its main disadvantage is the need to dedicate part of the memory address space for I/O devices.

2.4. PROGRAMMING EXAMPLES

Having introduced addressing modes and instruction types, we now move on to illustrate the use of these concepts through a number of programming examples. In presenting these examples, generic mnemonics will be used. This is done in order to emphasize the understanding of how to use different addressing modes in performing different operations independent of the machine used. Applications of similar principles using real-life machine examples are presented in Chapter 3.

Example 1   In this example, we would like to show a program segment that can be used to perform the task of adding 100 numbers stored at consecutive memory locations starting at location 1000. The results should be stored in memory location 2000.

$$
\begin{array}{lll}
& CLEAR\ R_0; & R_0 \leftarrow 0 \\
& MOVE\ \#\ 100,\ R_1; & R_1 \leftarrow 100 \\
& CLEAR\ R_2; & R_2 \leftarrow 0 \\
LOOP: & ADD\ 1000(R_2),\ R_0; & R_0 \leftarrow R_0 + M\ (1000 + R_2) \\
& INCREMENT\ R_2; & R_2 \leftarrow R_2 + 1 \\
& DECREMENT\ R_1; & R_1 \leftarrow R_1 - 1 \\
& BRANCH\text{-}IF > 0\ LOOP; & GO\ TO\ LOOP\ if\ contents\ of\ R_1 > 0 \\
& STORE\ R_0,\ 2000; & M(2000) \leftarrow R_0
\end{array}
$$

In this example, use has been made of immediate ($MOVE\ \#100,\ R_1$) and indexed (ADD $1000(R_2),\ R_0$) addressing.

Example 2   In this example autoincrement addressing will be used to perform the same task performed in Example 1.

$$
\begin{array}{lll}
& CLEAR\ R_0; & R_0 \leftarrow 0 \\
& MOVE\ \#100,\ R_1; & R_1 \leftarrow 100 \\
& CLEAR\ R_2; & R_2 \leftarrow 0 \\
LOOP: & ADD\ 1000(R_2)+,\ R_0; & R_0 \leftarrow R_0 + M\ (1000 + R_2)\ \&\ R_2 \leftarrow R_2 + 1 \\
& DECREMENT\ R_1; & R_1 \leftarrow R_1 - 1 \\
& BRANCH\text{-}IF > 0\ LOOP; & GO\ TO\ LOOP\ if\ contents\ of\ R_1 > 0 \\
& STORE\ R_0,\ 2000; & M(2000) \leftarrow R_0
\end{array}
$$

As can be seen, a given task can be performed using more than one programming methodology. The method used by the programmer depends on his/her experience

MAIN PROGRAM

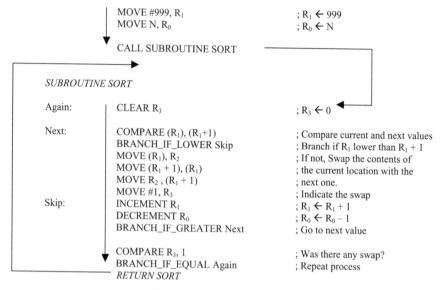

Figure 2.13 *SORT* subroutine

as well as the richness of the instruction set of the machine used. Note also that the use of the autoincrement addressing in Example 2 has led to a decrease in the number of instructions used to perform the same task.

Example 3 This example illustrates the use of a subroutine, *SORT*, to sort *N* values in ascending order (Fig. 2.13). The numbers are originally stored in a list starting at location 1000. The sorted values are also stored in the same list and again starting at location 1000. The subroutine sorts the data using the well-known "Bubble Sort" technique. The content of register R_3 is checked at the end of every loop to find out whether the list is sorted or not.

Example 4 This example illustrates the use of a subroutine, *SEARCH*, to search for a value *VAL* in a list of *N* values (Fig. 2.14). We assume that the list is not originally sorted and therefore a brute force search is used. In this search, the value *VAL* is compared with every element in the list from top to bottom. The content of register R_3 is used to indicate whether *VAL* was found. The first element of the list is located at address 1000.

Example 5 This example illustrates the use of a subroutine, *SEARCH*, to search for a value *VAL* in a list of *N* values (as in Example 4) (Fig. 2.15). Here, we make use of the stack to send the parameters *VAL* and *N*.

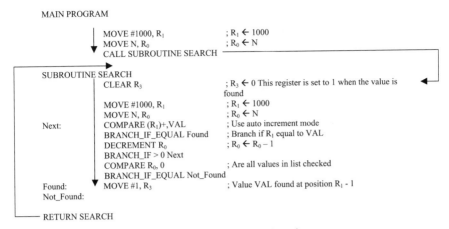

Figure 2.14 *SEARCH* subroutine

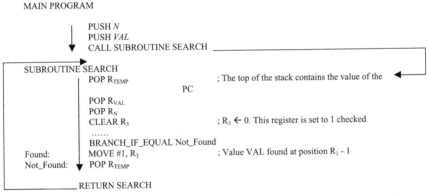

Figure 2.15 Subroutine *SEARCH* using stack to send parameters *VAL* and *N*

2.5. SUMMARY

In this chapter we considered the main issues relating to instruction set design and characteristics. We presented a model of the main memory in which the memory is abstracted as a sequence of cells, each capable of storing n bits. A number of addressing modes were presented. These include immediate, direct, indirect, indexed, autoincrement, and autodecrement. Examples showing how to use these addressing modes were then presented. We also presented a discussion on instruction types, which include data movement, arithmetic/logical, instruction sequencing, and Input/Output. Our discussion concluded with a presentation of a number of examples showing how to use the principles and concepts discussed in the chapter in programming the solution of a number of sample problems. In the next chapter, we will introduce the concepts involved in programming the solution of real-life problems using assembly language.

EXERCISES

1. Write a program using the addressing modes and the instruction types presented in Sections 2.2 and 2.3 to reverse the bits stored in a 16-bit register R_0.

2. Consider a computer that has a number of registers such that the three registers $R_0 = 1500$, $R_1 = 4500$, and $R_2 = 1000$. Show the effective address of memory and the registers' contents in each of the following instructions (assume that all numbers are decimal).
   (a) $ADD (R_0)+, R_2$
   (b) $SUBTRACT - (R_1), R_2$
   (c) $MOVE 500(R_0), R_2$
   (d) $LOAD \#5000, R_2$
   (e) $STORE R_0, 100(R_2)$

3. Assume that the top of the stack in a program is pointed to by the register SP. You are required to write program segments to perform each of the following tasks (assume that only the following addressing modes are available: indexed, autoincrement, and autodecrement).
   (a) Pop the top three elements of the stack, add them, and push the result back onto the stack.
   (b) Pop the top two elements of the stack, subtract them, and push the results back onto the stack.
   (c) Push five elements (one at a time) onto the stack.
   (d) Remove the top five elements from the top of the stack.
   (e) Copy the third element from the top of the stack into register R_0.

4. You are required to write a program segment that can perform the operation $C \leftarrow A + B$ where each of A and B represents a set of 100 memory locations each storing a value such that the set of values represented by A are stored starting at memory location 1000 and those represented by B are stored starting at memory location 2000. The results should be stored starting at memory location 3000. The above operation is to be performed using each of the following instruction classes.
   (a) A machine with one-address instructions
   (b) A machine with one-and-half instructions
   (c) A machine with two-address instructions
   (d) A machine with three-address instructions
   (e) A machine with zero-address instructions

5. Write program segments that perform the operation $C \leftarrow C + A \times B$ using each of the instruction classes indicated in Exercise 4 above. Assume that A, B, and C are memory addresses.

6. Assume that a series of five tests has been offered to a class consisting of 50 students. The score obtained by students in each of the five tests are stored sequentially in memory locations starting respectively at memory locations 1000, 2000, 3000, 4000, and 5000. You are required to write a program

that calculates the average score obtained by each student in the five tests and store the same in memory locations starting at memory location 6000. Each student is identified by his/her student ID. You may assume that students' IDs are sequential.

7. Repeat Exercise 6 above assuming that the memory used is byte addressable while each score occupies 32-bit.

8. Rewrite the same program as in Exercise 6 above assuming that the students' IDs are not sequential, that is, each student ID is to be used as a pointer to his/her test scores.

9. Repeat Exercise 6 above assuming that the students scores are stored in an array S(50,5), that is, each row holds the scores obtained by a student (each score in a column of the same row) and that the first element of the array, that is, S (0,0) is stored in memory location 4000. The scores are stored rowwise, that is, one row after the other. The average score obtained by each student is to be stored at a memory location pointed to by his/her ID.

10. Repeat Exercise 9 above assuming that your job is to write a subroutine to perform the same task as in Exercise 9. Assume that the number of students, the number of tests, and the location of the first element in the array are to be passed to the subroutine as parameters in registers R_1, R_2, and R_3, respectively.

REFERENCES AND FURTHER READING

C. M. Gilmore, *Microprocessors*: *Principles and Applications*, 2nd ed., McGraw-Hill, New York, 1996.

V. C. Hamacher, Z. G. Vranesic, and S. G. Zaky, *Computer Organization*, 5th ed., McGraw-Hill, New York, 2002

A. D. Patterson, J. L. Hennessy, *Computer Organization & Design*; *The Hardware/Software Interface*, Morgan Kaufmann, San Mateo, CA, 1994

B. Wilkinson, *Computer Architecture*: *Design and Performance*, 2nd ed., Prentice-Hall, Hertfordshire, UK, 1996.

CHAPTER 3

Assembly Language Programming

In Chapter 2 we introduced the basic concepts and principles involved in the design of an instruction set of a machine. This chapter considers the issues related to assembly language programming. Although high-level languages and compiler technology have witnessed great advances over the years, assembly language remains necessary in some cases. Programming in assembly can result in machine code that is much smaller and much faster than that generated by a compiler of a high-level language. Small and fast code could be critical in some embedded and portable applications, where resources may be very limited. In such cases, small portions of the program that may be heavily used can be written in assembly language. For the reader of this book, learning assembly languages and writing assembly code can be extremely helpful in understanding computer organization and architecture.

A computer program can be represented at different levels of abstraction. A program could be written in a machine-independent, high-level language such as Java or C++. A computer can execute programs only when they are represented in machine language specific to its architecture. A machine language program for a given architecture is a collection of machine instructions represented in binary form. Programs written at any level higher than the machine language must be translated to the binary representation before a computer can execute them. An assembly language program is a symbolic representation of the machine language program. Machine language is pure binary code, whereas assembly language is a direct mapping of the binary code onto a symbolic form that is easier for humans to understand and manage. Converting the symbolic representation into machine language is performed by a special program called the assembler. An assembler is a program that accepts a symbolic language program (source) and produces its machine language equivalent (target). In translating a program into binary code, the assembler will replace symbolic addresses by numeric addresses, replace symbolic operation codes by machine operation codes, reserve storage for instructions and data, and translate constants into machine representation.

The purpose of this chapter is to give the reader a general overview of assembly language and its programming. It is not meant to be a manual of the assembly language for any specific architecture. We start the chapter with a discussion of a

Fundamentals of Computer Organization and Architecture, by M. Abd-El-Barr and H. El-Rewini
ISBN 0-471-46741-3   Copyright © 2005 John Wiley & Sons, Inc.

simple hypothetical machine that will be referred to throughout the chapter. The machine has only five registers and its instruction set has only 10 instructions. We will use this simple machine to define a rather simple assembly language that will be easy to understand and will help explain the main issues in assembly programming. We will introduce instruction mnemonics and the syntax and assembler directives and commands. A discussion on the execution of assembly programs is then presented. We conclude the chapter by showing a real-world example of the assembly language for the *X86 Intel CISC family.*

3.1. A SIMPLE MACHINE

Machine language is the native language of a given processor. Since assembly language is the symbolic form of machine language, each different type of processor has its own unique assembly language. Before we study the assembly language of a given processor, we need first to understand the details of that processor. We need to know the memory size and organization, the processor registers, the instruction format, and the entire instruction set. In this section, we present a very simple hypothetical processor, which will be used in explaining the different topics in assembly language throughout the chapter.

Our simple machine is an accumulator-based processor, which has five 16-bit registers: Program Counter (PC), Instruction Register (IR), Address Register (AR), Accumulator (AC), and Data Register (DR). The PC contains the address of the next instruction to be executed. The IR contains the operation code portion of the instruction being executed. The AR contains the address portion (if any) of the instruction being executed. The AC serves as the implicit source and destination of data. The DR is used to hold data. The memory unit is made up of 4096 words of storage. The word size is 16 bits. The processor is shown in Figure 3.1.

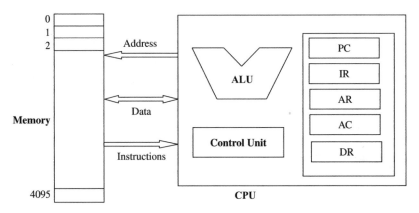

Figure 3.1 A simple machine

TABLE 3.1   Instruction Set of the Simple Processor

Operation code	Operand	Meaning of instruction
0000		Stop execution
0001	*adr*	Load operand from memory (location adr) into AC
0010	*adr*	Store contents of AC in memory (location adr)
0011		Copy the contents AC to DR
0100		Copy the contents of DR to AC
0101		Add DR to AC
0110		Subtract DR from AC
0111		And bitwise DR to AC
1000		Complement contents of AC
1001	*adr*	Jump to instruction with address adr
1010	*adr*	Jump to instruction adr if AC = 0

We assume that our simple processor supports three types of instructions: data transfer, data processing, and program control. The data transfer operations are load, store, and move data between the registers AC and DR. The data processing instructions are add, subtract, and, and not. The program control instructions are jump and conditional jump. The instruction set of our processor is summarized in Table 3.1. The instruction size is 16 bits, 4 bits for the operation code and 12 bits for the address (when appropriate).

Example 1   Let us write a machine language program that adds the contents of memory location 12 (00C-hex), initialized to 350 and memory location 14 (00E-hex), initialized to 96, and store the result in location 16 (010-hex), initialized to 0.

The program is given in binary instructions in Table 3.2. The first column gives the memory location in binary for each instruction and operand. The second column

TABLE 3.2   Simple Machine Language Program in Binary (Example 1)

Memory location (bytes)	Binary instruction	Description
0000 0000 0000	0001 0000 0000 1100	Load the contents of location 12 in AC
0000 0000 0010	0011 0000 0000 0000	Move contents of AC to DR
0000 0000 0100	0001 0000 0000 1110	Load the contents of location 14 into AC
0000 0000 0110	0101 0000 0000 0000	Add DR to AC
0000 0000 1000	0010 0000 0001 0000	Store contents of AC in location 16
0000 0000 1010	0000 0000 0000 0000	Stop
0000 0000 1100	0000 0001 0101 1110	Data value 350
0000 0000 1110	0000 0000 0110 0000	Data value is 96
0000 0001 0000	0000 0000 0000 0000	Data value is 0

TABLE 3.3   Simple Machine Language Program in Hexadecimal (Example 1)

Memory location (bytes)	Hex instruction
000	100C
002	3000
004	100E
006	5000
008	2010
00A	0000
00C	015E
00E	0060
010	0000

lists the contents of the memory locations. For example, the contents of location 0 is an instruction with opcode: 0001, and operand address: 0000 0000 1100. Please note that in the case of operations that do not require operand, the operand portion of the instruction is shown as zeros. The program is expected to be stored in the indicated memory locations starting at location 0 during execution. If the program will be stored at different memory locations, the addresses in some of the instructions need to be updated to reflect the new locations.

It is clear that programs written in binary code are very difficult to understand and, of course, to debug. Representing the instructions in hexadecimal will reduce the number of digits to only four per instruction. Table 3.3 shows the same program in hexadecimal.

3.2. INSTRUCTION MNEMONICS AND SYNTAX

Assembly language is the symbolic form of machine language. Assembly programs are written with short abbreviations called mnemonics. A mnemonic is an abbreviation that represents the actual machine instruction. Assembly language programming is the writing of machine instructions in mnemonic form, where each machine instruction (binary or hex value) is replaced by a mnemonic. Clearly the use of mnemonics is more meaningful than that of hex or binary values, which would make programming at this low level easier and more manageable.

An assembly program consists of a sequence of assembly statements, where statements are written one per line. Each line of an assembly program is split into the following four fields: label, operation code (opcode), operand, and comments. Figure 3.2 shows the four-column format of an assembly instruction.

Labels are used to provide symbolic names for memory addresses. A label is an identifier that can be used on a program line in order to branch to the labeled line. It can also be used to access data using symbolic names. The maximum length of a

Label (Optional)	Operation Code (Required)	Operand (Required in some instructions)	Comment (Optional)

Figure 3.2   Assembly instruction format

label differs from one assembly language to another. Some allow up to 32 characters in length, others may be restricted to six characters. Assembly languages for some processors require a colon after each label while others do not. For example, SPARC assembly requires a colon after every label, but Motorola assembly does not. The Intel assembly requires colons after code labels but not after data labels.

The operation code (opcode) field contains the symbolic abbreviation of a given operation. The operand field consists of additional information or data that the opcode requires. The operand field may be used to specify constant, label, immediate data, register, or an address. The comments field provides a space for documentation to explain what has been done for the purpose of debugging and maintenance.

For the simple processor described in the previous section, we assume that the label field, which may be empty, can be of up to six characters. There is no colon requirement after each label. Comments will be preceded by "/". The simple mnemonics of the ten binary instructions of Table 3.1 are summarized in Table 3.4.

Let us consider the following assembly instruction:

```
START    LD X    \ copy the contents of location X into AC
```

The label of the instruction LD X is START, which means that it is the memory address of this instruction. That label can be used in a program as a reference as shown in the following instruction:

```
BRA START    \ go to the statement with label START
```

TABLE 3.4   Assembly Language for the Simple Processor

Mnemonic	Operand	Meaning of instruction
STOP		Stop execution
LD	*x*	Load operand from memory (location x) into AC
ST	*x*	Store contents of AC in memory (location x)
MOVAC		Copy the contents AC to DR
MOV		Copy the contents of DR to AC
ADD		Add DR to AC
SUB		Subtract DR from AC
AND		And bitwise DR to AC
NOT		Complement contents of AC
BRA	*adr*	Jump to instruction with address *adr*
BZ	*adr*	Jump to instruction *adr* if AC = 0

The jump instruction will make the processor jump to the memory address associated with the label START, thus executing the instruction LD X immediately after the BRA instruction.

In addition to program instructions, an assembly program may also include pseudo instructions or assembler directives. Assembler directives are commands that are understood by the assembler and do not correspond to actual machine instructions. For example, the assembler can be asked to allocate memory storage. In our assembly language for the simple processor, we assume that we can use the pseudo instruction W to reserve a word (16 bits) in memory. For example, the following pseudo instruction reserves a word for the label X and initializing it to the decimal value 350:

```
X    W       350     \ reserve a word initialized to 350
```

Again, the label of the pseudo instruction W 350 is X, which means it is the memory address of this value. The following is the assembly code of the machine language program of Example 1 in the previous section.

```
     LD X              \ AC ← X
     MOVAC             \ DR ← AC
     LD Y              \ AC ← Y
     ADD               \ AC ← AC + DR
     ST Z              \ Z ← AC
     STOP
X    W       350      \ reserve a word initialized to 350
Y    W       96       \ reserve a word initialized to 96
Z    W       0        \ result stored here
```

Example 2 In this example, we will write an assembly program to perform the multiplication operation: $Z \leftarrow X*Y$, where X, Y, and Z are memory locations.

As you know, the assembly of the simple CPU does not have a multiplication operation. We will compute the product by applying the add operation multiple times. In order to add Y to itself X times, we will use N as a counter that is initialized to X and decremented by one after each addition step. The BZ instruction will be used to test for the case when N reaches 0. We will use a memory location to store N but it will need to be loaded into AC before the BZ instruction is executed. We will also use a memory location ONE to store the constant 1. Memory location Z will have the partial products and eventually the final result.

The following is the assembly program using the assembly language of our simple processor. We will assume that the values of X and Y are small enough to allow their product to be stored in a single word. For the sake of this example, let us assume that X and Y are initialized to 5 and 15, respectively.

```
            LD X                \ Load X in AC
            ST N                \ Store AC (X original value) in N
LOOP        LD N                \ AC ← N
            BZ EXIT             \ Go to EXIT if AC = 0 (N reached 0)
            LD ONE              \ AC ← 1
            MOVAC               \ DR ← AC
            LD N                \ AC ← N
            SUB                 \ subtract 1 from N
            ST N                \ store decrements N
            LD Y                \ AC ← Y
            MOVAC               \ DR ← AC
            LD Z                \ AC ← Z (partial product)
            ADD                 \ Add Y to Z
            ST Z                \ store the new value of Z
            BRA LOOP
EXIT        STOP
X           W        5          \ reserve a word initialized to 5
Y           W       15          \ reserve a word initialized to 15
Z           W        0          \ reserve a word initialized to 0
ONE         W        1          \ reserve a word initialized to 1
N           W        0          \ reserve a word initialized to 0
```

3.3. ASSEMBLER DIRECTIVES AND COMMANDS

In the previous section, we introduced the reader to assembly and machine languages. We provided several assembly code segments written using our simple machine model. In writing assembly language programs for a specific architecture, a number of practical issues need to be considered. Among these issues are the following:

- Assembler directives
- Use of symbols
- Use of synthetic operations
- Assembler syntax
- Interaction with the operating system

The use of assembler *directives*, also called *pseudo-operations*, is an important issue in writing assembly language programs. Assembler directives are commands that are understood by the assembler and do not correspond to actual machine instructions. Assembler directives affect the way the assembler performs the conversion of assembly code to machine code. For example, special assembler directives can be used to instruct the assembler to place data items such that they have proper alignment. Alignment of data in memory is required for efficient implementation of architectures. For proper alignment of data, data of *n*-bytes width must be stored at an address that is divisible by n, for example, a word that has a two-byte width has to be stored at locations having addresses divisible by two.

In assembly language programs symbols are used to represent numbers, for example, immediate data. This is done to make the code easier to read, understand, and debug. Symbols are translated to their corresponding numerical values by the assembler.

The use of synthetic operations helps assembly programmers to use instructions that are not directly supported by the architecture. These are then translated by the assembler to a set of instructions defined by the architecture. For example, assemblers can allow the use of (a synthetic) increment instruction on architectures for which an increment instruction is not defined through the use of some other instructions such as the add instruction.

Assemblers usually impose some conventions in referring to hardware components such as registers and memory locations. One such convention is the prefixing of immediate values with the special characters (#) or a register name with the character (%).

The underlying hardware in some machines cannot be accessed directly by a program. The operating system (OS) plays the role of mediating access to resources such as memory and I/O facilities. Interactions with operating systems (OS) can take place in the form of a code that causes the execution of a function that is part of the OS. These functions are called *system calls*.

3.4. ASSEMBLY AND EXECUTION OF PROGRAMS

As you know by now, a program written in assembly language needs to be translated into binary machine language before it can be executed. In this section, we will learn how to get from the point of writing an assembly program to the execution phase. Figure 3.3 shows three steps in the assembly and execution process. The assembler reads the source program in assembly language and generates the object program in binary form. The object program is passed to the linker. The linker will check the object file for calls to procedures in the link library. The linker will combine the required procedures from the link library with the object program and produce the executable program. The loader loads the executable program into memory and branches the CPU to the starting address. The program begins execution.

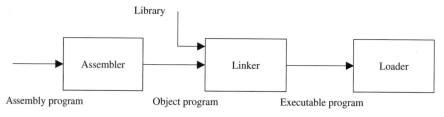

Figure 3.3   Assembly and execution process

3.4.1. Assemblers

Assemblers are programs that generate machine code instructions from a source code program written in assembly language. The assembler will replace symbolic addresses by numeric addresses, replace symbolic operation codes by machine operation codes, reserve storage for instructions and data, and translate constants into machine representation.

The functions of the assembler can be performed by scanning the assembly program and mapping its instructions to their machine code equivalent. Since symbols can be used in instructions before they are defined in later ones, a single scanning of the program might not be enough to perform the mapping. A simple assembler scans the entire assembly program twice, where each scan is called a pass. During the first pass, it generates a table that includes all symbols and their binary values. This table is called the symbol table. During the second pass, the assembler will use the symbol table and other tables to generate the object program, and output some information that will be needed by the linker.

3.4.2. Data Structures

The assembler uses at least three tables to perform its functions: symbol table, opcode table, and pseudo instruction table. The symbol table, which is generated in pass one, has an entry for every symbol in the program. Associated with each symbol are its binary value and other information. Table 3.5 shows the symbol table for the multiplication program segment of Example 2. We assume that the instruction LD X is starting at location 0 in the memory. Since each instruction takes two bytes, the value of the symbol LOOP is 4 (004 in hexadecimal). Symbol N, for example, will be stored at decimal location 40 (028 in hexadecimal). The values of the other symbols can be obtained in a similar way.

The opcode table provides information about the operation codes. Associated with each symbolic opcode in the table are its numerical value and other information about its type, its instruction length, and its operands. Table 3.6 shows the opcode

TABLE 3.5 Symbol Table for the Multiplication Segment (Example 2)

Symbol	Value (hexadecimal)	Other information
Loop	004	
EXIT	01E	
X	020	
Y	022	
Z	024	
ONE	026	
N	028	

TABLE 3.6   The Opcode Table for the Assembly of our Simple Processor

Opcode	Operand	Opcode value (binary)	Instruction length (bytes)	Instruction type
STOP	—	0000	2	Control
LD	Mem-adr	0001	2	Memory-reference
ST	Mem-adr	0010	2	Memory-reference
MOVAC	—	0011	2	Register-reference
MOV	—	0100	2	Register-reference
ADD	—	0101	2	Register-reference
SUB	—	0110	2	Register-reference
AND	—	0111	2	Register-reference
NOT	—	1000	2	Register-reference
BRA	Mem-adr	1001	2	Control
BZ	Mem-adr	1010	2	Control

table for the simple processor described in Section 3.1. As an example, we explain the information associated with the opcode LD. It has one operand, which is a memory address and its binary value is 0001. The instruction length of LD is 2 bytes and its type is memory-reference.

The entries of the pseudo instruction table are the pseudo instructions symbols. Each entry refers the assembler to a procedure that processes the pseudo instruction when encountered in the program. For example, if END is encountered, the translation process is terminated.

In order to keep track of the instruction locations, the assembler maintains a variable called instruction location counter (ILC). The ILC contains the value of memory location assigned to the instruction or operand being processed. The ILC is initialized to 0 and is incremented after processing each instruction. The ILC is incremented by the length of the instruction being processed, or the number of bytes allocated as a result of a data allocation pseudo instruction.

Figures 3.4 and 3.5 show simplified flowcharts of pass one and pass two in a two-pass assembler. Remember that the main function of pass one is to build the symbol table while pass two's main function is to generate the object code.

3.4.3. Linker and Loader

The linker is the entity that can combine object modules that may have resulted from assembling multiple assembly modules separately. The loader is the operating system utility that reads the executable into memory and start execution.

In summary, after assembly modules are translated into object modules, the functions of the linker and loader prepare the program for execution. These functions include combining object modules together, resolving addresses unknown at assembly time, allocating storage, and finally executing the program.

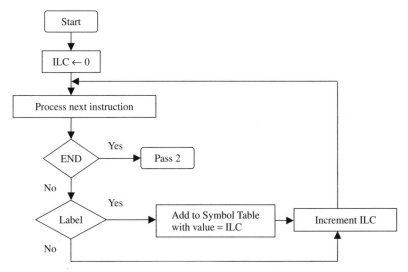

Figure 3.4 Simplified pass one in a two-pass assembler

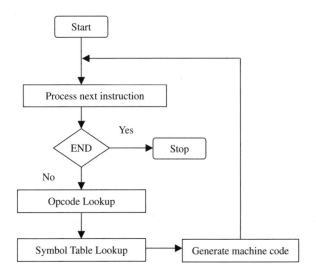

Figure 3.5 Simplified pass two in a two-pass assembler

3.5. EXAMPLE: THE *X86* FAMILY

In this section, we discuss the assembly language features and use of the *X86 family.* We present the basic organizational features of the system, the basic programming model, the addressing modes, sample of the different instruction types used, and finally examples showing how to use the assembly language of the system in programming sample real-life problems.

In the late 1970s, Intel introduced the 8086 as its first 16-bit microprocessor. This processor has a 16-bit external bus. The 8086 evolved into a series of faster and more powerful processors starting with the 80286 and ending with the *Pentium*. The latter was introduced in 1993. This Intel family of processors is usually called the *X86* family. Table 3.7 summarizes the main features of the main members of such a family.

The Intel *Pentium* processor has about three million transistors and its computational power ranges between two and five times that of its predecessor processor, the 80486. A number of new features were introduced in the *Pentium* processor, among which is the incorporation of a dual-pipelined superscalar architecture capable of processing more than one instruction per clock cycle.

The basic programming model of the 386, 486, and the *Pentium* is shown in Figure 3.6. It consists of three register groups. These are the general purpose registers, the segment registers, and the instruction pointer (program counter) and the flag register. The first set consists of general purpose registers A, B, C, D, SI (source index), DI (destination index), SP (stack pointer), and BP (base pointer). It should be noted that in naming these registers, we used *X* to indicate *eXtended*. The second set of registers consists of CS (code segment), SS (stack segment), and four data segment registers DS, ES, FS, and GS. The third set of registers consists of the instruction pointer (program counter) and the flags (status) register. The latter is shown in Figure 3.7. Among the status bits shown in Figure 3.7, the first five are identical to those bits introduced as early as in the 8085 8-bit microprocessor. The next 6–11 bits are identical to those introduced in the 8086. The flags in the bits 12–14 were introduced in the 80286 while the 16–17 bits were introduced in the 80386. The flag in bit 18 was introduced in the 80486. Table 3.8 shows the meaning of those flags.

In the *X86* family an instruction can perform an operation on one or two operands. In two-operand instructions, the second operand can be immediate data in

TABLE 3.7   Main Features of the Intel *X86* Microprocessor Family

Feature	8086	286	386	486	Pentium
Date introduced	1978	1982	1985	1991	1993
Data bus	8 bits	16 bits	32 bits	32 bits	64 bits
Address bus	20 bits	24 bits	32 bits	32 bits	32 bits
Operating speed	5,8,10 MHz	6,8,10, 12.5, 16, 20 MHz	16, 20,25, 33, 40, 50 MHz	25, 33, 50 MHz	50, 60, 66, 100 MHz
Instruction cache size	NA	NA	16 bytes	32 bytes	8 Kbytes
Data cache size	NA	NA	256 bytes	8 Kbytes	8 Kbytes
Physical memory	1 Mbytes	16 Mbytes	4 Gbytes	4 Gbytes	4 Gbytes
Data word size	16 bits	16 bits	16 bits	32 bits	32 bits

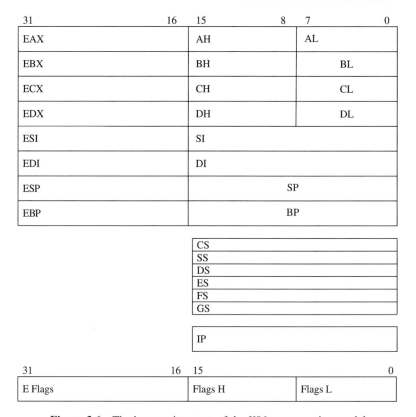

Figure 3.6 The base register sets of the *X86* programming model

Figure 3.7 The *X86* flag register

TABLE 3.8 *X86* Status Flags

Flag	Meaning	Processor	Flag	Meaning	Processor
C	Carry	All	P	Parity	All
A	Auxiliary	All	Z	Zero	All
S	Sign	All	T	Trap	All
I	Interrupt	All	D	Direction	All
O	Overflow	All	IOPL	I/O privilege level	286
NT	Nested task	286	RF	Resume	386
VM	Virtual mode	386	AC	Alignment check	486

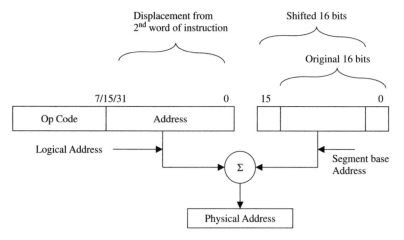

Figure 3.8 Direct addressing in the *X86* family

2's complement format. Data transfer, arithmetic and logical instructions can act on immediate data, registers, or memory locations.

In the *X86* family, direct and indirect memory addressing can be used. In direct addressing, a displacement address consisting of a 8-, 16-, or 32-bit word is used as the logical address. This logical address is added to the shifted contents of the segment register (segment base address) to give a physical memory address. Figure 3.8 illustrates the direct addressing process.

Address indirection in the *X86* family can be obtained using the content of a base pointer register (BPR), the content of an index register, or the sum of a base register and an index register. Figure 3.9 illustrates indirect addressing using the BPR.

The *X86* family of processors defines a number of instruction types. Using the naming convention introduced before, these instruction types are data movement, arithmetic and logic, and sequencing (control transfer). In addition, the *X86* family defines other instruction types such as string manipulation, bit manipulation, and high-level language support.

Data movement instructions in the *X86 family* include mainly four subtypes. These are the general-purpose, accumulator-specific, address-object, and flag instructions. A sample of these instructions is shown in Table 3.9.

Arithmetic and logic instructions in the *X86 family* include mainly five subtypes. These are addition, subtraction, multiplication, division, and logic instructions. A sample of the arithmetic instructions is shown in Table 3.10.

Logic instructions include the typical *AND, OR, NOT, XOR*, and *TEST*. The latter performs a logic compare of the source and the destination and sets the flags accordingly. In addition, the *X86* family has a set of shift and rotate instructions. A sample of these is shown in Table 3.11.

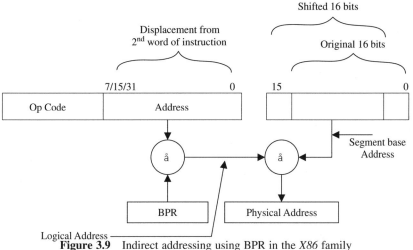

Figure 3.9   Indirect addressing using BPR in the *X86* family

Control transfer instructions in the *X86 family* include mainly four subtypes. These are conditional, iteration, interrupt, and unconditional. A sample of these instructions is shown in Table 3.12.

Processor control instructions in the *X86 family* include mainly three subtypes. These are external synchronization, flag manipulation, and general control instructions. A sample of these instructions is shown in Table 3.13.

Having introduced the basic features of the instruction set of the *X86* processor family, we now move on to present a number of programming examples to show

TABLE 3.9   Sample of the *X86* Data Movement Instructions

Mnemonic	Operation	Subtype
MOV	Move source to destination	General purpose
POP	Pop source from stack	General purpose
POPA	Pop all	General purpose
PUSH	Push source onto stack	General purpose
PUSHA	Push all	General purpose
XCHG	Exchange source with destination	General purpose
IN	Input to accumulator	Accumulator
OUT	Output from accumulator	Accumulator
XLAT	Table lookup to translate byte	Accumulator
LEA	Load effective address in register	Address-object
LMSW	Load machine status word	Address-object
SMSW	Store machine status word	Address-object
POPF	Pop flags off stack	Flag
PUSHF	Push flags onto stack	Flag

TABLE 3.10   Sample of the *X86* Arithmetic Instructions

Mnemonic	Operation	Subtype
ADD	Add source to destination	Addition
ADC	Add source to destination with carry	Addition
INC	Increment operand by 1	Addition
SUB	Subtract source from destination	Subtraction
SBB	Subtract source from destination with borrow	Subtraction
DEC	Decrement operand by 1	Subtraction
MUL	Unsigned multiply source by destination	Multiply
IMUL	Signed multiply source by destination	Multiply
DIV	Unsigned division accumulator by source	Division
IDIV	Signed division accumulator by source	Division

TABLE 3.11   Sample of the *X86* Shift and Rotate Instructions

Mnemonic	Operation
ROR	Rotate right
ROL	Rotate left
RCL	Rotate left through carry
RCR	Rotate right through carry
SAR	Arithmetic shift right
SAL	Arithmetic shift left
SHR	Logic shift right
SHL	Logic shift left

how the instruction set can be used. The examples presented are the same as those presented at the end of Chapter 2.

Example 3   Adding 100 numbers stored at consecutive memory locations starting at location 1000, the results should be stored in memory location 2000. *LIST* is

TABLE 3.12   Sample of the *X86* Control Transfer Instructions

Mnemonic	Operation	Subtype
SET	Set byte to true or false based on condition	Conditional
JS	Jump if sign	Conditional
LOOP	Loop if CX does not equal zero	Iteration
LOOPE	Loop if CX does not equal zero & ZF = 1	Iteration
INT	Interrupt	Interrupt
IRET	Interrupt return	Interrupt
JMP	Jump unconditional	Unconditional
RET	Return from procedure	Unconditional

TABLE 3.13   Sample of the *X86* Processor Control Instructions

Mnemonic	Operation	Subtype
HLT	Halt	External sync
LOCK	Lock the bus	External sync
CLC	Clear carry flag	Flag
CLI	Clear interrupt flag	Flag
STI	Set interrupt flag	Flag
INVD	Invalidate data cache	General control

defined as an array of *N* elements each of size byte. *FLAG* is a memory variable used to indicate whether the list has been sorted or not. The register *CX* is used as a counter with the *Loop* instruction. The *Loop* instruction decrements the *CX* register and branch if the result is not zero. The addressing mode used to access the array *List* [*BX* + 1] is called based addressing mode. It should be noted that since we are using BX and BX + 1 the *CX* counter is loaded with the value 999 in order not to exceed the list.

```
MOV CX, 1000 − 1      ; Counter = CX ← (1000 − 1)
MOV BX, Offset LIST   ; BX ← pointer to LIST
CALL SORT
.....
```

SORT PROC NEAR

```
Again:  MOV FLAG, 0          ; FLAG ← 0
Next:   MOV AL, [BX]
        CMP AL, [BX + 1]     ; Compare current and next values
        JLE Skip             ; Branch if current < next values
        XCHG AL, [BX + 1]    ; If not, Swap the contents of the
        MOV [BX + 1], AL     ; current location with the next one
        MOV FLAG, 1          ; Indicate the swap
Skip:   INC BX               ; BX ← BX + 1
        LOOP Next            ; Go to next value
        CMP FLAG, 1          ; Was there any swap
        JE Again             ; If yes Repeat process
        RET
```

SORT ENDP

Example 4   Here we implement the *SEARCH* algorithm in the 8086 instruction set. *LIST* is defined as an array of *N* elements each of size word. *FLAG* is a memory variable used to indicate whether the list has been sorted or not. The register *CX* is used as a counter with the loop instruction. The Loop instruction decrements the *CX* register and branch if the result is not zero. The addressing mode used to access the array List [BX + 1] is called based addressing mode.

```
MOV CX, 1000       ; Counter = CX ← 1000
MOV  BX,  Offset   ; BX ← pointer to LIST
LIST
MOV SI, 0          ; SI used as an index
MOV AX, VAL        ; AX ← VAL
CALL SEARCH

                   ; Test FLAG to check whether value found
.....
```

SEARCH PROC NEAR

```
              MOV FLAG, 0        ; FLAG ← 0
Next:         CMP AX, [BX + SI]  ; Compare current value to VAL
              JE Found           ; Branch if equal
              ADD SI, 2          ; SI ← SI + 2, next value
              LOOP Next          ; Go to next value
              JMP Not_Found
Found:        MOV FLAG, 1        ; Indicate value found
              MOV POSITION, SI   ; Return index of value in List
Not_Found:    RET
```

SEARCH ENDP

Example 5   This is the same as Example 4 but using the stack features of the *X86*.

```
PUSH DS                 ; See Table 3.9
MOV CX, 1000            ; Counter = CX ← 1000
MOV BX, OFFSET LIST     ; Point to beginning of LIST
PUSH BX
PUSH VAL                ; VAL is a word variable
CALL SEARCH

                        ; Test FLAG to check whether value found
                        ; If found get index from SI register
                          using
                        POP SI
.....
```

SEARCH PROC NEAR

```
POP TEMP       ; Save IP
POP AX         ; AX ← VAL. Value to search for
POP SI         ; SI ← OFFSET LIST and let BX = SI
```

```
          POP ES              ;Make ES = DS (See Table)
          CLD                 ;Set auto-increment mode
          REPNE SCASW         ;Scan LIST for value in AX if not
                               found; increment SI by 2,
                               decrement CX and if; not zero
                               scan next location in LIST.
                              ;If occurrence found Zero flag
                               is set
          JNZ Not_Found       ;If value not branch to
                               Not_Found?
          MOV FLAG, 1         ;Yes
          SUB SI, BX
          PUSH SI             ;Save position
Not_Found: PUSH TEMP          ;Restore IP
          RET
```

SEARCH ENDP

It should be noted in the above example that when a call to a procedure is initiated, the *IP* register is the last value to be pushed on top of the stack. Therefore, care should be made to avoid altering the value of the *IP* register. The top of the stack is thus saved to a temporary variable *TEMP* at procedure entry and restored before exit.

3.6. SUMMARY

A machine language is a collection of the machine instructions represented in 0s and 1s. Assembly language provides easier to use symbolic representation, in which an alphanumeric equivalent to machine language is used. There is a one-to-one correspondence between assembly language statements and machine instructions. An assembler is a program that accepts a symbolic language program (source program) and produces its machine language equivalent (target program). Although assembly language programming is difficult compared to programming in high-level languages, it is still important to learn assembly. In some applications, small portions of a program that are heavily used may need to be written in assembly language. Programming in assembly can result in machine code that is smaller and faster than that generated by a compiler of a high-level language. Assembly programmers have access to all the hardware features of the target machine that might not be accessible to high-level language programmers. In addition, learning assembly languages can be of great help in understanding the low level details of computer organization and architecture. In this chapter we provided a general overview of assembly language and its programming. The programmer view of the *X86 Intel microprocessor* family of processors was also introduced as a real-world example. Examples were then presented showing how to use the *X86* instruction set in writing sample programs similar to those presented in Chapter 2.

EXERCISES

1. What is the difference between each of the following pairs?
   - Compilers and assemblers
   - Source code and target code
   - Mnemonics and hexadecimal representation
   - Pseudo instructions and instructions
   - Labels and addresses
   - Symbol table and opcode table
   - Program counter (PC) and instruction location counter (ILC)

2. Using the assembly language of the simple processor in Section 3.1, write assembly code segments to do the following operation:
   - Swap two numbers
   - Logical OR
   - Negation

3. Add input/output instructions to the instruction set of the simple processor in Section 3.1 and write an assembly program to find the Fibonacci sequence.

4. Obtain the machine language code of the multiplication assembly program given in Section 3.2.

5. With the great advances in high-level languages and compilers, some people argue that assembly language is not important anymore. Give some arguments for and against this view.

6. Write a program segment using the instruction of the *X86 family* to compute $\sum_{i=1}^{200} X_i Y_i$, where X_i and Y_i are signed 8-bit numbers. Assume that no overflow will occur.

7. Write a subroutine using the *X86* instructions that can be called by a main program in a different code segment. The subroutine will multiply a signed 16-bit number in CX by a signed 8-bit number in AL. The main program will call this subroutine, store the result in two consecutive memory words, and stop. Assume that SI and DI contain the signed 8-bit and 16-bit numbers, respectively.

8. Write a program using the *X86* instructions to compare a source string of 100 words pointed to by an offset of 2000H in DS with a destination string pointed to by an offset 4000H in DS.

9. Write a program using the *X86* instructions to generate the first 10 numbers of the Fibonacci series, that is, to generate the series 1, 1, 2, 3, 5, 8, 13, 21, 34.

10. Write a program using the *X86* instructions to convert a word of text from upper case to lower case. Assume that the word consists of ASCII characters stored in successive memory locations starting at location *START* and ending at location *FINISH*.

REFERENCES AND FURTHER READING

C. M. Gilmore, *Microprocessors: Principles and Applications*, 2nd ed., McGraw-Hill, New York, 1996.

V. C. Hamacher, Z. G. Vranesic and S. G. Zaky, *Computer Organization*, 5th ed., McGraw-Hill, New York, 2002.

J. P. Hayes, *Computer Architecture and Organization*, McGraw-Hill, New York, 1998.

V. Heuring, and H. Jordan, *Computer Systems Design and Architecture*, Addison Wesley, NJ, 1997.

K. R. Irvine, *Assembly Language for Intel-Based Computers*, 4th ed., Prentice Hall, NJ, 2003.

A. D. Patterson and J. L. Hennessy, *Computer Organization & Design; The Hardware/ Software Interface*, Morgan Kaufmann, San Mafeo, 1994.

W. Stallings, *Computer Organization and Architectures: Designing for Performance*, 4th ed., Prentice-Hall, NJ, U.S.A, 1996.

A. Tanenbaum, *Structured Computer Organization*, 4th ed., Prentice Hall, Paramus, NJ, U.S.A, 1999.

J. Uffenbeck, *The 80 × 86 Family, Design, Programming, and Interfacing*, 3rd ed., Prentice Hall, Essex, UK, 2002.

B. Wilkinson, *Computer Architecture: Design and Performance*, 2nd ed., Prentice-Hall, Hertfordshire, UK, 1996.

CHAPTER 4

Computer Arithmetic

This chapter is dedicated to a discussion on computer arithmetic. Our goal is to introduce the reader to the fundamental issues related to the arithmetic operations and circuits used to support computation in computers. Our coverage starts with an introduction to number systems. In particular, we introduce issues such as number representations and base conversion. This is followed by a discussion on integer arithmetic. In this regard, we introduce a number of algorithms together with hardware schemes that are used in performing integer addition, subtraction, multiplication, and division. We end this chapter with a discussion on floating-point arithmetic. In particular, we introduce issues such as floating-point representation, floating-point operations, and floating-point hardware schemes. The IEEE floating-point standard is the last topic discussed in the chapter.

4.1. NUMBER SYSTEMS

A number system uses a specific radix (base). Radices that are power of 2 are widely used in digital systems. These radices include binary (base 2), quaternary (base 4), octagonal (base 8), and hexagonal (base 16). The base 2 *binary system* is dominant in computer systems.

An unsigned integer number A can be represented using n digits in base b: $A = (a_{n-1}a_{n-2}\ldots a_2a_1a_0)_b$. In this representation (called *positional representation*) each digit a_i is given by $0 \leq a_i \leq (b-1)$. Using positional representation, the decimal value of the unsigned integer number A is given by $A = \sum_{i=0}^{n-1} a_i \times b^i$. Consider, for example, the positional representation of the decimal number $A = 106$. Using 8 digits in base 2, A is represented as $A = 0 \times 2^7 + 1 \times 2^6 + 1 \times 2^5 + 0 \times 2^4 + 1 \times 2^3 + 0 \times 2^2 + 1 \times 2^1 + 0 \times 2^0$.

Using n digits, the largest value for an unsigned number A is given by $A_{max} = b^n - 1$. For example, the largest unsigned number that can be obtained using 4 digits in base 2 is $2^4 - 1 = 15$. In this case, decimal numbers ranging from 0 to 15 (corresponding to binary 0000 to 1111) can be represented. Similarly, the largest unsigned number that can be obtained using 4 digits in base 4 is

Fundamentals of Computer Organization and Architecture, by M. Abd-El-Barr and H. El-Rewini
ISBN 0-471-46741-3 Copyright © 2005 John Wiley & Sons, Inc.

$4^4 - 1 = 255$. In this case, decimal numbers ranging from 0 to 255 (corresponding to 0000 to 3333) can be represented.

Consider the use of n digits to represent a real number X in radix b such that the most significant k digits represent the integral part while the least significant m digits represents the fraction part. The value of X is given by

$$X = \sum_{i=-m}^{k-1} x_i \times b^i = x_{k-1}b^{k-1} + x_{k-2}b^{k-2} + \cdots + x_1 b^1$$

$$+ x_0 b^0 + x_{-1} b^{-1} + \cdots + x_{-m} b^{-m}$$

Consider, for example, the representation of the real number $X = 25.375$. This number can be represented in binary using $k = 5$ and $m = 3$ as follows.

$$X = \sum_{i=-3}^{4} x_i \times b^i = x_4 \times 2^4 + x_3 \times 2^3 + x_2 \times 2^2 + x_1 \times 2^1$$

$$+ x_0 \times 2^0 + x_{-1} \times 2^{-1} + x_{-2} \times 2^{-2} + x_{-3} 2^{-3}$$

with $x_4 = 1$, $x_3 = 1$, $x_2 = 0$, $x_1 = 0$, $x_0 = 1$, $x_{-1} = 0$, $x_{-2} = 1$, and $x_{-3} = 1$.

It is often necessary to convert the representation of a number from a given base to another, for example, from base 2 to base 10. This can be achieved using a number of methods (algorithms). An important tool in some of these algorithms is the division algorithm. The basis of the division algorithm is that of representing an integer a in terms of another integer c using a base b. The basic relation used is $a = c \times q + r$, where q is the quotient and r is the remainder, $0 \leq r \leq b - 1$ and $q = \lfloor a/c \rfloor$. Radix conversion is discussed below.

4.1.1. Radix Conversion Algorithm

A radix conversion algorithm is used to convert a number representation in a given radix, r_1, into another representation in a different radix, r_2. Consider the conversion of the integral part of a number X, X_{int}. The integral part X_{int} can be expressed as

$$X_{int} = \big\{ [\cdots (x_{k-1}r_2 + x_{k-2})r_2 + \cdots + x_2)r_2 + x_1] \big\} r_2 + x_0.$$

Dividing X_{int} by r_2 will result in a quotient $X_q = \{ [\cdots (x_{k-1}r_2 + x_{k-2})r_2 + \cdots + x_2)r_2 + x_1] \}$ and a remainder $X_{rem} = x_0$. Repeating the division process on the quotient and retaining the remainders as the required digits until a zero quotient is obtained will result in the required representation of X_{int} in the new radix r_2.

Using a similar argument, it is possible to show that a repeated multiplication of the fractional part of X (X_f) by r_2 retaining the obtained integers as the required digits, will result in the required representation of the fractional part in the new radix, r_2. It should, however, be noted that unlike the integral part conversion, the fractional part conversion may not terminate after a finite number of repeated multiplications. Therefore, the process may have to be terminated after a number of steps, thus leading to some acceptable approximation.

Example   Consider the conversion of the decimal number 67.575 into binary. Here $r_1 = 10$, $r_2 = 2$, $X_{int} = 67$, and $X_f = 0.575$. For the integral part X_{int}, a repeated division by 2 will result in the following quotients and remainders:

Quotient	33	16	8	4	2	1	0
Remainder	1	1	0	0	0	0	1

Therefore the integral part in radix $r_2 = 2$ is $X_{int} = (1000011)$. A similar method can be used to obtain the fractional part (through repeated multiplication):

Fractional part	0.150	0.300	0.600	0.200	0.400	0.800	0.600	0.200	...
Carry over bit	1	0	0	1	0	0	1	1	...

The fractional part is $X_f = (.10010011...)$. Therefore, the resultant representation of the number 67.575 in binary is given by $(1000011.10010011...)$.

4.1.2. Negative Integer Representation

There exist a number of methods for representation of negative integers. These include the *sign-magnitude*, *radix complement*, and *diminished radix complement*. These are briefly explained below.

4.1.3. Sign-Magnitude

According to this representation, the most significant bit (of the n bits used to represent the number) is used to represent the sign of the number such that a "1" in the most significant bit position indicates a negative number while a "0" in the most significant bit position indicates a positive number. The remaining $(n - 1)$ bits are used to represent the magnitude of the number. For example, the negative number (-18) is represented using 6 bits, base 2 in the sign-magnitude format, as follows (110010), while a $(+18)$ is represented as (010010). Although simple, the sign-magnitude representation is complicated when performing arithmetic operations. In particular, the sign bit has to be dealt with separately from the magnitude bits. Consider, for example, the addition of the two numbers $+18$ (010010) and -19 (110011) using the sign-magnitude representation. Since the two numbers carry different signs, then the result should carry the sign of the larger number in magnitude, in this case the (-19). The remaining 5-bit numbers are subtracted $(10011 - 10010)$ to produce (00001), that is, (-1).

4.1.4. Radix Complement

According to this system, a positive number is represented the same way as in the sign-magnitude. However, a negative number is represented using the b's complement (for base b numbers). Consider, for example, the representation of the number (-19) using 2's complement. In this case, the number 19 is first represented as (010011). Then each digit is complemented, hence the name radix complement to produce (101100). Finally a "1" is added at the least significant bit position to result in (101101). Now, consider the 2's complement representation of the number $(+18)$. Since the number is positive, then it is represented as (010010), the same as in the sign-magnitude case. Now, consider the addition of these two numbers. In this case, we add the corresponding bits without giving special treatment to the sign bit. The results of adding the two numbers produces (111111). This is the 2's complement representation of a (-1), as expected. The main advantage of the 2's complement representation is that no special treatment is needed for the sign of the numbers. Another characteristic of the 2's complement is the fact that a carry coming out of the most significant bit while performing arithmetic operations is ignored without affecting the correctness of the result. Consider, for example, adding -19 (101101) and $+26$ (011010). The result will be $(1)(000111)$, which is correct $(+7)$ if the carry bit is ignored.

4.1.5. Diminished Radix Complement

This representation is similar to the radix complement except for the fact that no "1" is added to the least significant bit after complementing the digits of the number, as is done in the radix complement. According to this number system representation, a (-19) is represented as (101100), while a $(+18)$ is represented as (010010). If we add these two numbers we obtain (111110), the 1's complement of a (-1). The main disadvantage of the diminished radix representation is the need for a correction factor whenever a carry is obtained from the most significant bit while performing arithmetic operations. Consider, for example, adding -3 (111100) to $+18$ (010010)

**TABLE 4.1   The 2's and the 1's Complement
Representation of an 8-Bit Number**

Number	Representation	Example
2's Complement		
$x = 0$	0	0 (00000000)
$0 < x < 256$	x	77 (01001101)
$-128 \leq x < 0$	$256 - |x|$	-56 (11001000)
1's Complement		
$x = 0$	0 or 255	(11111111)
$0 < x < 256$	x	77 (01001101)
$-127 \leq x < 0$	$255 - |x|$	-56 (11000111)

to obtain (1)(001110). If the carry bit is added to the least significant bit of the result, we obtain (001111), that is, (+15), which is a correct result.

Table 4.1 shows a comparison between the 2's complement and the 1's complement in the representation of an 8-bit number, x.

4.2. INTEGER ARITHMETIC

In this section, we introduce a number of techniques used to perform integer arithmetic using the radix complement representation of numbers. Our discussion will focus on the base "2" binary representation.

4.2.1. Two's Complement (2's) Representation

In order to represent a number in 2's complement, we perform the following two steps.

1. Perform the Boolean complement of each bit (including the sign bit);
2. Add 1 to the least significant bit (treating the number as an unsigned binary integer), that is, $-A = \overline{A} + 1$

Example   Consider the representation of (-22) using 2's complement.

$$22 = 00010110$$
$$\Downarrow$$
$$11101001 \ (1\text{'s complement})$$
$$+ \qquad 1$$

$$\overline{\qquad\qquad\qquad\qquad}$$

$$11101010 \ (-22)$$

4.2.2. Two's Complement Arithmetic

Addition   Addition of two n-bit numbers in 2's complement can be performed using an n-bit adder. Any carry-out bit can be ignored without affecting the correctness of the results, as long as the results of the addition is in the range -2^{n-1} to $+2^{n-1} - 1$.

Example   Consider the addition of the two 2's complement numbers (-7) and $(+4)$. This addition can be carried out as $(-7) + (+4) = -3$, that is, $1001 + (0100) = 1101$, a (-3) in 2's complement.

The condition that the result should be in the range -2^{n-1} to $+2^{n-1} - 1$ is important because a result outside this range will lead to an overflow and hence a wrong result. In simple terms, an overflow will occur if the result produced by a given operation is outside the range of the representable numbers. Consider the following two examples.

Example   Consider adding the two 2's complement numbers $(+7)$ and $(+6)$. The addition can be done as $(+7) + (+6) = +13$, that is, $0111 + (0110) = 1101$, a wrong result. This is because the result exceeds the largest value $(+7)$.

Example   Consider adding the two 2's complement numbers (-7) and (-4). The addition can be done as $(-7) + (-4) = -11$, that is, $1001 + (1100) = 0101$, a wrong result. This is because the result is less than the smallest value (-8). Notice that the original numbers are negative while the result is positive.

From these two examples, we can make the following observation: when two numbers (both positive or both negative) are added, then overflow can be detected if and only if the result has an opposite sign to the added numbers.

Subtraction   In 2's complement, subtraction can be performed in the same way addition is performed. For example, to perform $B - A = B + \bar{A} + 1$, that is, subtracting A from B is the same as addition to the complement of A to B.

Example   Consider the subtraction $2 - 7 = -5$. This can be performed as $2 + \bar{7} + 1 = 0010 + 1000 + 0001 = 1011\ (-5)$.

It should be noted that our earlier observation about the occurrence of overflow in the context of addition applies in the case of subtraction as well. This is because subtraction is after all addition to the complement. Consider the following illustrative example.

Example   Consider the subtraction $7 - (-7) = 14$. This can be performed as $7 + \bar{7} + 1 = 0111 + 1000 + 0001 = (1)\ 0000$, a wrong answer (result > 7).

Hardware Structures for Addition and Subtraction of Signed Numbers   The addition of two n-bit numbers A and B requires a basic hardware circuit that accepts three inputs, that is, a_i, b_i, and c_{i-1}. These three bits represent respectively the two current bits of the numbers A and B (at position i) and the carry bit from the previous bit position (at position $i - 1$). The circuit should produce two outputs, that is, s_i and c_i representing respectively the sum and the carry, according to the following truth-table.

a_i	0	0	0	0	1	1	1	1
b_i	0	0	1	1	0	0	1	1
c_{i-1}	0	1	0	1	0	1	0	1
s_i	0	1	1	0	1	0	0	1
c_i	0	0	0	1	0	1	1	1

The output logic functions are given by $s_i = a_i \oplus b_i \oplus c_{i-1}$ and $c_i = a_i b_i + a_i c_{i-1} + b_i c_{i-1}$. The circuit used to implement these two functions is called a *full-adder* (FA) and is shown in Figure 4.1.

Addition of two n-bit numbers A and B can be carried out using n consecutive FAs in an arrangement known as a *carry-ripple through adder (CRT)*, see Figure 4.2.

The n-bit CRT adder shown in Figure 4.2 can be used to add 2's complement numbers A and B in which the b_{n-1} and a_{n-1} represent the sign bits. The same circuit can be used to perform subtraction using the relation $B - A = B + \bar{A} + 1$. Figure 4.3 shows the structure of a binary addition/subtraction logic network.

In this figure, the two inputs A and B represent the arguments to be added/subtracted. The control input determines whether an add or a subtract operation is to be performed such that if the control input is 0 then an add operation is performed while if the control input is 1 then a subtract operation is performed. A simple circuit that can implement the Add/Sub block in Figure 4.3 is shown in Figure 4.4 for the case of 4-bit inputs.

One of the main drawbacks of the CRT circuit is the expected long delay between the time the inputs are presented to the circuit until the final output is obtained. This is because of the dependence of each stage on the carry output produced by the previous stage. This chain of dependence makes the CRT adder's delay $O(n)$, where n is the number of stages in the adder. In order to speed up the addition process, it is necessary to introduce addition circuits in which the chain of dependence among the adder stages must be broken. A number of fast addition circuits exist in the literature. Among these the *carry-look-ahead* (CLA) adder is well known. The CLA adder is introduced below.

Consider the CRT adder circuit. The two logic functions realized are $s_i = a_i \oplus b_i \oplus c_{i-1}$ and $c_i = a_i b_i + a_i c_{i-1} + b_i c_{i-1}$. These two functions can be rewritten in terms of two new subfunctions, the *carry generate*, $G_i = a_i b_i$ and the *carry propagate*, $P_i = a_i \oplus b_i$. Using these two new subfunctions, we can rewrite the logic equation for the carry output of any stage as $c_i = G_i + P_i c_{i-1}$. Now, we can write

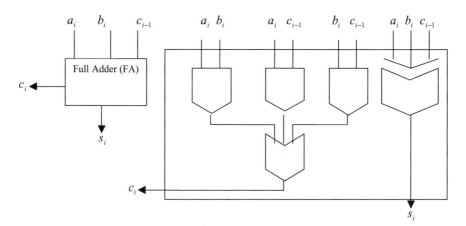

Figure 4.1 The full-adder (FA) circuit

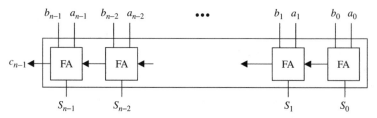

Figure 4.2 *n*-Bit carry-ripple through (CRT) adder

the series of carry outputs from the different stages as follows.

$$c_0 = G_0 + P_0 c_{-1}$$
$$c_1 = G_1 + P_1 c_0 = G_1 + P_1(G_0 + P_0 c_{-1}) = G_1 + G_0 P_1 + P_0 P_1 c_{-1}$$
$$c_2 = G_2 + P_2 c_1 = G_2 + P_2(G_1 + G_0 P_1 + P_0 P_1 c_{-1})$$
$$= G_2 + G_0 P_1 P_2 + G_1 P_2 + P_0 P_1 P_2 c_{-1}$$
$$c_3 = G_3 + P_3 c_2 = G_3 + P_3(G_2 + G_1 P_2 + G_0 P_1 P_2 + P_0 P_1 P_2 c_{-1})$$
$$= G_3 + G_2 P_3 + G_1 P_2 P_3 + G_0 P_1 P_2 P_3 + P_0 P_1 P_2 P_3 c_{-1}$$
$$\vdots$$

The sequence of carry outputs shows total independence among the different carries (broken carry chain). Figure 4.5 shows the overall architecture of a 4-bit CLA adder. There are basically three blocks in a CLA. The first one is used to generate the G_is and the P_is, while the second is used to create all the carry output. The third block is used to generate all the sum outputs. Regardless of the number of bits in the CLA, the delay through the first block is equivalent to a one gate delay, the delay through the second block is equivalent to a two gate delay and the delay through the third block is equivalent to a one gate delay. In Figure 4.5, we show the generation of some carry and sum outputs. The reader is encouraged to complete the design (see the Chapter Exercises).

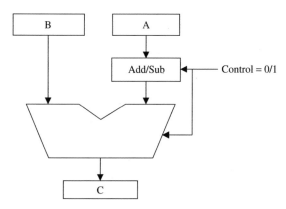

Figure 4.3 Addition/subtraction logic network

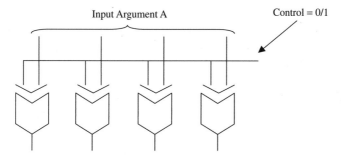

Figure 4.4 The Add/Sub circuit

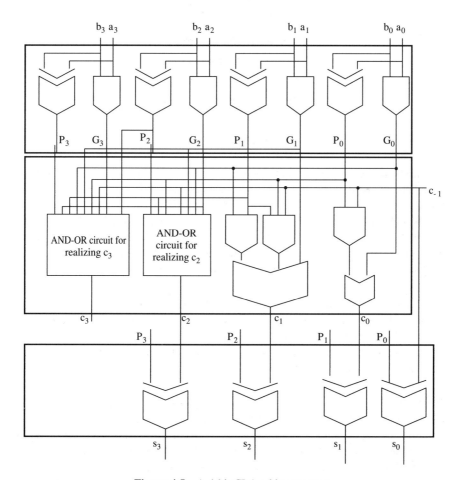

Figure 4.5 A 4-bit CLA adder structure

Multiplication In discussing multiplication, we shall assume that the two input arguments are the multiplier Q given by $Q = q_{n-1}q_{n-2} \cdots q_1 q_0$ and the multiplicand M given by $M = m_{n-1}m_{m-2} \cdots m_1 m_0$. A number of methods exist for performing multiplication. Some of these methods are discussed below.

The Paper and Pencil Method (for Unsigned Numbers) This is the simplest method for performing multiplication of two unsigned numbers. The method is illustrated through the example shown below.

Example Consider the multiplication of the two unsigned numbers 14 and 10. The process is shown below using the binary representation of the two numbers.

$$1110 \ (14) \ \text{Multiplicand(M)}$$
$$1010 \ (10) \ \text{Multiplier(Q)}$$

0000	(Partial Product)
1110	(Partial Product)
0000	(Partial Product)
1110	(Partial Product)

$$\overline{\overline{}}$$
$$10001100 \ (140) \ \text{Final Product(P)}$$

The above multiplication can be performed using an array of cells each consisting of an FA and an AND. Each cell computes a given partial product. Figure 4.6 shows the basic cell and an example array for a 4×4 multiplier array.

What characterizes this method is the need for adding n partial products regardless of the values of the multiplier bits. It should be noted that if a given bit of the multiplier is 0, then there should be no need for computing the corresponding partial product. The following method makes use of this observation.

The Add-Shift Method In this case, multiplication is performed as a series of (n) conditional addition and shift operations such that if the given bit of the multiplier is 0 then only a shift operation is performed, while if the given bit of the multiplier is 1 then addition of the partial products and a shift operation are performed. The following example illustrates this method.

Example Consider multiplication of the two unsigned numbers 11 and 13. The process is shown below in a tabular form. In this process, A is a 4-bit register and is initialized to 0s and C is the carry bit from the most significant bit position. The process is repeated $n = 4$ times (the number of bits in the multiplier Q). If the bit of the multiplier is "1", then $A \leftarrow A + M$ and the concatenation of AQ is shifted one bit position to the right. If, on the other hand, the bit is "0", then only a shift operation is performed on AQ. The structure required to perform such an

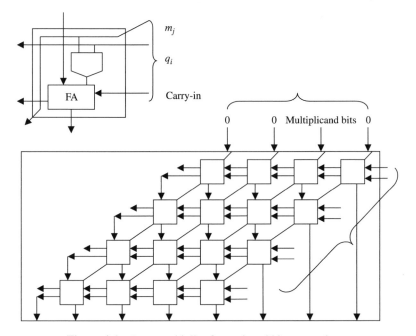

Figure 4.6   Array multiplier for unsigned binary numbers

M	C	A	Q		
1011	0	0000	1101	Initial values	
1011	0	1011	1101	Add	First cycle
1011	0	0101	1110	Shift	
1011	0	0010	1111	Shift	Second cycle
1011	0	1101	1111	Add	Third cycle
1011	0	0110	1111	Shift	
1011	1	0001	1111	Add	Fourth cycle
1011	0	1000	1111	Shift	

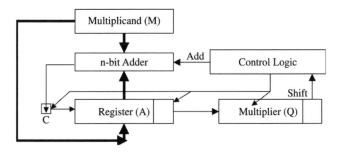

Figure 4.7   Hardware structure for add-shift multiplication

operation is shown in Figure 4.7. In this figure, the control logic is used to determine the operation to be performed depending on the least significant bit in Q. An n-bit adder is used to add the contents of registers A and M.

In order to speed up the multiplication operation, a number of other techniques can be used. These techniques are based on the observation that the larger the number of consecutive zeros and ones, the fewer partial products that have to be generated. A group of consecutive zeros in the multiplier requires no generation of new partial product. A group of k consecutive ones in the multiplier requires the generation of fewer than k new partial products. One technique that makes use of the above observation is the Booth's algorithm. We discuss below the 2-bit Booth's algorithm.

The Booth's Algorithm   In this technique, two bits of the multiplier, $Q(i)Q(i-1)$, $(0 \leq i \leq n-1)$, are inspected at a time. The action taken depends on the binary values of the two bits, such that if the two values are respectively 01, then $A \leftarrow A + M$; if the two values are 10, then $A \leftarrow A - M$. No action is needed if the values are 00 or 11. In all four cases, an arithmetic shift right operation on the concatenation of AQ is performed. The whole process is repeated n times (n is the number of bits in the multiplier). The Booth's algorithm requires the inclusion of a bit $Q(-1) = 0$ as the least significant bit in the multiplier Q at the beginning of the multiplication process. The Booth's algorithm is illustrated in Figure 4.8.

The following examples show how to apply the steps of the Booth's algorithm.

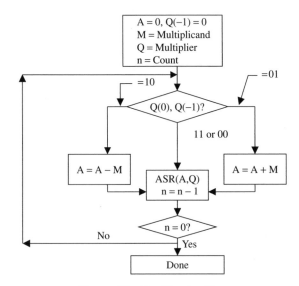

Figure 4.8   Booth's algorithm

Example   Consider the multiplication of the two positive numbers $M = 0111$ (7) and $Q = 0011$ (3) and assuming that $n = 4$. The steps needed are tabulated below.

M	A	Q	Q(−1)		
0111	0000	0011	0	Initial value	
0111	1001	0011	0	$A = A - M$	
0111	1100	1001	1	ASR	End cycle #1
0111	1110	0100	1	ASR	End cycle #2
0111	0101	0100	1	$A = A + M$	
0111	0010	1010	0	ASR	End cycle #3
0111	0001	0101	1	ASR	End cycle #4

$$+21 \text{ (correct result)}$$

Example   Consider the multiplication of the two numbers $M = 0111$ (7) and $Q = 1101$ (−3) and assuming that $n = 4$. The steps needed are tabulated below.

M	A	Q	Q(−1)		
0111	0000	1101	0	Initial value	
0111	1001	1101	0	$A = A - M$	
0111	1100	1110	1	ASR	End cycle #1
0111	0011	1110	1	$A = A + M$	
0111	0001	1111	0	ASR	End cycle #2
0111	1010	1111	0	$A = A - M$	
0111	1101	0111	1	ASR	End cycle #3
0111	1110	1011	1	ASR	End cycle #4

$$-21 \text{ (correct result)}$$

The hardware structure shown in Figure 4.9 can be used to perform the operations required by the Booth's algorithm. It consists of an ALU that can perform the add/sub operation depending on the two bits $Q(0)Q(-1)$. A control circuitry is also required to perform the ASR (AQ) and to issue the appropriate signals needed to control the number of cycles.

The main drawbacks of the Booth's algorithm are the variability in the number of add/sub operations and the inefficiency of the algorithm when the bit pattern in Q

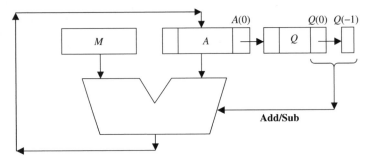

Figure 4.9 Hardware structure implementing Booth's algorithm

becomes a repeated pair of a 0 (1) followed by a 1(0). This last situation can be improved if three rather than two bits are inspected at a time.

Division Among the four basic arithmetic operations, division is considered the most complex and most time consuming. In its simplest form, an integer division operation takes two arguments, the dividend X and the divisor D. It produces two outputs, the quotient Q and the remainder R. The four quantities satisfy the relation $X = Q \times D + R$ where $R < D$. A number of complications arise when dealing with division. The most obvious among these is the case $D = 0$. Another subtle difficulty is the requirement that the resulting quotient should not exceed the capacity of the register holding it. This can be satisfied if $Q < 2^{n-1}$, where n is the number of bits in the register holding the quotient. This implies that the relation $X < 2^{n-1}D$ must also be satisfied. Failure to satisfy any of the above conditions will lead to an *overflow* condition.

We will start by showing the division algorithm assuming that all values involved, that is, divided, divisor, quotient, and remainder are interpreted as fractions. The process is also valid for integer values as will be shown later.

In order to obtain a positive fractional quotient $Q = 0q_1q_2\cdots q_{n-1}$, the division operation is performed as a sequence of repeated subtractions and shifts. In each step, the remainder should be compared with the divisor D. If the remainder is larger, then the quotient bit is set to "1"; otherwise the quotient bit is set to "0". This can be represented by the following equation $r_i = 2r_{i-1} - q_i \times D$ where r_i and r_{i-1} are the current and the previous remainder, respectively, with $r_0 = X$ and $i = 1, 2, \ldots, (n-1)$.

Example Consider the division of a dividend $X = 0.5 = (0.100000)$ and a divisor $D = 0.75 = (0.1100)$. The process is illustrated in the following table.

$r_0 = X$			0	•	1	0	0	0	0	0	Initial values
$2r_0$		0	1	•	0	0	0	0	0		Set $q_1 = 1$
$-D$	+	1	1	•	0	1	0				
$r_1 = 2r_0 - D$		0	0	•	0	1	0	0	0		
$2r_1$		0	0	•	1	0	0	0			Set $q_2 = 0$

$r_2 = 2r_1$		0	0	•	1	0	0	0	
$2r_2$		0	1	•	0	0	0		Set $q_3 = 1$
$-D$	+	1	1	•	0	1	0		
$r_3 = 2r_2 - D$		0	0	•	0	1	0		

The resultant quotient $Q = (0 \cdot 101) = (5/8)$ and remainder $R = (1/32)$. These values are correct since $X = QD + R = (5/8)(3/4) + 1/32 = 1/2$.

Now we show the validity of the above process in the case of integer values. In this case, the equation $X = QD + R$ can be rewritten as $2^{2n-2}X_f = 2^{n-1}Q_f \times 2^{n-1}D_f + 2^{n-1}R_f$, leading to $X_f = Q_f \times D_f + 2^{-(n-1)}R_f$ where X_f, D_f, Q_f, and R_f are fractions. We offer the following illustrative example.

Example   Consider the division of a dividend $X = 32 = (0100000)$ and a divisor $D = 6 = (0110)$. The process is illustrated in the following table.

$r_0 = X$			0	1	0	0	0	0	0	Initial values
$2r_0$		0	1	0	0	0	0	0		Set $q_1 = 1$
$-D$	+	1	1	0	1	0				
$r_1 = 2r_0 - D$		0	0	0	1	0	0	0		
$2r_1$		0	0	1	0	0	0			Set $q_2 = 0$
$r_2 = 2r_1$		0	0	1	0	0	0			
$2r_2$		0	1	0	0	0				Set $q_3 = 1$
$-D$	+	1	1	0	1	0				
$r_3 = 2r_2 - D$		0	0	0	1	0				
$2r_3$		0	0	1	0					Set $q_4 = 0$

The resultant quotient is $Q = 0101 = (5)$ and the remainder $R = 0010$ (2). These are correct values.

A hardware structure for binary division is shown in Figure 4.10. In this figure, the divisor (D) and the contents of register A are added using an $(n + 1)$-bit adder. A control logic is used to perform the required shift left operation (see Exercises).

The comparison between the remainder and the divisor is considered to be the most difficult step in the division process. The way used above to perform such comparison is to subtract D from $2r_{i-1}$ and if the result is negative, then we set $q_i = 0$. This required restoring the previous value by adding back the subtracted value (*restoring division*).

The alternative is to use a *non-restoring division* algorithm:

Step #1: Do the following n times
   1. If the sign of A is 0, shift left AQ and subtract D from A; otherwise shift left AQ and add D to A.
   2. If the sign of A is 0, set $q_0 = 1$; otherwise set $q_0 = 0$.
Step #2: If the sign of A is 1, add D to A.

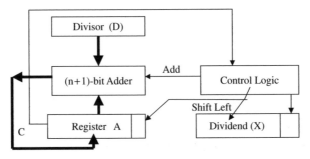

Figure 4.10   Binary division structure

Example   Consider the division of a dividend $X = 8 = (1000)$ and a divisor $D = 3 = (0011)$ using the non-restoring algorithm. The process is illustrated in the following table.

Initially	0	0	0	0	0	1	0	0	0	
	0	0	0	1	1					
Shift	0	0	0	0	1	0	0	0		First cycle
Subtract	1	1	1	0	1					
Set x_0	1	1	1	0		0	0	0	0	
Shift	1	1	1	0	0	0	0	0		
Add	0	0	0	1	1					Second cycle
Set x_0	1	1	1	1	1	0	0	0	0	
Shift	1	1	1	1	0	0	0	0		
Add	0	0	0	1	1					Third cycle
Set x_0	0	0	0	0	1	0	0	0	1	
Shift	0	0	0	1	0	0	0	1		
Subtract	1	1	1	0	1					Fourth cycle
Set x_0	1	1	1	1	1	0	0	1	0	
								Quotient		
Add	1	1	1	1	1					
	0	0	0	1	1	Restore remainder				
	0	0	0	1	0					
			Remainder							

4.3. FLOATING-POINT ARITHMETIC

Having considered integer representation and arithmetic, we consider in this section floating-point representation and arithmetic.

4.3.1. Floating-Point Representation (Scientific Notation)

A floating-point (FP) number can be represented in the following form: $\pm m * b^{e}$, where m, called the *mantissa*, represents the fraction part of the number and is

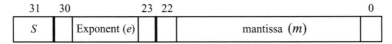

Figure 4.11 Representation of a floating-point number

normally represented as a signed binary fraction, e represents the exponent, and b represents the base (radix) of the exponent.

Example Figure 4.11 is a representation of a floating-point number having $m = 23$ bits, $e = 8$ bits, and S (sign bit) $= 1$ bit. If the value stored in S is 0, the number is positive and if the value stored in S is 1, the number is negative.

The *exponent* in the above example, can only represent positive numbers 0 through 255. To represent both positive and negative exponents, a fixed value, called a *bias*, is subtracted from the exponent field to obtain the true exponent. Assume that in the above example a bias $= 128$ is used, then true exponents in the range -128 (stored as 0 in the exponent field) to $+127$ (stored as 255 in the exponent field) can be represented. Based on this representation, the exponent $+4$ can be represented by storing 132 in the exponent field, while the exponent -12 can be represented by storing 116 in the exponent field.

Assuming that $b = 2$, then an FP number such as 1.75 can be represented in any of the forms shown in Figure 4.12.

To simplify performing operations on FP numbers and to increase their precision, they are always represented in what is called *normalized forms*. An FP number is said to be *normalized* if the leftmost bit of the mantissa is 1. Therefore, among the three above possible representations for 1.75, the first representation is normalized and should be used.

Since the most significant bit (MSB) in a normalized FP number is always 1, then this bit is often not stored and is assumed to be a hidden bit to the left of the radix point, that is, the stored mantissa is $1.m$. Therefore, a nonzero normalized number represents the value $(-1)^s * (1.m) * 2^{e-128}$.

Floating-Point Arithmetic Addition/Subtraction The difficulty in adding two FP numbers stems from the fact that they may have different exponents. Therefore, before adding two FP numbers, their exponents must be equalized, that is, the mantissa of the number that has smaller magnitude of exponent must be *aligned*.

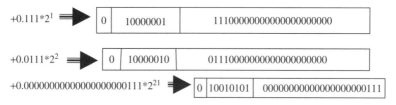

Figure 4.12 Different representation of an FP number

Steps Required to Add/Subtract Two Floating-Point Numbers

1. Compare the magnitude of the two exponents and make suitable *alignment* to the number with the smaller magnitude of exponent.
2. Perform the addition/subtraction.
3. Perform *normalization* by shifting the resulting mantissa and adjusting the resulting exponent.

Example   Consider adding the two FP numbers $1.1100 * 2^4$ and $1.1000 * 2^2$.

1. Alignment: $1.1000 * 2^2$ has to be aligned to $0.0110 * 2^4$
2. Addition: Add the two numbers to get $10.0010 * 2^4$.
3. Normalization: The final normalized result is $0.1000 * 2^6$ (assuming 4 bits are allowed after the radix point).

Addition/subtraction of two FP numbers can be illustrated using the schematic shown in Figure 4.13.

Multiplication   Multiplication of a pair of FP numbers $X = m_x * 2^a$ and $Y = m_y * 2^b$ is represented as $X * Y = (m_x * m_y) * 2^{a+b}$.

A general algorithm for multiplication of FP numbers consists of three basic steps. These are:

1. Compute the exponent of the product by adding the exponents together.
2. Multiply the two mantissas.
3. Normalize and round the final product.

Example   Consider multiplying the two FP numbers $X = 1.000 * 2^{-2}$ and $Y = -1.010 * 2^{-1}$.

1. Add exponents: $-2 + (-1) = -3$.
2. Multiply mantissas: $1.000 * -1.010 = -1.010000$.

The product is $-1.0100 * 2^{-3}$.

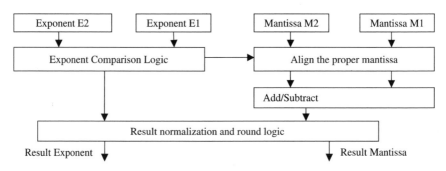

Figure 4.13   Addition/subtraction of FP numbers

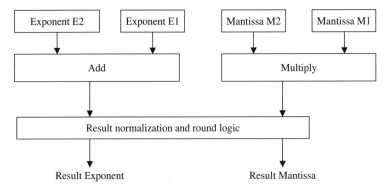

Figure 4.14   FP multiplication

Multiplication of two FP numbers can be illustrated using the schematic shown in Figure 4.14.

Division   Division of a pair of FP numbers $X = m_x * 2^a$ and $Y = m_y * 2^b$ is represented as $X/Y = (m_x/m_y) * 2^{a-b}$.

A general algorithm for division of FP numbers consists of three basic steps:

1. Compute the exponent of the result by subtracting the exponents.
2. Divide the mantissa and determine the sign of the result.
3. Normalize and round the resulting value, if necessary.

Example   Consider the division of the two FP numbers $X = 1.0000 * 2^{-2}$ and $Y = -1.0100 * 2^{-1}$.

1. Subtract exponents: $-2 - (-1) = -1$.
2. Divide the mantissas: $1.0000 \div -1.0100 = -0.1101$.
3. The result is $-0.1101 * 2^{-1}$.

Division of two FP numbers can be illustrated using the schematic shown in Figure 4.15.

4.3.3. The IEEE Floating-Point Standard

There are essentially two IEEE standard floating-point formats. These are the *basic* and the *extended* formats. In each of these, IEEE defines two formats, that is, the single-precision and the double-precision formats. The single-precision format is 32-bit and the double-precision is 64-bit. The single extended format should have at least 44 bits and the double extended format should have at least 80 bits.

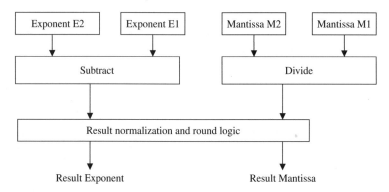

Figure 4.15 FP division

In the single-precision format, base 2 is used, thus allowing the use of a hidden bit. The exponent field is 8 bits. The IEEE single-precision representation is shown in Figure 4.16.

The 8-bit exponent allows for any of 256 combinations. Among these, two combinations are reserved for special values:

1. $e = 0$ is reserved for zero (with fraction $m = 0$) and denormalized numbers (with fraction $m \neq 0$).
2. $e = 255$ is reserved for $\pm\infty$ (with fraction $m = 0$) and not a number (NaN) (with fraction $m \neq 0$).

	$m = 0$	$m \neq 0$
$e = 0$	0	Denormalized
$e = 255$	$\pm\infty$	NaN

The single extended IEEE format extends the exponent field from 8 to 11 bits and the mantissa field from $23 + 1$ to 32 or more bits (without a hidden bit). This results in a total length of at least 44 bits. The single extended format is used in calculating intermediate results.

4.3.4. Double-Precision IEEE Format

Here the exponent field is 11 bits and the significant field is 52 bits. The format is shown in Figure 4.17.

Similar to the single-precision format, the extreme values of e (0 and 2047) are reserved for the same purpose.

S	8 bits (biased exponent) e	23 bits (unbiased fraction) m

Figure 4.16 IEEE single-precision representation

S	11 bits (biased exponent) e	52 bits (unbiased fraction) m

Figure 4.17   Double-precision representation

TABLE 4.2   Characteristics of the IEEE Single and Double Floating-Point Formats

Characteristic	Single-precision	Double-precision
Length in bits	32	64
Fraction part in bits	23	52
Hidden bits	1	1
Exponent length in bits	8	11
Bias	127	1023
Approximate range	$2^{128} \approx 3.8 \times 10^{38}$	$2^{1024} \approx 9.0 \times 10^{307}$
Smallest normalized number	$2^{-126} \approx 10^{-38}$	$2^{-1022} \approx 10^{-308}$

A number of attributes characterizing the IEEE single- and double-precision formats are summarized in Table 4.2.

4.4. SUMMARY

In this chapter, we have discussed a number of issues related to computer arithmetic. Our discussion started with an introduction to number representation and radix conversion techniques. We then discussed integer arithmetic and, in particular, we discussed the four main operations, that is, addition, subtraction, multiplication, and division. In each case, we have shown basic architectures and organization. The last topic discussed in the chapter has been floating-point representation and arithmetic. We have also shown the basic architectures needed to perform basic floating-point operations such as addition, subtraction, multiplication, and division. We ended our discussion in the chapter with the IEEE floating-point number representation.

EXERCISES

1. Represent the decimal values 26, -123 as signed, 10-bit numbers using each of the following binary formats:
   (a) Sign-and-magnitude;
   (b) 2's complement.
2. Compute the decimal value of the binary number 1011 1101 0101 0110 if the given number represents unsigned integer. Repeat if the number represents 2's complement. Repeat if the number represents sign-magnitude integer.

3. Consider the binary numbers in the following addition and subtraction problems to be signed 6-bit values in the 2's complement representation. Perform each of the following operations, specifying whether overflow occurs.

010110	011001	110111	100001	111111	011010
+001001	+010000	+101011	−011101	−000111	−100010

4. Multiply each of the following pairs of signed 2's complement numbers using the 2-bit Booth algorithm.

$M = 010111$	$M = 110011$	$M = 110101$	$M = 1111$
$Q = 110110$	$Q = 101100$	$Q = 011011$	$Q = 1111$

5. Divide each of the following pairs of signed 2's complement numbers using both the restoring and the nonrestoring algorithms.

$X = 010111$	$X = 110011$	$X = 110101$	$X = 1111$
$D = 110110$	$D = 101100$	$D = 011011$	$D = 1111$

6. Show how to perform addition, subtraction, multiplication, and division of the following floating numbers.

$A =$	0	10001	011011
$B =$	1	01111	101010

The numbers are represented in a 12-bit format using a base $b = 2$, a 5-bit exponent e with a bias $= 16$, and 6-bit normalized mantissa m.

7. Show a complete design (in terms of the logic equations) for a 4-bit adder/ subtractor using carry-look-ahead technique for all carries c_1, c_2, c_3, c_4. Assume that the two 4-bit input numbers are $A = a_4a_3a_2a_1$ and $B = b_4b_3b_2b_1$.

8. Design a BCD adder using a 4-bit binary adder and the least number of logic gates. The adder should receive two 4-bit numbers A and B and should produce 4-bit sum and a carry output.

9. Show a design of a 16-bit CLA that uses the 4-bit CLA block shown in Figure 4.5. Compute the delay and the area (in terms of the number of logic gates required).

10. Compare the longest path delay from input to output of a 32-bit adder using 4-bit CLA adder blocks in a multilevel architecture with that of a 32-bit CRT adder. Assume that a gate delay is given by T_g.

11. Convert each of the following decimal numbers to their IEEE single-precision floating-point counterparts.
    (a) −76
    (b) 0.92
    (c) 5.3125

   (d) -0.000072
   (e) 8.04×10^{21}

12. Convert the following IEEE single-precision floating-point numbers to their decimal counterparts.
   (a) 6589 00000
   (b) 807B 00000H
   (c) CDEF 0000H

13. Complete the logic design of the array multiplier shown in Figure 4.6.

14. Design the control logic shown in Figure 4.7.

15. Provide a complete logic design for the Control Logic indicated in Figure 4.10.

REFERENCES AND FURTHER READING

C. Hamacher, Z. Vranesic and S. Zaky, *Computer Organization*, 5th ed., McGraw-Hill, New York, 2002.

V. Heuring and H. Jordan, *Computer Systems Design and Archiecture*, Addison Wesley Longman, NJ, USA, 1997.

K. Israel, *Computer Arithmetic Algorithms*, 2nd ed., A. K. Peters, Ltd., Massachusetts, 2002.

W. Stallings, *Computer Organization and Architectures: Designing for Performance*, 4th ed., Prentice-Hall, NJ, USA, 1996.

B. Wilkinson, *Computer Architecture: Design and Performance*, 2nd ed., Prentice-Hall, Hertfordshire, UK, 1996.

CHAPTER 5

Processing Unit Design

In previous chapters, we studied the history of computer systems and the fundamental issues related to memory locations, addressing modes, assembly language, and computer arithmetic. In this chapter, we focus our attention on the main component of any computer system, the central processing unit (CPU). The primary function of the CPU is to execute a set of instructions stored in the computer's memory. A simple CPU consists of a set of registers, an arithmetic logic unit (ALU), and a control unit (CU). In what follows, the reader will be introduced to the organization and main operations of the CPU.

5.1. CPU BASICS

A typical CPU has three major components: (1) register set, (2) arithmetic logic unit (ALU), and (3) control unit (CU). The register set differs from one computer architecture to another. It is usually a combination of general-purpose and special-purpose registers. General-purpose registers are used for any purpose, hence the name general purpose. Special-purpose registers have specific functions within the CPU. For example, the program counter (PC) is a special-purpose register that is used to hold the address of the instruction to be executed next. Another example of special-purpose registers is the instruction register (IR), which is used to hold the instruction that is currently executed. The ALU provides the circuitry needed to perform the arithmetic, logical and shift operations demanded of the instruction set. In Chapter 4, we have covered a number of arithmetic operations and circuits used to support computation in an ALU. The control unit is the entity responsible for fetching the instruction to be executed from the main memory and decoding and then executing it. Figure 5.1 shows the main components of the CPU and its interactions with the memory system and the input/output devices.

The CPU fetches instructions from memory, reads and writes data from and to memory, and transfers data from and to input/output devices. A typical and

Fundamentals of Computer Organization and Architecture, by M. Abd-El-Barr and H. El-Rewini
ISBN 0-471-46741-3 Copyright © 2005 John Wiley & Sons, Inc.

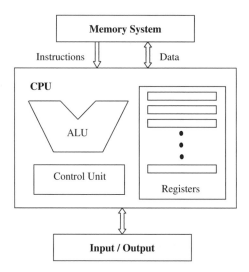

Figure 5.1   Central processing unit main components and interactions with the memory and I/O

simple execution cycle can be summarized as follows:

1. The next instruction to be executed, whose address is obtained from the PC, is fetched from the memory and stored in the IR.
2. The instruction is decoded.
3. Operands are fetched from the memory and stored in CPU registers, if needed.
4. The instruction is executed.
5. Results are transferred from CPU registers to the memory, if needed.

The execution cycle is repeated as long as there are more instructions to execute. A check for pending interrupts is usually included in the cycle. Examples of interrupts include I/O device request, arithmetic overflow, or a page fault (see Chapter 7). When an interrupt request is encountered, a transfer to an interrupt handling routine takes place. Interrupt handling routines are programs that are invoked to collect the state of the currently executing program, correct the cause of the interrupt, and restore the state of the program.

The actions of the CPU during an execution cycle are defined by micro-orders issued by the control unit. These micro-orders are individual control signals sent over dedicated control lines. For example, let us assume that we want to execute an instruction that moves the contents of register X to register Y. Let us also assume that both registers are connected to the data bus, D. The control unit will issue a control signal to tell register X to place its contents on the data bus D. After some delay, another control signal will be sent to tell register Y to read from data bus D. The activation of the control signals is determined using either hardwired control or microprogramming. These concepts are explained later in this chapter.

The remainder of this chapter is organized as follows. Section 5.2 presents the register set and explains the different types of registers and their functions. In Section 5.3, we will understand what is meant by datapath and control. CPU instruction cycle and the control unit will be covered in Sections 5.4 and 5.5, respectively.

5.2. REGISTER SET

Registers are essentially extremely fast memory locations within the CPU that are used to create and store the results of CPU operations and other calculations. Different computers have different register sets. They differ in the number of registers, register types, and the length of each register. They also differ in the usage of each register. General-purpose registers can be used for multiple purposes and assigned to a variety of functions by the programmer. Special-purpose registers are restricted to only specific functions. In some cases, some registers are used only to hold data and cannot be used in the calculations of operand addresses. The length of a data register must be long enough to hold values of most data types. Some machines allow two contiguous registers to hold double-length values. Address registers may be dedicated to a particular addressing mode or may be used as address general purpose. Address registers must be long enough to hold the largest address. The number of registers in a particular architecture affects the instruction set design. A very small number of registers may result in an increase in memory references. Another type of registers is used to hold processor status bits, or flags. These bits are set by the CPU as the result of the execution of an operation. The status bits can be tested at a later time as part of another operation.

5.2.1. Memory Access Registers

Two registers are essential in memory write and read operations: the *memory data register* (MDR) and *memory address register* (MAR). The MDR and MAR are used exclusively by the CPU and are not directly accessible to programmers.

In order to perform a write operation into a specified memory location, the MDR and MAR are used as follows:

1. The word to be stored into the memory location is first loaded by the CPU into MDR.

2. The address of the location into which the word is to be stored is loaded by the CPU into a MAR.

3. A write signal is issued by the CPU.

Similarly, to perform a memory read operation, the MDR and MAR are used as follows:

1. The address of the location from which the word is to be read is loaded into the MAR.

2. A read signal is issued by the CPU.

3. The required word will be loaded by the memory into the MDR ready for use by the CPU.

5.2.2. Instruction Fetching Registers

Two main registers are involved in fetching an instruction for execution: the *program counter* (PC) and the *instruction register* (IR). The PC is the register that contains the address of the next instruction to be fetched. The fetched instruction is loaded in the IR for execution. After a successful instruction fetch, the PC is updated to point to the next instruction to be executed. In the case of a branch operation, the PC is updated to point to the branch target instruction after the branch is resolved, that is, the target address is known.

5.2.3. Condition Registers

Condition registers, or flags, are used to maintain status information. Some architectures contain a special program status word (PSW) register. The PSW contains bits that are set by the CPU to indicate the current status of an executing program. These indicators are typically for arithmetic operations, interrupts, memory protection information, or processor status.

5.2.4. Special-Purpose Address Registers

Index Register   As covered in Chapter 2, in index addressing, the address of the operand is obtained by adding a constant to the content of a register, called the *index register*. The index register holds an address displacement. Index addressing is indicated in the instruction by including the name of the index register in parentheses and using the symbol X to indicate the constant to be added.

Segment Pointers   As we will discuss in Chapter 6, in order to support segmentation, the address issued by the processor should consist of a segment number (base) and a displacement (or an offset) within the segment. A segment register holds the address of the base of the segment.

Stack Pointer   As shown in Chapter 2, a stack is a data organization mechanism in which the last data item stored is the first data item retrieved. Two specific operations can be performed on a stack. These are the *Push* and the *Pop* operations. A specific register, called the *stack pointer* (SP), is used to indicate the stack location that can be addressed. In the stack push operation, the SP value is used to indicate the location (called the top of the stack). After storing (pushing) this value, the SP is incremented (in some architectures, e.g. *X86*, the SP is decremented as the stack grows low in memory).

5.2.5. 80×86 Registers

As discussed in Chapter 3, the Intel basic programming model of the 386, 486, and the *Pentium* consists of three register groups. These are the general-purpose registers, the segment registers, and the instruction pointer (program counter) and the flag register.

Figure 5.2 (which repeats Fig. 3.6) shows the three sets of registers. The first set consists of general purpose registers A, B, C, D, SI (source index), DI (destination index), SP (stack pointer), and BP (base pointer). The second set of registers consists of CS (code segment), SS (stack segment), and four data segment registers DS, ES, FS, and GS. The third set of registers consists of the instruction pointer (program counter) and the flags (status) register. Among the status bits, the first five are identical to those bits introduced as early as in the 8085 8-bit microprocessor. The next 6–11 bits are identical to those introduced in the 8086. The flags in the bits 12–14 were introduced in the 80286 while the 16–17 bits were introduced in the 80386. The flag in bit 18 was introduced in the 80486.

5.2.6. MIPS Registers

The MIPS CPU contains 32 general-purpose registers that are numbered 0–31. Register x is designated by $x. Register $zero always contains the hardwired value 0. Table 5.1 lists the registers and describes their intended use. Registers $at (1), $k0 (26), and $k1 (27) are reserved for use by the assembler and operating system. Registers $a0–$a3 (4–7) are used to pass the first four arguments to routines

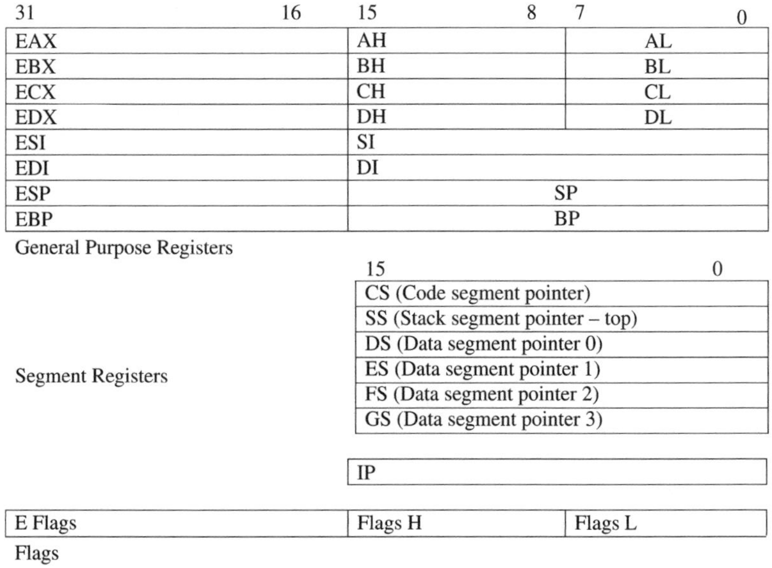

31	16	15	8	7	0
EAX		AH		AL	
EBX		BH		BL	
ECX		CH		CL	
EDX		DH		DL	
ESI		SI			
EDI		DI			
ESP		SP			
EBP		BP			

General Purpose Registers

15	0
CS (Code segment pointer)	
SS (Stack segment pointer – top)	
DS (Data segment pointer 0)	
ES (Data segment pointer 1)	
FS (Data segment pointer 2)	
GS (Data segment pointer 3)	

Segment Registers

IP

E Flags	Flags H	Flags L

Flags

Figure 5.2   The main register sets in 80×86 (80386 and above extended all 16 bit registers except segment registers)

TABLE 5.1 MIPS General-Purpose Registers

Name	Number	Usage	Name	Number	Usage
zero	0	Constant 0	s0	16	Saved temporary (preserved across call)
at	1	Reserved for assembler	s1	17	Saved temporary (preserved across call)
v0	2	Expression evaluation and	s2	18	Saved temporary (preserved across call)
v1	3	results of a function	s3	19	Saved temporary (preserved across call)
a0	4	Argument 1	s4	20	Saved temporary (preserved across call)
a1	5	Argument 2	s5	21	Saved temporary (preserved across call)
a2	6	Argument 3	s6	22	Saved temporary (preserved across call)
a3	7	Argument 4	s7	23	Saved temporary (preserved across call)
t0	8	Temporary (not preserved across call)	t8	24	Temporary (not preserved across call)
t1	9	Temporary (not preserved across call)	t9	25	Temporary (not preserved across call)
t2	10	Temporary (not preserved across call)	k0	26	Reserved for OS kernel
t3	11	Temporary (not preserved across call)	k1	27	Reserved for OS kernel
t4	12	Temporary (not preserved across call)	gp	28	Pointer to global area
t5	13	Temporary (not preserved across call)	sp	29	Stack pointer
t6	14	Temporary (not preserved across call)	fp	30	Frame pointer
t7	15	Temporary (not preserved across call)	ra	31	Return address (used by function call)

(remaining arguments are passed on the stack). Registers $v0 and $v1 (2, 3) are used to return values from functions. Registers $t0–$t9 (8–15, 24, 25) are caller-saved registers used for temporary quantities that do not need to be preserved across calls. Registers $s0–$s7 (16–23) are calle-saved registers that hold long-lived values that should be preserved across calls.

Register $sp(29) is the stack pointer, which points to the last location in use on the stack. Register $fp(30) is the frame pointer. Register $ra(31) is written with the return address for a function call. Register $gp(28) is a global pointer that points into the middle of a 64 K block of memory in the heap that holds constants and global variables. The objects in this heap can be quickly accessed with a single load or store instruction.

5.3. DATAPATH

The CPU can be divided into a data section and a control section. The data section, which is also called the datapath, contains the registers and the ALU. The datapath is capable of performing certain operations on data items. The control section is basically the control unit, which issues control signals to the datapath. Internal to the CPU, data move from one register to another and between ALU and registers. Internal data movements are performed via local buses, which may carry data, instructions, and addresses. Externally, data move from registers to memory and I/O devices, often by means of a system bus. Internal data movement among registers and between the ALU and registers may be carried out using different organizations including one-bus, two-bus, or three-bus organizations. Dedicated datapaths may also be used between components that transfer data between themselves more frequently. For example, the contents of the PC are transferred to the MAR to fetch a new instruction at the beginning of each instruction cycle. Hence, a dedicated datapath from the PC to the MAR could be useful in speeding up this part of instruction execution.

5.3.1. One-Bus Organization

Using one bus, the CPU registers and the ALU use a single bus to move outgoing and incoming data. Since a bus can handle only a single data movement within one clock cycle, two-operand operations will need two cycles to fetch the operands for the ALU. Additional registers may also be needed to buffer data for the ALU. This bus organization is the simplest and least expensive, but it limits the amount of data transfer that can be done in the same clock cycle, which will slow down the overall performance. Figure 5.3 shows a one-bus datapath consisting of a set of general-purpose registers, a memory address register (MAR), a memory data register (MDR), an instruction register (IR), a program counter (PC), and an ALU.

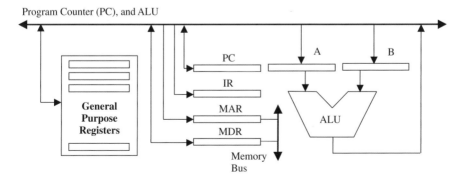

Figure 5.3 One-bus datapath

5.3.2. Two-Bus Organization

Using two buses is a faster solution than the one-bus organization. In this case, general-purpose registers are connected to both buses. Data can be transferred from two different registers to the input point of the ALU at the same time. Therefore, a two-operand operation can fetch both operands in the same clock cycle. An additional buffer register may be needed to hold the output of the ALU when the two buses are busy carrying the two operands. Figure 5.4a shows a two-bus organization. In some cases, one of the buses may be dedicated for moving data into registers (*in-bus*), while the other is dedicated for transferring data out of the registers (*out-bus*). In this case, the additional buffer register may be used, as one of the ALU inputs, to hold one of the operands. The ALU output can be connected directly to the in-bus, which will transfer the result into one of the registers. Figure 5.4b shows a two-bus organization with in-bus and out-bus.

5.3.3. Three-Bus Organization

In a three-bus organization, two buses may be used as source buses while the third is used as destination. The source buses move data out of registers (*out-bus*), and

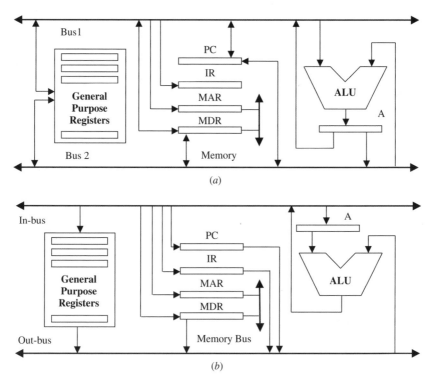

Figure 5.4 Two-bus organizations. (*a*) An Example of Two-Bus Datapath. (*b*) Another Example of Two-Bus Datapath with in-bus and out-bus

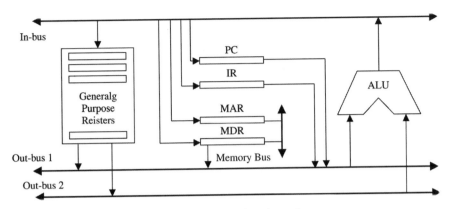

Figure 5.5   Three-bus datapath

the destination bus may move data into a register (*in-bus*). Each of the two out-buses is connected to an ALU input point. The output of the ALU is connected directly to the in-bus. As can be expected, the more buses we have, the more data we can move within a single clock cycle. However, increasing the number of buses will also increase the complexity of the hardware. Figure 5.5 shows an example of a three-bus datapath.

5.4. CPU INSTRUCTION CYCLE

The sequence of operations performed by the CPU during its execution of instructions is presented in Fig. 5.6. As long as there are instructions to execute, the next instruction is fetched from main memory. The instruction is executed based on the operation specified in the opcode field of the instruction. At the completion of the instruction execution, a test is made to determine whether an interrupt has occurred. An interrupt handling routine needs to be invoked in case of an interrupt.

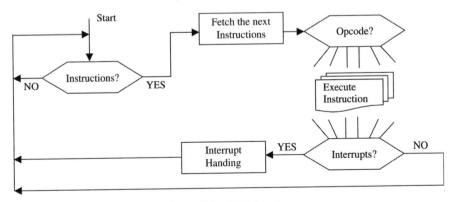

Figure 5.6   CPU functions

The basic actions during fetching an instruction, executing an instruction, or handling an interrupt are defined by a sequence of micro-operations. A group of control signals must be enabled in a prescribed sequence to trigger the execution of a micro-operation. In this section, we show the micro-operations that implement instruction fetch, execution of simple arithmetic instructions, and interrupt handling.

5.4.1. Fetch Instructions

The sequence of events in fetching an instruction can be summarized as follows:

1. The contents of the PC are loaded into the MAR.
2. The value in the PC is incremented. (This operation can be done in parallel with a memory access.)
3. As a result of a memory read operation, the instruction is loaded into the MDR.
4. The contents of the MDR are loaded into the IR.

Let us consider the one-bus datapath organization shown in Fig. 5.3. We will see that the fetch operation can be accomplished in three steps as shown in the table below, where $t_0 < t_1 < t_2$. Note that multiple operations separated by ";" imply that they are accomplished in parallel.

Step	Micro-operation
t_0	MAR $\leftarrow$ (PC); A $\leftarrow$ (PC)
t_1	MDR $\leftarrow$ Mem[MAR]; PC $\leftarrow$ (A) + 4
t_2	IR $\leftarrow$ (MDR)

Using the three-bus datapath shown in Figure 5.5, the following table shows the steps needed.

Step	Micro-operation
t_0	MAR $\leftarrow$ (PC); PC $\leftarrow$ (PC) + 4
t_1	MDR $\leftarrow$ Mem[MAR]
t_2	IR $\leftarrow$ (MDR)

5.4.2. Execute Simple Arithmetic Operation

Add R_1, R_2, R_0   This instruction adds the contents of source registers R_1 and R_2, and stores the results in destination register R_0. This addition can be executed as follows:

1. The registers R_0, R_1, R_2, are extracted from the IR.
2. The contents of R_1 and R_2 are passed to the ALU for addition.
3. The output of the ALU is transferred to R_0.

Using the one-bus datapath shown in Figure 5.3, this addition will take three steps as shown in the following table, where $t_0 < t_1 < t_2$.

Step	Micro-operation
t_0	$A \leftarrow (R_1)$
t_1	$B \leftarrow (R_2)$
t_2	$R_0 \leftarrow (A) + (B)$

Using the two-bus datapath shown in Figure 5.4a, this addition will take two steps as shown in the following table, where $t_0 < t_1$.

Step	Micro-operation
t_0	$A \leftarrow (R_1) + (R_2)$
t_1	$R_0 \leftarrow (A)$

Using the two-bus datapath with in-bus and out-bus shown in Figure 5.4b, this addition will take two steps as shown below, where $t_0 < t_1$.

Step	Micro-operation
t_0	$A \leftarrow (R_1)$
t_1	$R_0 \leftarrow (A) + (R_2)$

Using the three-bus datapath shown in Figure 5.5, this addition will take only one step as shown in the following table.

Step	Micro-operation
t_0	$R_0 \leftarrow (R_1) + (R_2)$

Add X, R_0 This instruction adds the contents of memory location X to register R_0 and stores the result in R_0. This addition can be executed as follows:

1. The memory location X is extracted from IR and loaded into MAR.

2. As a result of memory read operation, the contents of X are loaded into MDR.

3. The contents of MDR are added to the contents of R_0.

Using the one-bus datapath shown in Figure 5.3, this addition will take five steps as shown below, where $t_0 < t_1 < t_2 < t_3 < t_4$.

Step	Micro-operation
t_0	MAR $\leftarrow$ X
t_1	MDR $\leftarrow$ Mem[MAR]
t_2	A $\leftarrow$ (R_0)
t_3	B $\leftarrow$ (MDR)
t_4	R_0 $\leftarrow$ $(A) + (B)$

Using the two-bus datapath shown in Figure 5.4a, this addition will take four steps as shown below, where $t_0 < t_1 < t_2 < t_3$.

Step	Micro-operation
t_0	MAR $\leftarrow$ X
t_1	MDR $\leftarrow$ Mem[MAR]
t_2	A $\leftarrow$ $(R_0) + (MDR)$
t_3	R_0 $\leftarrow$ (A)

Using the two-bus datapath with in-bus and out-bus shown in Figure 5.4b, this addition will take four steps as shown below, where $t_0 < t_1 < t_2 < t_3$.

Step	Micro-operation
t_0	MAR $\leftarrow$ X
t_1	MDR $\leftarrow$ Mem[MAR]
t_2	A $\leftarrow$ (R_0)
t_3	R_0 $\leftarrow$ $(A) + (MDR)$

Using the three-bus datapath shown in Figure 5.5, this addition will take three steps as shown below, where $t_0 < t_1 < t_2$.

Step	Micro-operation
t_0	MAR $\leftarrow$ X
t_1	MDR $\leftarrow$ Mem[MAR]
t_2	R_0 $\leftarrow$ $R_0 + (MDR)$

5.4.3. Interrupt Handling

After the execution of an instruction, a test is performed to check for pending interrupts. If there is an interrupt request waiting, the following steps take place:

1. The contents of PC are loaded into MDR (to be saved).
2. The MAR is loaded with the address at which the PC contents are to be saved.
3. The PC is loaded with the address of the first instruction of the interrupt handling routine.

4. The contents of MDR (old value of the PC) are stored in memory.
The following table shows the sequence of events, where $t_1 < t_2 < t_3$.

Step	Micro-operation	
t_1	MDR ←	(PC)
t_2	MAR ←	address1 (where to save old PC);
	PC ←	address2 (interrupt handling routine)
t_3	Mem[MAR] ←	(MDR)

5.5. CONTROL UNIT

The control unit is the main component that directs the system operations by sending control signals to the datapath. These signals control the flow of data within the CPU and between the CPU and external units such as memory and I/O. Control buses generally carry signals between the control unit and other computer components in a clock-driven manner. The system clock produces a continuous sequence of pulses in a specified duration and frequency. A sequence of steps $t_0, t_1, t_2, \ldots,$

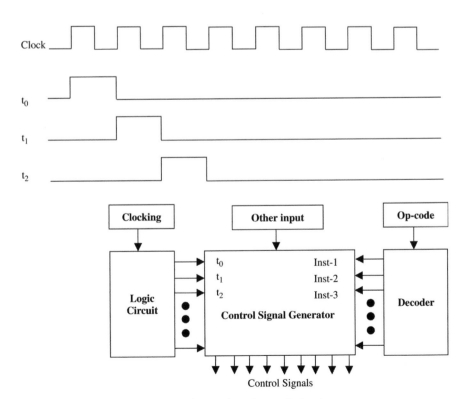

Figure 5.7 Timing of control signals

$(t_0 < t_1 < t_2 < \cdots)$ are used to execute a certain instruction. The op-code field of a fetched instruction is decoded to provide the control signal generator with information about the instruction to be executed. Step information generated by a logic circuit module is used with other inputs to generate control signals. The signal generator can be specified simply by a set of Boolean equations for its output in terms of its inputs. Figure 5.7 shows a block diagram that describes how timing is used in generating control signals.

There are mainly two different types of control units: *microprogrammed* and *hardwired*. In microprogrammed control, the control signals associated with operations are stored in special memory units inaccessible by the programmer as control words. A control word is a microinstruction that specifies one or more microoperations. A sequence of microinstructions is called a microprogram, which is stored in a ROM or RAM called a control memory CM.

In hardwired control, fixed logic circuits that correspond directly to the Boolean expressions are used to generate the control signals. Clearly hardwired control is faster than microprogrammed control. However, hardwired control could be very expensive and complicated for complex systems. Hardwired control is more economical for small control units. It should also be noted that microprogrammed control could adapt easily to changes in the system design. We can easily add new instructions without changing hardware. Hardwired control will require a redesign of the entire systems in the case of any change.

Example 1 Let us revisit the add operation in which we add the contents of source registers R_1, R_2, and store the results in destination register R_0. We have shown earlier that this operation can be done in one step using the three-bus datapath shown in Figure 5.5.

Let us try to examine the control sequence needed to accomplish this addition at step t_0. Suppose that the op-code field of the current instruction was decoded to Inst-x type. First we need to select the source registers and the destination register, then we select Add as the ALU function to be performed. The following table shows the needed step and the control sequence.

Step	Instruction type	Micro-operation	Control
t_0	Inst-x	$R_0 \leftarrow (R_1) + (R_2)$	Select R_1 as source 1 on out-bus1 (R_1 out-bus1) Select R_2 as source 2 on out-bus2 (R_2 out-bus2) Select R_0 as destination on in-bus (R_0 in-bus) Select the ALU function Add (Add)

Figure 5.8 shows the signals generated to execute Inst-x during time period t_0. The AND gate ensures that these signals will be issued when the op-code is decoded into Inst-x and during time period t_0. The signals (R_1 out-bus 1), (R_2 out-bus2),

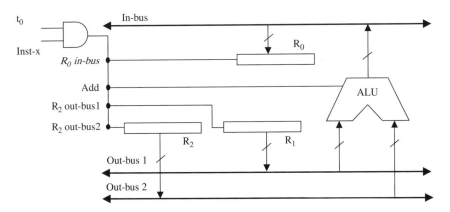

Figure 5.8   Signals generated to execute Inst-x on three-bus datapath during time period t_0

(R_0 in-bus), and (Add) will select R_1 as a source on out-bus1, R_2 as a source on out-bus2, R_0 as destination on in-bus, and select the ALUs add function, respectively.

Example 2   Let us repeat the operation in the previous example using the one-bus datapath shown in Fig. 5.3. We have shown earlier that this operation can be carried out in three steps using the one-bus datapath. Suppose that the op-code field of the current instruction was decoded to Inst-x type. The following table shows the needed steps and the control sequence.

Step	Instruction type	Micro-operation	
t_0	Inst-x	$A \leftarrow (R_1)$	Select R_1 as source (R_1 out)
			Select A as destination (A in)
t_1	Inst-x	$B \leftarrow (R_2)$	Select R_2 as source (R_2 out)
			Select B as destination (B in)
t_2	Inst-x	$R_0 \leftarrow (A) + (B)$	Select the ALU function Add (Add)
			Select R_0 as destination (R_0 in)

Figure 5.9 shows the signals generated to execute Inst-x during time periods t_0, t_1, and t_2. The AND gates ensure that the appropriate signals will be issued when the op-code is decoded into Inst-x and during the appropriate time period. During t_0, the signals (R_1 out) and (A in) will be issued to move the contents of R_1 into A. Similarly during t_1, the signals (R_2 out) and (B in) will be issued to move the contents of R_2 into B. Finally, the signals (R_0 in) and (Add) will be issued during t_2 to add the contents of A and B and move the results into R_0.

5.5.1. Hardwired Implementation

In hardwired control, a direct implementation is accomplished using logic circuits. For each control line, one must find the Boolean expression in terms of the input to the control signal generator as shown in Figure 5.7. Let us explain the

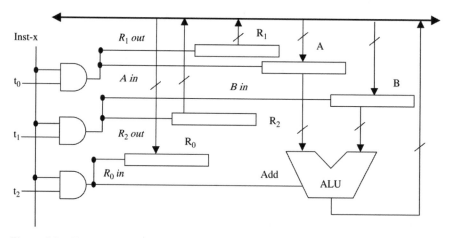

Figure 5.9 Signals generated to execute Inst-x on one-bus datapath during time period t_0, t_1, t_2

implementation using a simple example. Assume that the instruction set of a machine has the three instructions: Inst-x, Inst-y, and Inst-z; and A, B, C, D, E, F, G, and H are control lines. The following table shows the control lines that should be activated for the three instructions at the three steps t_0, t_1, and t_2.

Step	Inst-x	Inst-y	Inst-z
t_0	D, B, E	F, H, G	E, H
t_1	C, A, H	G	D, A, C
t_2	G, C	B, C	

The Boolean expressions for control lines A, B, and C can be obtained as follows:

$$A = \text{Inst-x} \cdot t_1 + \text{Inst-z} \cdot t_1 = (\text{Inst-x} + \text{Inst-z}) \cdot t_1$$
$$B = \text{Inst-x} \cdot t_0 + \text{Inst-y} \cdot t_2$$
$$C = \text{Inst-x} \cdot t_1 + \text{Inst-x} \cdot t_2 + \text{Inst-y} \cdot t_2 + \text{Inst-z} \cdot t_1$$
$$= (\text{Inst-x} + \text{Inst-z}) \cdot t_1 + (\text{Inst-x} + \text{Inst-y}) \cdot t_2$$

Figure 5.10 shows the logic circuits for these control lines. Boolean expressions for the rest of the control lines can be obtained in a similar way. Figure 5.11 shows the state diagram in the execution cycle of these instructions.

5.5.2. Microprogrammed Control Unit

The idea of microprogrammed control units was introduced by M. V. Wilkes in the early 1950s. Microprogramming was motivated by the desire to reduce the complexities involved with hardwired control. As we studied earlier, an instruction is

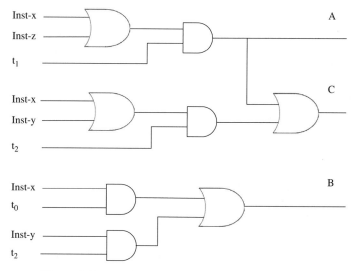

Figure 5.10   Logic circuits for control lines A, B, and C

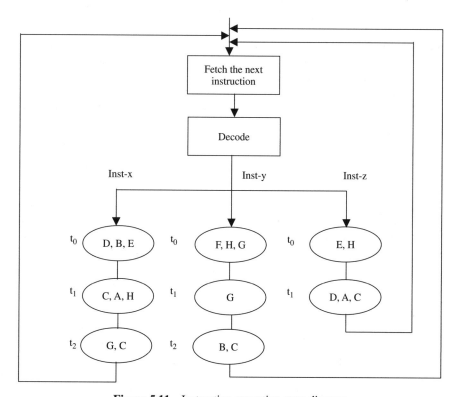

Figure 5.11   Instruction execution state diagram

implemented using a set of micro-operations. Associated with each micro-operation is a set of control lines that must be activated to carry out the corresponding micro-operation. The idea of microprogrammed control is to store the control signals associated with the implementation of a certain instruction as a microprogram in a special memory called a control memory (CM). A microprogram consists of a sequence of microinstructions. A microinstruction is a vector of bits, where each bit is a control signal, condition code, or the address of the next microinstruction. Microinstructions are fetched from CM the same way program instructions are fetched from main memory (Fig. 5.12).

When an instruction is fetched from memory, the op-code field of the instruction will determine which microprogram is to be executed. In other words, the op-code is mapped to a microinstruction address in the control memory. The microinstruction processor uses that address to fetch the first microinstruction in the microprogram. After fetching each microinstruction, the appropriate control lines will be enabled. Every control line that corresponds to a "1" bit should be turned *on.* Every control line that corresponds to a "0" bit should be left *off.* After completing the execution of one microinstruction, a new microinstruction will be fetched and executed. If the condition code bits indicate that a branch must be taken, the next microinstruction is specified in the address bits of the current microinstruction. Otherwise, the next microinstruction in the sequence will be fetched and executed.

The length of a microinstruction is determined based on the number of micro-operations specified in the microinstructions, the way the control bits will be interpreted, and the way the address of the next microinstruction is obtained. A microinstruction may specify one or more micro-operations that will be activated simultaneously. The length of the microinstruction will increase as the number of parallel micro-operations per microinstruction increases. Furthermore, when each control bit in the microinstruction corresponds to exactly one control line, the length of microinstruction could get bigger. The length of a microinstruction could be reduced if control lines are coded in specific fields in the microinstruction. Decoders will be needed to map each field into the individual control lines. Clearly, using the decoders will reduce the number of control lines that can be activated simultaneously. There is a tradeoff between the length of the microinstructions and the amount of parallelism. It is important that we reduce the length of microinstructions to reduce the cost and access time of the control memory. It may also be desirable that more micro-operations be performed in parallel and more control lines can be activated simultaneously.

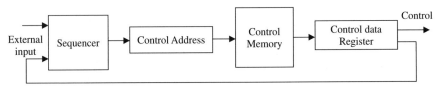

Figure 5.12   Fetching microinstructions (control words)

Horizontal Versus Vertical Microinstructions Microinstructions can be classified as *horizontal* or *vertical*. Individual bits in horizontal microinstructions correspond to individual control lines. Horizontal microinstructions are long and allow maximum parallelism since each bit controls a single control line. In vertical microinstructions, control lines are coded into specific fields within a microinstruction. Decoders are needed to map a field of k bits to 2^k possible combinations of control lines. For example, a 3-bit field in a microinstruction could be used to specify any one of eight possible lines. Because of the encoding, vertical microinstructions are much shorter than horizontal ones. Control lines encoded in the same field cannot be activated simultaneously. Therefore, vertical microinstructions allow only limited parallelism. It should be noted that no decoding is needed in horizontal microinstructions while decoding is necessary in the vertical case.

Example 3 Consider the three-bus datapath shown in Figure 5.5. In addition to the PC, IR, MAR, and MDR, assume that there are 16 general-purpose registers numbered R_0-R_{15}. Also, assume that the ALU supports eight functions (add, subtract, multiply, divide, AND, OR, shift left, and shift right). Consider the add operation Add R_1, R_2, R_0, which adds the contents of source registers R_1, R_2, and store the results in destination register R_0. In this example, we will study the format of the microinstruction under horizontal organization.

We will use horizontal microinstructions, in which there is a control bit for each control line. The format of the microinstruction should have control bits for the following:

- ALU operations
- Registers that output to out-bus1 (source 1)
- Registers that output to out-bus2 (source 2)
- Registers that input from in-bus (destination)
- Other operations that are not shown here

The following table shows the number of bits needed for ALU, Source 1, Source 2, and destination:

Purpose	Number of bits	Explanations
ALU	8 bits	8 functions
Source 1	20 bits	16 general-purpose registers + 4 special-purpose registers
Source 2	16 bits	16 general-purpose registers
Destination	20 bits	16 general-purpose registers + 4 special-purpose registers

Figure 5.13 is the microinstruction for Add R_1, R_2, R_0 on the three-bus datapath.

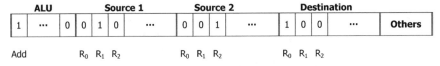

Figure 5.13 Microinstruction for Add R_1, R_2, R_0

Example 4 In this example, we will use vertical microinstructions, in which decoders will be needed. We will use a three-bus datapath as shown in Figure 5.5. Assume that there are 16 general-purpose registers and that the ALU supports eight functions. The following tables show the encoding for ALU functions, registers connected to out-bus 1 (Source 1), registers connected to out-bus 2 (Source 2), and registers connected to in-bus (Destination).

Purpose	Number of bits	Explanations
ALU	4 bits	8 functions + none
Source 1	5 bits	16 general-purpose registers + 4 special-purpose registers + none
Source 2	5 bits	16 general-purpose registers + none
Destination	5 bits	16 general-purpose registers + 4 special-purpose registers + none

Encoding	ALU function
0000	None (ALU will connect out-bus1 to in-bus)
0001	Add
0010	Subtract
0011	Multiple
0100	Divide
0101	AND
0110	OR
0111	Shift left
1000	Shift right

Encoding	Source 1	Destination	Encoding	Source 2
00000	R_0	R_0	00000	R_0
00001	R_1	R_1	00001	R_1
00010	R_2	R_2	00010	R_2
00011	R_3	R_3	00011	R_3
00100	R_4	R_4	00100	R_4
00101	R_5	R_5	00101	R_5
00110	R_6	R_6	00110	R_6
00111	R_7	R_7	00111	R_7
01000	R_8	R_8	01000	R_8
01001	R_9	R_9	01001	R_9
01010	R_{10}	R_{10}	01010	R_{10}

Encoding	Source 1	Destination	Encoding	Source 2
01011	R_{11}	R_{11}	01011	R_{11}
01100	R_{12}	R_{12}	01100	R_{12}
01101	R_{13}	R_{13}	01101	R_{13}
01110	R_{14}	R_{14}	01110	R_{14}
01111	R_{15}	R_{15}	01111	R_{15}
10000	PC	PC	10000	None
10001	IR	IR		
10010	MAR	MAR		
10011	MDR	MDR		
10100	NONE	NONE		

Figure 5.14 is the microinstruction for Add R_1, R_2, R_0 using the three-bus data-path under vertical organization:

Example 5   Using the same encoding of Example 4, let us find vertical microinstructions used in fetching an instruction.

MAR ← *PC*   First, we need to select PC as source 1 by using "10000" for source 1 field. Similarly, we select MAR as our destination by using "10010" in the destination field. We also need to use "0000" for the ALU field, which will be decoded to "NONE". As shown in the ALU encoding table (Example 4), "NONE" means that out-bus1 will be connected to in-bus. The field source 2 will be set to "10000", which means none of the registers will be selected. The microinstruction is shown in Figure 5.15.

Memory Read and Write   Memory operations can easily be accommodated by adding 1 bit for read and another for write. The two microinstructions in Figure 5.16 perform memory read and write, respectively.

Fetch   Fetching an instruction can be done using the three microinstructions of Figure 5.17.
    The first and second microinstructions have been shown above. The third microinstruction moves the contents of the MDR to IR (IR ← MDR). MDR is selected as source 1 by using "10011" for source 1 field. Similarly, IR is selected as the destination by using "10001" in the destination field. We also need to use "0000" ("NONE")

ALU				Source 1					Source 2					Destination					
0	0	0	1	0	0	0	0	1	0	0	0	1	0	0	0	0	0	0	Others

Figure 5.14   Microinstruction for Add R_1, R_2, R_0

ALU				Source 1					Source 2					Destination					
0	0	0	0	1	0	0	0	0	1	0	0	0	0	1	0	0	1	0	Others

Figure 5.15   Microinstruction for *MAR* ← *PC*

				R	W	
ALU	**Source 1**	**Source 2**	**Destination**	1	0	**Others**

MDR ← Mem[MAR]

				R	W	
ALU	**Source 1**	**Source 2**	**Destination**	0	1	**Others**

Mem[MAR] ← MDR

Figure 5.16 Microinstructions for memory read and write

	ALU	Source 1	Source 2	Destination	R	W	
MAR ← (PC)	0 0 0 0 1	0 0 0 0 1	0 0 0 0 1	1 0 0 1	0	0	**Others**
MDR ← Mem[MAR]	0 0 0 0 0	0 0 0 0 0	0 0 0 0 0	0 0 0 0	1	0	**Others**
IR ← MDR	0 0 0 0 1	0 0 1 1 1	1 0 0 0 0	1 0 0 0	1	0	**Others**

Figure 5.17 Microinstructions for fetching an instruction

in the ALU field, which means that out-bus1 will be connected to in-bus. The field source 2 will be set to "10000", which means none of the registers will be selected.

5.6. SUMMARY

The CPU is the part of a computer that interprets and carries out the instructions contained in the programs we write. The CPU's main components are the register file, ALU, and the control unit. The register file contains general-purpose and special registers. General-purpose registers may be used to hold operands and intermediate results. The special registers may be used for memory access, sequencing, status information, or to hold the fetched instruction during decoding and execution. Arithmetic and logical operations are performed in the ALU. Internal to the CPU, data may move from one register to another or between registers and ALU. Data may also move between the CPU and external components such as memory and I/O. The control unit is the component that controls the state of the instruction cycle. As long as there are instructions to execute, the next instruction is fetched from main memory. The instruction is executed based on the operation specified in the op-code field of the instruction. The control unit generates signals that control the flow of data within the CPU and between the CPU and external units such as memory and I/O. The control unit can be implemented using hardwired or microprogramming techniques.

EXERCISES

1. How many instruction bits are required to specify the following:
    (a) Two operand registers and one result register in a machine that has 64 general-purpose registers?

   (b) Three memory addresses in a machine with 64 KB of main memory?

2. Show the micro-operations of the *load*, *store*, and *jump* instructions using:
   (a) One-bus system
   (b) Two-bus system
   (c) Three-bus system

3. Add control signals to all the tables in Section 5.4.

4. Data movement within the CPU can be performed in several different ways. Contrast the following methods in terms of their advantages and disadvantages:
   (a) Dedicated connections
   (b) One-bus datapath
   (c) Two-bus datapath
   (d) Three-bus datapath

5. Find a method of encoding the microinstructions described by the following table so that the minimum number of control bits is used and all inherent parallelism among the microoperations is preserved.

Microinstruction	Control signals activated
I_1	a, b, c, d, e
I_2	a, d, f, g
I_3	b, h
I_4	c
I_5	c, e, g, i
I_6	a, h, j

6. Suppose that the instruction set of a machine has three instructions: Inst-1, Inst-2, and Inst-3; and A, B, C, D, E, F, G, and H are the control lines. The following table shows the control lines that should be activated for the three instructions at the three steps T0, T1, and T2.

Step	Inst-1	Inst-2	Inst-3
T0	D, B, E	F, H, G	E, H
T1	C, A, H	G	D, A, C
T2	G, C	B, C	

   (a) Hardwired approach:
      (i) Write Boolean expressions for all the control lines A–G.
      (ii) Draw the logic circuit for each control line.
   (b) Microprogramming approach:
      (i) Assuming a horizontal representation, write down the microprogram for instructions Inst-1. Indicate the microinstruction size.

(ii) If we allow both horizontal and vertical representation, what would be the best grouping? What is the microinstruction size? Write the microprogram of Inst-1.

7. A certain processor has a microinstruction format containing 10 separate control fields C_0: C_9. Each C_i can activate any one of n_i distinct control lines, where n_i is specified as follows:

$$i: \quad 0 \quad 1 \quad 2 \quad 3 \quad 4 \quad 5 \quad 6 \quad 7 \quad 8 \quad 9$$
$$n_i: \quad 4 \quad 4 \quad 3 \quad 11 \quad 9 \quad 16 \quad 7 \quad 1 \quad 8 \quad 22$$

(a) What is the minimum number of control bits needed to represent the 10 control fields?

(b) What is the maximum number of control bits needed if a purely horizontal format is used for all control information?

8. What are the main differences between the following pairs?

(a) Vertical and horizontal microinstructions

(b) Microprogramming and hardwired control

9. Using the single-bus architecture, generate the necessary control signals, in the proper order (with minimum number of micro-instructions), for *conditional branch* instruction.

10. Write a micro-program for the fetch instruction using the one-bus datapath and the two-bus datapath.

REFERENCES AND FURTHER READING

R. J. Baron and L. Higbie, *Computer Architecture*, Addison Wesley, Canada, 1992.

M. J. Flynn, *Computer Architecture*, Jones and Barlett, MA, USA, 1995.

J. P. Hayes, *Computer Architecture and Organization*, McGraw-Hill, New York, 1998.

J. Hennessy and D. Patterson, *Computer Architecture: A Quantitative Approach*, Morgan Kaufmann, San Francisco, *CA*, 2003.

V. P. Heuring and H. F. Jordan, *Computer Systems Design and Architecture*, Addison Wesley, NJ, 1997.

M. Murdocca and V. Heuring, *Principles of Computer Architecture*, Prentice Hall, NJ, USA, 2000.

D. Patterson and J. Hennessy, *Computer Organization and Design*, Morgan Kaufmann, San Mateo, CA, 1998.

W. Stallings, *Computer Organization and Architecture: Designing for Performance*, NJ, 1996.

A. S. Tanenbaum, *Structured Computer Organization*, Prentice Hall, NJ, USA, 1999.

CHAPTER 6

Memory System Design I

In this chapter, we study the computer memory system. It was stated in Chapter 3 that without a memory no information can be stored or retrieved in a computer. It is interesting to observe that as early as 1946 it was recognized by Burks, Goldstine, and Von Neumann that a computer memory has to be organized in a hierarchy. In such a hierarchy, larger and slower memories are used to supplement smaller and faster ones. This observation has since then proven essential in constructing a computer memory. If we put aside the set of CPU registers (as the first level for storing and retrieving information inside the CPU, see Chapter 5), then a typical memory hierarchy starts with a small, expensive, and relatively fast unit, called the *cache*. The cache is followed in the hierarchy by a larger, less expensive, and relatively slow *main memory* unit. Cache and main memory are built using solid-state semiconductor material. They are followed in the hierarchy by far larger, less expensive, and much slower magnetic memories that consist typically of the (hard) disk and the tape. Our deliberation in this chapter starts by discussing the characteristics and factors influencing the success of a memory hierarchy of a computer. We then direct our attention to the design and analysis of cache memory. Discussion on the (main) memory unit is conducted in Chapter 7. Also discussed in Chapter 7 are the issues related to *virtual memory* design. A brief coverage of the different *read-only memory* (ROM) implementations is also provided in Chapter 7.

6.1. BASIC CONCEPTS

In this section, we introduce a number of fundamental concepts that relate to the memory hierarchy of a computer.

6.1.1. Memory Hierarchy

As mentioned above, a typical memory hierarchy starts with a small, expensive, and relatively fast unit, called the *cache*, followed by a larger, less expensive, and relatively slow *main memory* unit. Cache and main memory are built using solid-state

Fundamentals of Computer Organization and Architecture, by M. Abd-El-Barr and H. El-Rewini
ISBN 0-471-46741-3   Copyright © 2005 John Wiley & Sons, Inc.

semiconductor material (typically CMOS transistors). It is customary to call the fast memory level the *primary memory*. The solid-state memory is followed by larger, less expensive, and far slower magnetic memories that consist typically of the (hard) disk and the tape. It is customary to call the disk the *secondary memory*, while the tape is conventionally called the *tertiary memory*. The objective behind designing a memory hierarchy is to have a memory system that performs as if it consists entirely of the fastest unit and whose cost is dominated by the cost of the slowest unit.

The memory hierarchy can be characterized by a number of parameters. Among these parameters are the *access type, capacity, cycle time, latency, bandwidth*, and *cost*. The term *access* refers to the action that physically takes place during a *read* or *write* operation. The capacity of a memory level is usually measured in bytes. The cycle time is defined as the time elapsed from the start of a read operation to the start of a subsequent read. The latency is defined as the time interval between the request for information and the access to the first bit of that information. The bandwidth provides a measure of the number of bits per second that can be accessed. The cost of a memory level is usually specified as dollars per megabytes. Figure 6.1 depicts a typical memory hierarchy. Table 6.1 provides typical values of the memory hierarchy parameters.

The term *random access* refers to the fact that any access to any memory location takes the same fixed amount of time regardless of the actual memory location and/or the sequence of accesses that takes place. For example, if a *write* operation to memory location 100 takes 15 ns and if this operation is followed by a *read* operation to memory location 3000, then the latter operation will also take 15 ns. This is to be compared to sequential access in which if access to location 100 takes 500 ns, and if a consecutive access to location 101 takes 505 ns, then it is expected that an access to location 300 may take 1500 ns. This is because the memory has to cycle through locations 100 to 300, with each location requiring 5 ns.

The effectiveness of a memory hierarchy depends on the principle of moving information into the fast memory infrequently and accessing it many times before replacing it with new information. This principle is possible due to a phenomenon called *locality of reference*; that is, within a given period of time, programs tend to reference a relatively confined area of memory repeatedly. There exist two forms of locality: spatial and temporal locality. *Spatial locality* refers to the

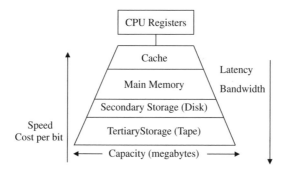

Figure 6.1 Typical memory hierarchy

TABLE 6.1   Memory Hierarchy Parameters

	Access type	Capacity	Latency	Bandwidth	Cost/MB
CPU registers	Random	64–1024 bytes	1–10 ns	System clock rate	High
Cache memory	Random	8–512 KB	15–20 ns	10–20 MB/s	$500
Main memory	Random	16–512 MB	30–50 ns	1–2 MB/s	$20–50
Disk memory	Direct	1–20 GB	10–30 ms	1–2 MB/s	$0.25
Tape memory	Sequential	1–20 TB	30–10,000 ms	1–2 MB/s	$0.025

phenomenon that when a given address has been referenced, it is most likely that addresses near it will be referenced within a short period of time, for example, consecutive instructions in a straightline program. *Temporal locality*, on the other hand, refers to the phenomenon that once a particular memory item has been referenced, it is most likely that it will be referenced next, for example, an instruction in a program loop.

The sequence of events that takes place when the processor makes a request for an item is as follows. First, the item is sought in the first memory level of the memory hierarchy. The probability of finding the requested item in the first level is called the *hit ratio*, h_1. The probability of not finding (missing) the requested item in the first level of the memory hierarchy is called the *miss ratio*, $(1 - h_1)$. When the requested item causes a "*miss*," it is sought in the next subsequent memory level. The probability of finding the requested item in the second memory level, the hit ratio of the second level, is h_2. The miss ratio of the second memory level is $(1 - h_2)$. The process is repeated until the item is found. Upon finding the requested item, it is brought and sent to the processor. In a memory hierarchy that consists of three levels, the average memory access time can be expressed as follows:

$$t_{av} = h_1 \times t_1 + (1 - h_1)[t_1 + h_2 \times t_2 + (1 - h_2)(t_2 + t_3)]$$
$$= t_1 + (1 - h_1)[t_2 + (1 - h_2)t_3]$$

The average access time of a memory level is defined as the time required to access one word in that level. In this equation, t_1, t_2, t_3 represent, respectively, the access times of the three levels.

6.2. CACHE MEMORY

Cache memory owes its introduction to Wilkes back in 1965. At that time, Wilkes distinguished between two types of main memory: The conventional and the *slave memory*. In Wilkes terminology, a slave memory is a second level of unconventional high-speed memory, which nowadays corresponds to what is called *cache memory* (the term cache means a safe place for hiding or storing things).

The idea behind using a cache as the first level of the memory hierarchy is to keep the information expected to be used more frequently by the CPU in the cache (a small high-speed memory that is near the CPU). The end result is that at any given time some active portion of the main memory is duplicated in the cache. Therefore, when the processor makes a request for a memory reference, the request is first sought in the cache. If the request corresponds to an element that is currently residing in the cache, we call that a cache hit. On the other hand, if the request corresponds to an element that is not currently in the cache, we call that a cache miss. A *cache hit ratio*, h_c, is defined as the probability of finding the requested element in the cache. A *cache miss ratio* $(1 - h_c)$ is defined as the probability of not finding the requested element in the cache.

In the case that the requested element is not found in the cache, then it has to be brought from a subsequent memory level in the memory hierarchy. Assuming that the element exists in the next memory level, that is, the main memory, then it has to be brought and placed in the cache. In expectation that the next requested element will be residing in the neighboring locality of the current requested element (spatial locality), then upon a cache miss what is actually brought to the main memory is a *block* of elements that contains the requested element. The advantage of transferring a block from the main memory to the cache will be most visible if it could be possible to transfer such a block using one main memory access time. Such a possibility could be achieved by increasing the rate at which information can be transferred between the main memory and the cache. One possible technique that is used to increase the bandwidth is *memory interleaving*. To achieve best results, we can assume that the block brought from the main memory to the cache, upon a cache miss, consists of elements that are stored in different memory modules, that is, whereby consecutive memory addresses are stored in successive memory modules. Figure 6.2 illustrates the simple case of a main memory consisting of eight memory modules. It is assumed in this case that the block consists of 8 bytes.

Having introduced the basic idea leading to the use of a cache memory, we would like to assess the impact of temporal and spatial locality on the performance of the memory hierarchy. In order to make such an assessment, we will limit our

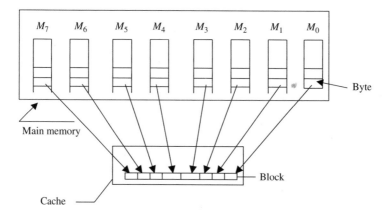

Figure 6.2 Memory interleaving using eight modules

deliberation to the simple case of a hierarchy consisting only of two levels, that is, the cache and the main memory. We assume that the main memory access time is t_m and the cache access time is t_c. We will measure the impact of locality in terms of the average access time, defined as the average time required to access an element (a word) requested by the processor in such a two-level hierarchy.

6.2.1. Impact of Temporal Locality

In this case, we assume that instructions in program loops, which are executed many times, for example, n times, once loaded into the cache, are used more than once before they are replaced by new instructions. The average access time, t_{av}, is given by

$$t_{av} = \frac{nt_c + t_m}{n} = t_c + \frac{t_m}{n}$$

In deriving the above expression, it was assumed that the requested memory element has created a cache miss, thus leading to the transfer of a main memory block in time t_m. Following that, n accesses were made to the same requested element, each taking t_c. The above expression reveals that as the number of repeated accesses, n, increases, the average access time decreases, a desirable feature of the memory hierarchy.

6.2.2. Impact of Spatial Locality

In this case, it is assumed that the size of the block transferred from the main memory to the cache, upon a cache miss, is m elements. We also assume that due to spatial locality, all m elements were requested, one at a time, by the processor. Based on these assumptions, the average access time, t_{av}, is given by

$$t_{av} = \frac{mt_c + t_m}{m} = t_c + \frac{t_m}{m}$$

In deriving the above expression, it was assumed that the requested memory element has created a cache miss, thus leading to the transfer of a main memory block, consisting of m elements, in time t_m. Following that, m accesses, each for one of the elements constituting the block, were made. The above expression reveals that as the number of elements in a block, m, increases, the average access time decreases, a desirable feature of the memory hierarchy.

6.2.3. Impact of Combined Temporal and Spatial Locality

In this case, we assume that the element requested by the processor created a cache miss leading to the transfer of a block, consisting of m *elements*, to the cache (that take t_m). Now, due to spatial locality, all m elements constituting a block were requested, one at a time, by the processor (requiring mt_c). Following that, the originally requested element was accessed $(n-1)$ times (temporal locality), that is, a total of n times access to that element. Based on these assumptions, the average access time, t_{av}, is given by

$$t_{av} = \frac{\left(\frac{mt_c + t_m}{m}\right) + (n-1)t_c}{n} = \frac{t_c + \left(\frac{t_m}{m}\right) + (n-1)t_c}{n} = \frac{t_m}{nm} + t_c$$

A further simplifying assumption to the above expression is to assume that $t_m = mt_c$. In this case the above expression will simplify to

$$t_{av} = \frac{mt_c}{nm} + t_c = t_c + \frac{t_c}{n} = \frac{n+1}{n}t_c$$

The above expression reveals that as the number of repeated accesses n increases, the average access time will approach t_c. This is a significant performance improvement.

It should be clear from the above discussion that as more requests for items that do not exist in the cache (cache miss) occur, more blocks would have to be brought to the cache. This should raise two basic questions: Where to place an incoming main memory block in the cache? And in the case where the cache is totally filled, which cache block should the incoming main memory block replace? Placement of incoming blocks and replacement of existing blocks are performed according to specific protocols (algorithms). These protocols are strongly related to the internal organization of the cache. Cache internal organization is discussed in the following subsections. However, before discussing cache organization, we first introduce the cache-mapping function.

6.2.4. Cache-Mapping Function

Without loss of generality, we present cache-mapping function taking into consideration the interface between two successive levels in the memory hierarchy: primary level and secondary level. If the focus is on the interface between the cache and main memory, then the cache represents the primary level, while the main memory represents the secondary level. The same principles apply to the interface between any two memory levels in the hierarchy. In the following discussion, we focus our attention to the interface between the cache and the main memory.

It should be noted that a request for accessing a memory element is made by the processor through issuing the address of the requested element. The address issued by the processor may correspond to that of an element that exists currently in the cache (cache hit); otherwise, it may correspond to an element that is currently residing in the main memory. Therefore, address translation has to be made in order to determine the whereabouts of the requested element. This is one of the functions performed by the memory management unit (MMU). A schematic of the address mapping function is shown in Figure 6.3.

In this figure, the system address represents the address issued by the processor for the requested element. This address is used by an address translation function inside the MMU. If address translation reveals that the issued address corresponds to an element currently residing in the cache, then the element will be made

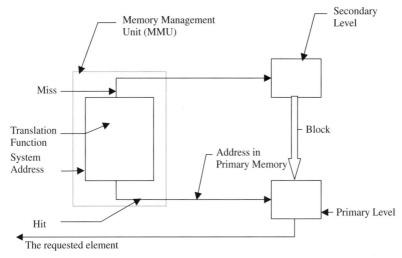

Figure 6.3   Address mapping operation

available to the processor. If, on the other hand, the element is not currently in the cache, then it will be brought (as part of a block) from the main memory and placed in the cache and the element requested is made available to the processor.

6.2.5. Cache Memory Organization

There are three main different organization techniques used for cache memory. The three techniques are discussed below. These techniques differ in two main aspects:

1. The criterion used to place, in the cache, an incoming block from the main memory.
2. The criterion used to replace a cache block by an incoming block (on cache full).

Direct Mapping   This is the simplest among the three techniques. Its simplicity stems from the fact that it places an incoming main memory block into a specific fixed cache block location. The placement is done based on a fixed relation between the incoming block number, i, the cache block number, j, and the number of cache blocks, N:

$$j = i \bmod N$$

Example 1   Consider, for example, the case of a main memory consisting of 4K blocks, a cache memory consisting of 128 blocks, and a block size of 16 words. Figure 6.4 shows the division of the main memory and the cache according to the direct-mapped cache technique.

As the figure shows, there are a total of 32 main memory blocks that map to a given cache block. For example, main memory blocks 0, 128, 256, 384, ... , 3968 map to cache block 0. We therefore call the direct-mapping technique a

Tag		Cache		Main Memory				
3	0	384	0	128	256	384		3968
1	1	129	1	129	257	385		
0	2		2	130	258	386		
	126							
31	127	4095	127	255	383			4095
			0	1	2	3		31

Figure 6.4 Mapping main memory blocks to cache blocks

many-to-one mapping technique. The main advantage of the direct-mapping technique is its simplicity in determining where to place an incoming main memory block in the cache. Its main disadvantage is the inefficient use of the cache. This is because according to this technique, a number of main memory blocks may compete for a given cache block even if there exist other empty cache blocks. This disadvantage should lead to achieving a low cache hit ratio.

According to the direct-mapping technique the MMU interprets the address issued by the processor by dividing the address into three fields as shown in Figure 6.5. The lengths, in bits, of each of the fields in Figure 6.5 are:

1. Word field $= \log_2 B$, where B is the size of the block in words.
2. Block field $= \log_2 N$, where N is the size of the cache in blocks.
3. Tag field $= \log_2 (M/N)$, where M is the size of the main memory in blocks.
4. The number of bits in the main memory address $= \log_2 (B \times M)$

It should be noted that the total number of bits as computed by the first three equations should add up to the length of the main memory address. This can be used as a check for the correctness of your computation.

Example 2 Compute the above four parameters for Example 1.

Word field $= \log_2 B = \log_2 16 = \log_2 2^4 = 4$ bits
Block field $= \log_2 N = \log_2 128 = \log_2 2^7 = 7$ bits
Tag field $= \log_2(M/N) = \log_2(2^2 \times 2^{10}/2^7) = 5$ bits

The number of bits in the main memory address $= \log_2 (B \times M) = \log_2 (2^4 \times 2^{12}) = 16$ bits.

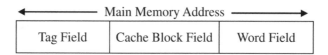

Figure 6.5 Direct-mapped address fields

Having shown the division of the main memory address, we can now proceed to explain the protocol used by the MMU to satisfy a request made by the processor for accessing a given element. We illustrate the protocol using the parameters given in the example presented above (Fig. 6.6).

The steps of the protocol are:

1. Use the *Block field* to determine the cache block that should contain the element requested by the processor. The *Block field* is used directly to determine the cache block sought, hence the name of the technique: direct-mapping.

2. Check the corresponding *Tag memory* to see whether there is a match between its content and that of the *Tag field*. A match between the two indicates that the targeted cache block determined in step 1 is currently holding the main memory element requested by the processor, that is, a *cache hit*.

3. Among the elements contained in the cache block, the targeted element can be selected using the *Word field*.

4. If in step 2, no match is found, then this indicates a *cache miss*. Therefore, the required block has to be brought from the main memory, deposited in the cache, and the targeted element is made available to the processor. The cache *Tag memory* and the cache block memory have to be updated accordingly.

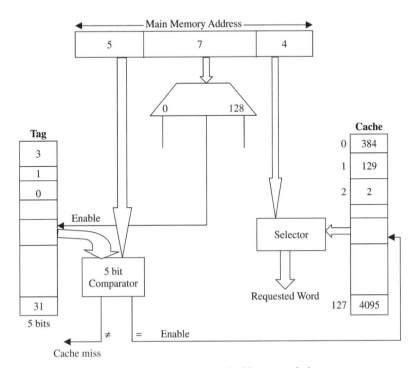

Figure 6.6   Direct-mapped address translation

The direct-mapping technique answers not only the placement of the incoming main memory block in the cache question, but it also answers the replacement question. Upon encountering a totally filled cache while a new main memory block has to be brought, the replacement is trivial and determined by the equation $j = i \bmod N$.

The main advantages of the direct-mapping technique is its simplicity measured in terms of the direct determination of the cache block; no search is needed. It is also simple in terms of the replacement mechanism. The main disadvantage of the technique is its expected poor utilization of the cache memory. This is represented in terms of the possibility of targeting a given cache block, which requires frequent replacement of blocks while the rest of the cache is not used. Consider, for example, the sequence of requests made by the processor for elements held in the main memory blocks 1, 33, 65, 97, 129, and 161. Consider also that the cache size is 32 blocks. It is clear that all the above blocks map to cache block number 1. Therefore, these blocks will compete for that same cache block despite the fact that the remaining 31 cache blocks are not used.

The expected poor utilization of the cache by the direct mapping technique is mainly due to the restriction on the placement of the incoming main memory blocks in the cache (the many-to-one property). If such a restriction is relaxed, that is, if we make it possible for an incoming main memory block to be placed in any empty (available) cache block, then the resulting technique would be so flexible that efficient utilization of the cache would be possible. Such a flexible technique, called the *Associative Mapping* technique, is explained next.

Fully Associative Mapping   According to this technique, an incoming main memory block can be placed in any available cache block. Therefore, the address issued by the processor need only have two fields. These are the *Tag* and *Word* fields. The first uniquely identifies the block while residing in the cache. The second field identifies the element within the block that is requested by the processor. The MMU interprets the address issued by the processor by dividing it into two fields as shown in Figure 6.7. The length, in bits, of each of the fields in Figure 6.7 are given by:

1. Word field $= \log_2 B$, where B is the size of the block in words
2. Tag field $= \log_2 M$, where M is the size of the main memory in blocks
3. The number of bits in the main memory address $= \log_2 (B \times M)$

It should be noted that the total number of bits as computed by the first two equations should add up to the length of the main memory address. This can be used as a check for the correctness of your computation.

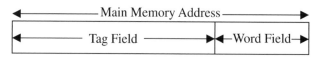

Figure 6.7   Associative-mapped address fields

Example 3 Compute the above three parameters for a memory system having the following specification: size of the main memory is 4K blocks, size of the cache is 128 blocks, and the block size is 16 words. Assume that the system uses associative mapping.

Word field $= \log_2 B = \log_2 16 = \log_2 2^4 = 4$ bits
Tag field $= \log_2 M = \log_2 2^7 \times 2^{10} = 12$ bits

The number of bits in the main memory address $= \log_2 (B \times M) = \log_2 (2^4 \times 2^{12}) = 16$ bits.

Having shown the division of the main memory address, we can now proceed to explain the protocol used by the MMU to satisfy a request made by the processor for accessing a given element. We illustrate the protocol using the parameters given in the example presented above (see Fig. 6.8). The steps of the protocol are:

1. Use the *Tag field* to search in the *Tag memory* for a match with any of the tags stored.
2. A match in the tag memory indicates that the corresponding targeted cache block determined in step 1 is currently holding the main memory element requested by the processor, that is, a *cache hit*.

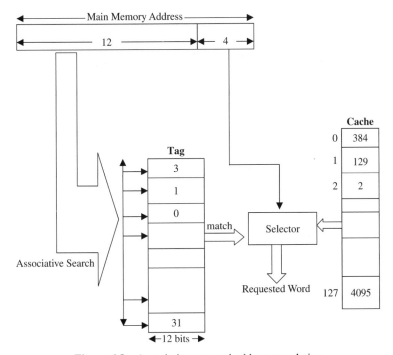

Figure 6.8 Associative-mapped address translation

3. Among the elements contained in the cache block, the targeted element can be selected using the *Word field*.

4. If in step 2, no match is found, then this indicates a *cache miss*. Therefore, the required block has to be brought from the main memory, deposited in the first available cache block, and the targeted element (word) is made available to the processor. The cache *Tag memory* and the cache block memory have to be updated accordingly.

It should be noted that the search made in step 1 above requires matching the *tag field* of the address with each and every entry in the *tag memory*. Such a search, if done sequentially, could lead to a long delay. Therefore, the *tags* are stored in an *associative (content addressable) memory*. This allows the entire contents of the tag memory to be searched in parallel (associatively), hence the name, associative mapping.

It should be noted that, regardless of the cache organization used, a mechanism is needed to ensure that any accessed cache block contains *valid* information. The validity of the information in a cache block can be checked via the use of a single bit for each cache block, called the *valid bit*. The valid bit of a cache block should be updated in such a way that if *valid bit* = 1, then the corresponding cache block carries valid information; otherwise, the information in the cache block is invalid. When a computer system is powered up, all valid bits are made equal to 0, indicating that they carry invalid information. As blocks are brought to the cache, their statuses are changed accordingly to indicate the validity of the information contained.

The main advantage of the associative-mapping technique is the efficient use of the cache. This stems from the fact that there exists no restriction on where to place incoming main memory blocks. Any unoccupied cache block can potentially be used to receive those incoming main memory blocks. The main disadvantage of the technique, however, is the hardware overhead required to perform the associative search conducted in order to find a match between the tag field and the tag memory as discussed above.

A compromise between the simple but inefficient direct cache organization and the involved but efficient associative cache organization can be achieved by conducting the search over a limited set of cache blocks while knowing ahead of time where in the cache an incoming main memory block is to be placed. This is the basis for the set-associative mapping technique explained next.

Set-Associative Mapping   In the set-associative mapping technique, the cache is divided into a number of sets. Each set consists of a number of blocks. A given main memory block maps to a specific cache set based on the equation $s = i \bmod S$, where S is the number of sets in the cache, i is the main memory block number, and s is the specfic cache set to which block i maps. However, an incoming block maps to any block in the assigned cache set. Therefore, the address issued by the processor is divided into three distinct fields. These are the *Tag*, *Set*, and *Word* fields. The *Set* field is used to uniquely identify the specific cache set that ideally should hold the targeted block. The *Tag* field uniquely identifies the targeted block within the determined set. The *Word* field identifies the element (word) within the block that is requested by the processor. According to the set-associative mapping technique, the MMU interprets the address issued by the processor by dividing it into three fields as shown in Figure 6.9. The length, in bits, of each of the fields of Figure 6.9 is given by

1. Word field $= \log_2 B$, where B is the size of the block in words
2. Set field $= \log_2 S$, where S is the number of sets in the cache
3. Tag field $= \log_2 (M/S)$, where M is the size of the main memory in blocks. $S = N/B_s$, where N is the number of cache blocks and B_s is the number of blocks per set
4. The number of bits in the main memory address $= \log_2 (B \times M)$

It should be noted that the total number of bits as computed by the first three equations should add up to the length of the main memory address. This can be used as a check for the correctness of your computation.

Example 4 Compute the above three parameters (Word, Set, and Tag) for a memory system having the following specification: size of the main memory is 4K blocks, size of the cache is 128 blocks, and the block size is 16 words. Assume that the system uses set-associative mapping with four blocks per set.

$$S = \frac{128}{4} = 32 \text{ sets.}$$

1. Word field $= \log_2 B = \log_2 16 = \log_2 2^4 = 4$ bits
2. Set field $= \log_2 32 = 5$ bits
3. Tag field $= \log_2 (4 \times 2^{10}/32) = 7$ bits

The number of bits in the main memory address $= \log_2 (B \times M) = \log_2 (2^4 \times 2^{12}) = 16$ bits.

Having shown the division of the main memory address, we can now proceed to explain the protocol used by the MMU to satisfy a request made by the processor for accessing a given element. We illustrate the protocol using the parameters given in the example presented above (see Fig. 6.10). The steps of the protocol are:

1. Use the *Set field* (5 bits) to determine (directly) the specified set (1 of the 32 sets).

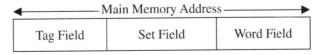

Figure 6.9   Set-associative-mapped address fields

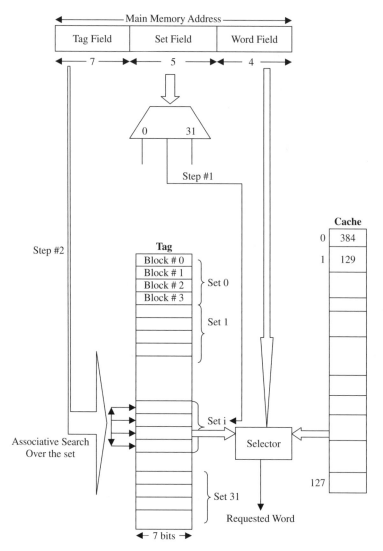

Figure 6.10   Set-associative-mapped address translation

2. Use the *Tag field* to find a match with any of the (four) blocks in the determined set. A match in the tag memory indicates that the specified set determined in step 1 is currently holding the targeted block, that is, a *cache hit*.

3. Among the 16 words (elements) contained in hit cache block, the requested word is selected using a selector with the help of the *Word field*.

4. If in step 2, no match is found, then this indicates a *cache miss*. Therefore, the required block has to be brought from the main memory, deposited in the specified set first, and the targeted element (word) is made available to the processor. The cache *Tag memory* and the cache block memory have to be updated accordingly.

It should be noted that the search made in step 2 above requires matching the *tag field* of the address with each and every entry in the *tag memory* for the specified set. Such a search is performed in parallel (associatively) over the set, hence the name, set-associative mapping. The hardware overhead required to performing the associative search within a set in order to find a match between the tag field and the tag memory is not as complex as that used in the case of the fully associative technique.

The set-associative-mapping technique is expected to produce a moderate cache utilization efficiency, that is, not as efficient as the fully associative technique and not as poor as the direct technique. However, the technique inherits the simplicity of the direct mapping technique in terms of determining the target set.

An overall qualitative comparison among the three mapping techniques is shown in Table 6.2. Owing to its moderate complexity and moderate cache utilization, the set-associative technique is used in the Intel Pentium line of processors.

The discussion above shows how the associative-mapping and the set-associative techniques answer the question about the placement of the incoming main memory block in the cache. The other important question that was posed at the beginning of the discussion on cache memory is that of replacement. Specifically, upon encountering a totally filled cache while a new main memory block has to be brought, which of the cache blocks should be selected for replacement? This is discussed below.

6.2.6. Replacement Techniques

A number of replacement techniques can be used. These include a randomly selected block (*random selection*), the block that has been in the cache the longest (*first-in-first-out, FIFO*), and the block that has been used the least while residing in the cache (*least recently used, LRU*).

Let us assume that when a computer system is powered up, a random number generator starts generating numbers between 0 and $(N - 1)$. As the name indicates,

TABLE 6.2   Qualitative Comparison Among Cache Mapping Techniques

Mapping technique	Simplicity	Associative tag search	Expected cache utilization	Replacement technique
Direct	Yes	None	Low	Not needed
Associative	No	Involved	High	Yes
Set-associative	Moderate	Moderate	Moderate	Yes

random selection of a cache block for replacement is done based on the output of the random number generator at the time of replacement. This technique is simple and does not require much additional overhead. However, its main shortcoming is that it does not take locality into consideration. Random techniques have been found effective enough such that they have been first used by Intel in its *iAPX* microprocessor series.

The FIFO technique takes the time spent by a block in the cache as a measure for replacement. The block that has been in the cache the longest is selected for replacement regardless of the recent pattern of access to the block. This technique requires keeping track of the lifetime of a cache block. Therefore, it is not as simple as the random selection technique. Intuitively, the FIFO technique is reasonable to use for straightline programs where locality of reference is not of concern.

According to the LRU replacement technique, the cache block that has been recently used the least is selected for replacement. Among the three replacement techniques, the LRU technique is the most effective. This is because the history of block usage (as the criterion for replacement) is taken into consideration. The LRU algorithm requires the use of a cache controller circuit that keeps track of references to all blocks while residing in the cache. This can be achieved through a number of possible implementations. Among these implementations is the use of counters. In this case each cache block is assigned a counter. Upon a cache hit, the counter of the corresponding block is set to 0, all other counters having a smaller value than the original value in the counter of the hit block are incremented by 1, and all counters having a larger value are kept unchanged. Upon a cache miss, the block whose counter is showing the maximum value is chosen for replacement, the counter is set to 0, and all other counters are incremented by 1.

Having introduced the above three cache mapping technique, we offer the following example, which illustrates the main observations made about the three techniques.

Example 5 Consider the case of a 4×8 two-dimensional array of numbers, A. Assume that each number in the array occupies one word and that the array elements are stored column-major order in the main memory from location 1000 to location 1031. The cache consists of eight blocks each consisting of just two words. Assume also that whenever needed, *LRU* replacement policy is used. We would like to examine the changes in the cache if each of the above three mapping techniques is used as the following sequence of requests for the array elements are made by the processor:

$a_{0,0}, a_{0,1}, a_{0,2}, a_{0,3}, a_{0,4}, a_{0,5}, a_{0,6}, a_{0,7}$

$a_{1,0}, a_{1,1}, a_{1,2}, a_{1,3}, a_{1,4}, a_{1,5}, a_{1,6}, a_{1,7}$

Solution The distribution of the array elements in the main memory is shown in Figure 6.11. Shown also is the status of the cache before the above requests were made.

Direct Mapping Table 6.3 shows that there were 16 cache misses (not a single cache hit) and that the number of replacements made is 12 (these are shown

Main Memory

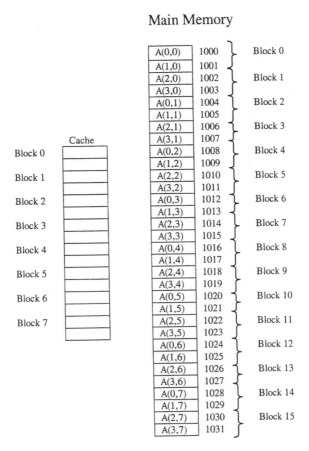

Figure 6.11   Array elements in the main memory

tinted). It also shows that out of the available eight cache blocks, only four (0, 2, 4, and 6) are used, while the remaining four are inactive all the time. This represents a 50% cache utilization.

Fully Associative Mapping   Table 6.4 shows that there were eight cache hits (50% of the total number of requests) and that there were no replacements made. It also shows a 100% cache utilization.

Set-Associative Mapping (With Two Blocks per Set)   Table 6.5 shows that there were 16 cache misses (not a single cache hit) and that the number of replacements made is 12 (these are shown tinted). It also shows that of the available four cache sets, only two sets are used, while the remaining two are inactive all the time. This represents a 50% cache utilization.

TABLE 6.3   Direct Mapping

Request	Cache hit/miss	MM block number (i)	Cache block number (j)	BL0	BL1	BL2	BL3	BL4	BL5	BL6	BL7
A(0,0)	Miss	0	0	0 1							
				0 0							
A(0,1)	Miss	2	2	0 1		0 1					
				0 0		1 1					
A(0,2)	Miss	4	4	0 1		0 1		0 1			
				0 0		1 1		2 2			
A(0,3)	Miss	6	6	0 1		0 1		0 1		0 1	
				0 0		1 1		2 2		3 3	
A(0,4)	Miss	8	0	0 1		0 1		0 1		0 1	
				4 4		1 1		2 2		3 3	
A(0,5)	Miss	10	2	0 1		0 1		0 1		0 1	
				4 4		5 5		2 2		3 3	
A(0,6)	Miss	12	4	0 1		0 1		0 1		0 1	
				4 4		5 5		6 6		3 3	
A(0,7)	Miss	14	6	0 1		0 1		0 1		0 1	
				4 4		5 5		6 6		7 7	
A(1,0)	Miss	0	0	0 1		0 1		0 1		0 1	
				0 0		5 5		6 6		7 7	
A(1,1)	Miss	2	2	0 1		0 1		0 1		0 1	
				0 0		1 1		6 6		6 6	
A(1,2)	Miss	4	4	0 1		0 1		0 1		0 1	
				0 0		1 1		2 2		6 6	
A(1,3)	Miss	6	6	0 1		0 1		0 1		0 1	
				0 0		1 1		2 2		3 3	
A(1,4)	Miss	8	0	0 1		0 1		0 1		0 1	
				4 4		1 1		2 2		3 3	
A(1,5)	Miss	10	2	0 1		0 1		0 1		0 1	
				4 4		5 5		2 2		3 3	
A(1,6)	Miss	12	4	0 1		0 1		0 1		0 1	
				4 4		5 5		6 6		3 3	
A(1,7)	Miss	14	6	0 1		0 1		0 1		0 1	
				4 4		5 5		6 6		7 7	

6.2.7. Cache Write Policies

Having discussed the main issues related to cache mapping techniques and the replacement policies, we would like to address a very important related issue, that is, cache coherence. Coherence between a cache word and its copy in the main memory should be maintained at all times, if at all possible. A number of policies (techniques) are used in performing write operations to the main memory blocks while residing in the cache. These policies determine the degree of coherence that

TABLE 6.4 Fully Associative Mapping

Request	Cache hit/miss	MM block number (i)	Cache block number	BL0	BL1	BL2	BL3	BL4	BL5	BL6	BL7
A(0,0)	Miss	0	0	0 1							
				0 0							
A(0,1)	Miss	2	1	0 1	0 1						
				0 0	1 1						
A(0,2)	Miss	4	2	0 1	0 1	0 1					
				0 0	1 1	2 2					
A(0,3)	Miss	6	3	0 1	0 1	0 1	0 1				
				0 0	1 1	2 2	3 3				
A(0,4)	Miss	8	4	0 1	0 1	0 1	0 1	0 1			
				0 0	1 1	2 2	3 3	4 4			
A(0,5)	Miss	10	5	0 1	0 1	0 1	0 1	0 1	0 1		
				0 0	1 1	2 2	3 3	4 4	5 5		
A(0,6)	Miss	12	6	0 1	0 1	0 1	0 1	0 1	0 1	0 1	
				0 0	1 1	2 2	3 3	4 4	5 5	6 6	
A(0,7)	Miss	14	7	0 1	0 1	0 1	0 1	0 1	0 1	0 1	0 1
				0 0	1 1	2 2	3 3	4 4	5 5	6 6	7 7
A(1,0)	Hit	0	0	0 1	0 1	0 1	0 1	0 1	0 1	0 1	0 1
				0 0	1 1	2 2	3 3	4 4	5 5	6 6	7 7
A(1,1)	Hit	2	1	0 1	0 1	0 1	0 1	0 1	0 1	0 1	0 1
				0 0	1 1	2 2	3 3	4 4	5 5	6 6	7 7
A(1,2)	Hit	4	2	0 1	0 1	0 1	0 1	0 1	0 1	0 1	0 1
				0 0	1 1	2 2	3 3	4 4	5 5	6 6	7 7
A(1,3)	Hit	6	3	0 1	0 1	0 1	0 1	0 1	0 1	0 1	0 1
				0 0	1 1	2 2	3 3	4 4	5 5	6 6	7 7
A(1,4)	Hit	8	4	0 1	0 1	0 1	0 1	0 1	0 1	0 1	0 1
				0 0	1 1	2 2	3 3	4 4	5 5	6 6	7 7
A(1,5)	Hit	10	5	0 1	0 1	0 1	0 1	0 1	0 1	0 1	0 1
				0 0	1 1	2 2	3 3	4 4	5 5	6 6	7 7
A(1,6)	Hit	12	6	0 1	0 1	0 1	0 1	0 1	0 1	0 1	0 1
				0 0	1 1	2 2	3 3	4 4	5 5	6 6	7 7
A(1,7)	Hit	14	7	0 1	0 1	0 1	0 1	0 1	0 1	0 1	0 1
				0 0	1 1	2 2	3 3	4 4	5 5	6 6	7 7

can be maintained between cache words and their counterparts in the main memory. In the following paragraphs, we discuss these write policies. In particular, we discuss two main cases: cache write policies upon a cache hit and the cache write policies upon a cache miss. We also discuss the cache read policy upon a cache miss. Cache read upon a cache hit is straightforward.

Cache Write Policies Upon a Cache Hit   There are essentially two possible write policies upon a cache hit. These are the *write-through* and the *write-back*.

TABLE 6.5 Set-Associative Mapping

Request	Cache hit/miss	MM block number (i)	Cache block number	Set # 0 BL0	BL1	Set # 1 BL2	BL3	Set # 2 BL4	BL5	Set # 3 BL6	BL7
A(0,0)	Miss	0	0	0	1						
				0	0						
A(0,1)	Miss	2	2	0	1			0	1		
				0	0			1	1		
A(0,2)	Miss	4	0	0	1	0	1	0	1		
				0	0	2	2	1	1		
A(0,3)	Miss	6	2	0	1	0	1	0	1	0	1
				0	0	2	2	1	1	3	3
A(0,4)	Miss	8	0	0	1	0	1	0	1	0	1
				4	4	2	2	1	1	3	3
A(0,5)	Miss	10	2	0	1	0	1	0	1	0	1
				4	4	2	2	5	5	3	3
A(0,6)	Miss	12	0	0	1	0	1	0	1	0	1
				4	4	6	6	5	5	3	3
A(0,7)	Miss	14	2	0	1	0	1	0	1	0	1
				4	4	6	6	5	5	7	7
A(1,0)	Miss	0	0	0	1	0	1	0	1	0	1
				0	0	6	6	5	5	7	7
A(1,1)	Miss	2	2	0	1	0	1	0	1	0	1
				0	0	6	6	1	1	7	7
A(1,2)	Miss	4	0	0	1	0	1	0	1	0	1
				0	0	2	2	1	1	7	7
A(1,3)	Miss	6	2	0	1	0	1	0	1	0	1
				0	0	2	2	1	1	3	3
A(1,4)	Miss	8	0	0	1	0	1	0	1	0	1
				4	4	2	2	1	1	3	3
A(1,5)	Miss	10	2	0	1	0	1	0	1	0	1
				4	4	2	2	5	5	3	3
A(1,6)	Miss	12	0	0	1	0	1	0	1	0	1
				4	4	6	6	5	5	3	3
A(1,7)	Miss	14	2	0	1	0	1	0	1	0	1
				4	4	6	6	4	4	2	2

In the write-through policy, every write operation to the cache is repeated to the main memory at the same time. In the write-back policy, all writes are made to the cache. A write to the main memory is postponed until a replacement is needed. Every cache block is assigned a bit, called the *dirty bit*, to indicate that at least one write operation has been made to the block while residing in the cache. At replacement time, the dirty bit is checked; if it is set, then the block is written back to the main memory, otherwise, it is simply overwritten by the incoming block. The write-through policy maintains coherence between the cache blocks and their counterparts in the main memory at the expense of the extra time needed to write to the main memory. This leads to an increase in the average access time. On the other hand, the write-back policy eliminates the increase in the average access time. However, coherence is only guaranteed at the time of replacement.

Cache Write Policy Upon a Cache Miss Two main schemes can be used. These are *write-allocate* whereby the main memory block is brought to the cache and then updated. The other scheme is called *write-no-allocate* whereby the missed main memory block is updated while in the main memory and not brought to the cache.

In general, *write-through* caches use *write-no-allocate* policy while *write-back* caches use *write-allocate policy*.

Cache Read Policy Upon a Cache Miss Two possible strategies can be used. In the first, the main memory missed block is brought to the cache while the required word is forwarded immediately to the CPU as soon as it is available. In the second strategy, the missed main memory block is entirely stored in the cache and the required word is then forwarded to the CPU.

Having discussed the issues related to the design and analysis of cache memory, we briefly present formulae for the average access time of a memory hierarchy under different cache write policies.

Case No. 1: Cache Write-Through Policy

Write-allocate In this case, the average access time for a memory system is given by

$$t_a = t_c + (1 - h)t_b + w(t_m - t_c)$$

where t_b is the time required to transfer a block to the cache, $(t_m - t_c)$ is the additional time incurred due to the write operations, w is the fraction of write operations. It should be noted that if the data path and organization allow, then $t_b = t_m$; otherwise, $t_b = Bt_m$, where B is the block size in words.

Write-no-allocate In this case, the average access time can be expressed as

$$t_a = t_c + (1 - w)(1 - h)t_b + w(t_m - t_c)$$

Case No. 2: Cache Write-Back Policy The average access time for a system that uses a write-back policy is given by $t_a = t_c + (1 - h)t_b + w_b(1 - h)t_b$, where w_b is the probability that a block has been altered while being in the cache.

6.2.8. Real-Life Cache Organization Analysis

Intel's Pentium IV Processor Cache   Intel's Pentium 4 processor uses a two-level cache organization as shown schematically in Figure 6.12. In this figure, L1 represents an 8 KB data cache. This is a four-way set-associative. The block size is 64 bytes. Consider the following example (tailored after the L1 Pentium cache).

Example 6

Cache organization	Set-associative
Main Memory size	16 MB
Cache L1 size	8 KB
Number of blocks per set	Four
CPU addressing	Byte addressable

The main memory address should be divided into three fields: Word, Set, and Tag (Fig. 6.13). The length of each field is computed as follows.

Number of main memory blocks $M = 2^{24}/2^6 = 2^{18}$ blocks

Number of cache blocks $N = 2^{13}/2^6 = 128$ blocks

$S = 128/4 = 32$ sets

Set field $= \log_2 32 = 5$ bits

Word field $= \log_2 B = \log_2 64 = \log_2 2^6 = 6$ bits

Tag field $= \log_2 (2^{18}/2^5) = 13$ bits

Main memory address $= \log_2 (B \times M) = \log_2 (2^6 \times 2^{18}) = 24$ bits

The second cache level in Figure 6.11 is L2. This is called the *advanced transfer cache*. It is organized as an eight-way set-associative cache having a 256 KB total size and 128-byte block size. Following a similar set of steps as shown above for the L1 level, we obtain the following:

Number of main memory blocks $M = 2^{24}/2^7 = 2^{17}$ blocks

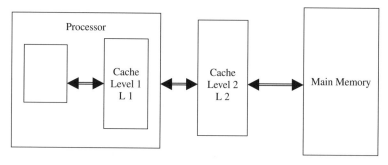

Figure 6.12   Pentium IV two-level cache

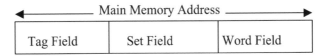

Figure 6.13 Division of main memory address

Number of cache blocks $N = 2^{18}/2^7 = 2^{11}$ blocks
$S = 2^{11}/2^3 = 2^8$ sets
Set field $= \log_2 2^8 = 8$ bits
Word field $= \log_2 B = \log_2 128 = \log_2 2^7 = 7$ bits
Tag field $= \log_2 (2^{17}/2^8) = 9$ bits

The following tables summarize the L1 and L2 Pentium 4 cache performance in terms of the cache hit ratio and cache latency.

CPU	L1 Hit ratio	L2 Hit ratio	L1 Latency	L2 Latency	Average latency
Pentium 4 at 1.5 GHz	90%	99%	1.33 ns	6.0 ns	1.8 ns

PowerPC 604 Processor Cache   The PowerPC cache is divided into data and instruction caches, called *Harvard Organization*. Both the instruction and the data caches are organized as 16 KB four-way set-associative. The following table summarizes the PowerPC 604 cache basic characteristics.

Cache organization	Set-associative
Block size	32 bytes
Main memory size	4 GB ($M = 128$ Mega blocks)
Cache size	16 KB ($N = 512$ blocks)
Number of blocks per set	Four
Number of cache sets (S)	128 sets

The main memory address should be divided into three fields: Word, Set, and Tag (Fig. 6.13). The length of each field is computed as follows:

Number of main memory blocks $M = 2^{32}/2^5 = 2^{27}$ blocks
Number of cache blocks $N = 2^{14}/2^5 = 512$ blocks
$S = 512/4 = 128$ sets
Set field $= \log_2 128 = 7$ bits
Word field $= \log_2 B = \log_2 32 = \log_2 2^5 = 5$ bits
Tag field $= \log_2 (2^{27}/2^7) = 20$ bits
Main memory address $= \log_2 (B \times M) = \log_2 (2^5 \times 2^{27}) = 32$ bits

PMC-Sierra RM7000A 64-bit MIPS RISC Processor   The RM7000 uses a different cache organization compared to that of the Intel and the PowerPC. In this case, three separate caches are included. These are:

1. Primary instruction cache: A 16 KB, four-way set-associative cache with 32-byte block size (eight instructions)
2. Primary data cache: A 16 KB, four-way set-associative cache with 32 bytes block size (eight words)
3. Secondary cache: A 256 KB, four-way set-associative cache for both instructions and data

In addition to the three on-chip caches, the RM7000 provides a dedicated tertiary cache interface, which supports tertiary cache sizes of 512 KB, 2 MB, and 8 MB. This tertiary cache is only accessed after a secondary cache miss.

The primary caches require one cycle each to access. Each of these caches has 64-bit read data path and 128-bit write data path. Both caches can be accessed simultaneously, giving an aggregate bandwidth of over 4 GB per second. The secondary cache has a 64-bit data path and is accessed only on a primary cache miss. It has a three-cycle miss penalty. Owing to the unusual cache organization of the RM7000, it uses the two cache access schemes described below.

Non-Blocking Caches   In this scheme, the caches do not stall on a miss, rather the processor continues to operate out of the primary caches until one of the following events takes place:

1. Two cache misses are outstanding and a third load/store instruction appears on the instruction bus.
2. A subsequent instruction requires data from either of the instructions that caused a cache miss.

The use of nonblocking caches improves the overall performance by allowing the cache to continue operating even though a cache miss has occurred.

Cache Locking   In this scheme, critical code or data segments are locked into the primary and secondary caches. The locked contents can be updated on a write hit, but cannot be selected for replacement on a miss. RM7000 allows each of the three caches to be locked separately. However, only two of the available four sets of each cache can be locked. In particular, RM7000 allows a maximum of 128 KB of data or code to be locked in the secondary cache, a maximum of 8 KB of code to be locked in the instruction cache, and a maximum of 8 KB of data to be locked in the data cache.

6.3. SUMMARY

In this chapter, we consider the design and analysis of the first level of a memory hierarchy, that is, the cache memory. In this context, the locality issues were discussed and their effect on the average access time was explained. Three cache mapping techniques, namely direct, associative, and set-associative mappings were analyzed and their performance measures compared. We have also introduced three replacement techniques: Random, FIFO, and LRU replacement. The impact of the three techniques on the cache hit ratio was analyzed. Cache writing policies were also introduced and analyzed. Our discussion on cache ended with a presentation of the cache memory organization and characteristics of three real-life examples: Pentium IV, PowerPC, and PMC-Sierra RM7000, processors. In Chapter 7, we will discuss the issues related to the design aspects of the internal and external organization of the main memory. We will also discuss the issues related to virtual memory.

EXERCISES

1. Determine the memory interleaving factor required to obtain an average access time of less that 60 ns given that the main memory has an access time of 100 ns and the cache has an access time of 20 ns. What is the average access time of the resulting system?
2. What is the average access time of a system having three levels of memory, a cache memory, a semiconductor main memory, and a magnetic disk secondary memory, if the access times of the memories are 20 ns, 100 ns, and 1 ms, respectively. The cache hit ratio is 90% and the main memory hit ratio is 95%.
3. A computer system has an MM consisting of 16 MB 32-bit words. It also has an 8 KB cache. Assume that the computer uses a byte-addressable mechanism. Determine the number of bits in each field of the address in each of the following organizations:
   (a) Direct mapping with block size of one word
   (b) Direct mapping with a block size of eight words
   (c) Associative mapping with a block size of eight words
   (d) Set-associative mapping with a set size of four block and a block size of one word.
4. Consider the execution of the following program segment on an 8×8 array A.

```
For i: = 0 to 7 do
SUM: = 0
    For j: = 0 to 7 do
        SUM: = SUM + A(i,j)
    End for
AVE(i): = SUM/8
End for
```

Assume that the main memory is divided into eight interleaved memory blocks and that each cache memory block consists of eight elements. Assume also that the cache memory access time is 10 ns and that the memory access time is ten times the cache memory access time. Compute the average access time per element of the array A.

5. Consider the execution of the following program segment on a 4×10 array A. The two-dimensional array A is stored in the main memory in a column-major order. Assume that there are eight blocks in the cache, each is just one word, and that the LRU is used for replacement. Show a trace of the contents of the cache memory blocks for the different values of indices j and k assuming three different cache memory organizations, that is, *direct*, *associative*, and *set-associative mapping*. Provide your observations on the results obtained.

```
SUM: = 0
For j: = 0 to 9 do
     SUM: = SUM + A(0,j)
End for
AVE: = SUM/10
For k: = 0 to 9 do
     A(0,k): = A(0, k)/AVE
End for
```

6. Consider the case of a 4×8 two-dimensional array of numbers, A. Assume that each number in the array occupies one word and that the array elements are stored row-major in the main memory for location 1000 to location 1031. The cache consists of eight blocks each consisting of four words. Assume also that whenever needed, LRU replacement policy is used. We would like to examine the changes in the cache if each of the above three mapping techniques is used as the following sequence of requests for the array elements is made:

$a_{0,0}, a_{0,1}, a_{0,2}, a_{0,3}, a_{0,4}, a_{0,5}, a_{0,6}, a_{0,7}$

$a_{1,0}, a_{1,1}, a_{1,2}, a_{1,3}, a_{1,4}, a_{1,5}, a_{1,6}, a_{1,7}$

$a_{2,0}, a_{2,1}, a_{2,2}, a_{2,3}, a_{2,4}, a_{2,5}, a_{2,6}, a_{2,7}$

$a_{3,0}, a_{3,1}, a_{3,2}, a_{3,3}, a_{3,4}, a_{3,5}, a_{3,6}, a_{3,7}$

Show the status of the cache before and after the given requests were made, the number of replacements made, and an estimate of the cache utilization.

7. A computer system has an MM consisting of 1 M 16-bit words. It also has a 4 K word cache organized in the block-set-associative manner, with four blocks per set and 64 words per block. Assume that the cache is initially empty. Suppose that the CPU fetches 4352 words from locations 0, 1, 2, ..., 4351 (in that order). It then repeats this fetch sequence nine more times. If the cache is 10 times faster than the MM, estimate the improvement factor resulting from the use of the cache. Assume that whenever a block is to be brought from the MM and the correspondence set in the cache is full, the new block replaces the least recently used block of this set. Repeat for the case of using the *most recently used* replacement technique; that is, if the cache is full, then the new block will replace the most recently used block in the cache. Note: This example is quoted from Reference #3.

REFERENCES AND FURTHER READING

S. D. Burd, *Systems Architecture*, 3rd ed., Thomson Learning Ltd, Boston, USA, 2001.

H. Cragon, *Memory Systems and Pipelined Processors*, Jones and Bartlett: Sudbury, MA, 1996.

V. C. Hamacher, Z. G. Vranesic, and S. G. Zaky, *Computer Organization*, 5th ed., McGraw-Hill, New York, 2002.

J. L. Hennessy, and D. A. Patterson, *Computer Architecture: A Quantitative Approach*, Morgan Kaufmann, San Francisco, CA, 1996.

V. P. Heuring, and H. F. Jordan, *Computer Systems Design and Architecture*, Addison-Wesley, NJ, USA, 1997.

D. A. Patterson, and J. L. Hennessy, *Computer Organization & Design: The Hardware/Software Interface*, Morgan Kaufmann, San Mateo, CA, 1994.

H. S. Stone, *High-Performance Computer Architecture*, Addison-Wesley, Amsterdam, Netherlands, 1987.

M. Wilkes, Slave memories and dynamic storage allocation, IEEE Trans. Electron. Comput., EC-14(2), 270–271, (1965).

B. Wilkinson, *Computer Architecture: Design and Performance*, Prentice-Hall, Hertfordshire, UK, 1996.

Websites

http://www.sysopt.com

http://www.intel.com

http://www.AcerHardware.com

http://www.pmc-sierra.com/products/details/rm7000a

http://physinfo.ulb.ac.be/divers_html/PowerPC_Programming_Info/into_to_ppc/ppc2_hardware.html

CHAPTER 7

Memory System Design II

In Chapter 6 we introduced the concept of memory hierarchy. We have also character-ized a memory hierarchy in terms of the locality of reference and its impact on the aver-age access time. We then moved on to cover the different issues related to the first level of the hierarchy, that is, the cache memory (the reader is advised to carefully review Chapter 6 before proceeding with this chapter). In this chapter, we continue our cover-age of the different levels of the memory hierarchy. In particular, we start our discus-sion with the issues related to the design and analysis of the (main) memory unit. Issues related to *virtual memory* design are then discussed. A brief coverage of the different *read-only memory* (ROM) implementations is provided at the end of the chapter.

7.1. MAIN MEMORY

As the name implies, the main memory provides the main storage for a computer. Figure 7.1 shows a typical interface between the main memory and the CPU. Two CPU registers are used to interface the CPU to the main memory. These are the memory address register (MAR) and the memory data register (MDR). The MDR is used to hold the data to be stored and/or retrieved in/from the memory location whose address is held in the MAR.

It is possible to visualize a typical internal main memory structure as consisting of rows and columns of basic cells. Each cell is capable of storing one bit of infor-mation. Figure 7.2 provides a conceptual internal organization of a memory chip. In this figure, cells belonging to a given row can be assumed to form the bits of a given memory word. Address lines $A_{n-1}A_{n-2}\ldots A_1A_0$ are used as inputs to the address decoder in order to generate the word select lines $W_{2^n-1}\ldots W_1W_0$. A given word select line is common to all memory cells in the same row. At any given time, the address decoder activates only one word select line while deactivating the remaining lines. A word select line is used to enable all cells in a row for read or write. Data (bit) lines are used to input or output the contents of cells. Each memory cell is connected to two data lines. A given data line is common to all cells in a given column.

Fundamentals of Computer Organization and Architecture, by M. Abd-El-Barr and H. El-Rewini
ISBN 0-471-46741-3 Copyright © 2005 John Wiley & Sons, Inc.

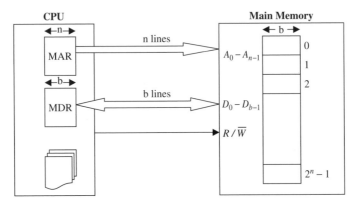

Figure 7.1 A typical CPU and main memory interface

In static CMOS technology, each main memory cell consists of six transistors as shown in Figure 7.3. The six transistor static CMOS memory cell consists of two inverters back to back. It should be noted that the cell could exist in one of the two stable states. For example, if in Figure 7.3 $A = 1$, then transistor N_2 will be on and point $B = 0$, which in turn will cause transistor P_1 to be on, thus causing point $A = 1$. This represents a cell stable state, call it state 1. In a similar way

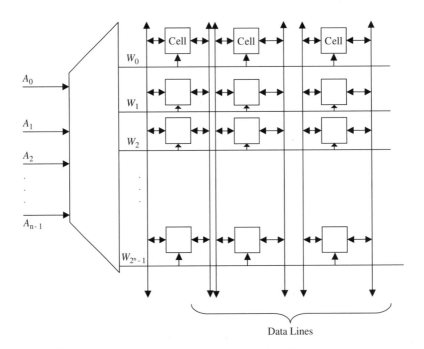

Figure 7.2 A conceptual internal organization of a memory chip

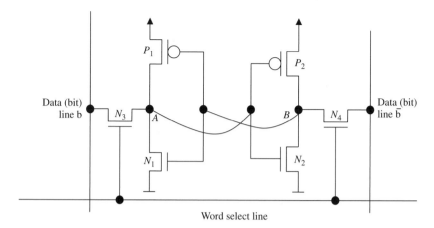

Figure 7.3 Static CMOS memory cell

one can show that if $A = 0$, then $B = 1$, which represents the other cell stable state, call it state 0. The two transistors N_3 and N_4 are used to connect the cell to the two data (bit) lines. Normally (if the word select is not activated) these two transistors are turned off, thus protecting the cell from the signal values carried by the data lines. The two transistors are turned on when the word select line is activated. What takes place when the two transistors are turned on will depend on the intended memory operation as shown below.

Read operation:

1. Both lines b and $\bar{b}$ are precharged high.
2. The word select line is activated, thus turning on both transistors N_3 and N_4.
3. Depending on the internal value stored in the cell, point $A(B)$ will lead to the discharge of line $b(\bar{b})$.

Write operation:

1. The bit lines are precharged such that $b(\bar{b}) = 1(0)$.
2. The word select line is activated, thus turning on both transistors N_3 and N_4.
3. The bit line precharged with 0 will have to force the point $A(B)$, which has 1, to 0.

The internal organization of the memory array should satisfy an important memory design factor, that is, efficient utilization of the memory chip. Consider, for example, a 1K×4 memory chip. Using the organization shown in Figure 7.2, the memory array should be organized as 1K rows of cells, each consisting of four cells. The chip will then have to have 10 pins for the address and four pins for the data. However, this may not lead to the best utilization of the chip area.

Another possible organization of the memory cell array is as a 64×64, that is, to organize the array in the form of 64 rows, each consisting of 64 cells. In this case, six address lines (forming what is called the row address) will be needed in order to select one of the 64 rows. The remaining four address lines (called the column address) will be used to select the appropriate 4 bits among the available 64 bits constituting a row. Figure 7.4 illustrates this organization.

Another important factor related to the design of the main memory subsystem is the number of chip pins required in an integrated circuit. Consider, for example, the design of a memory subsystem whose capacity is 4K bits. Different organization of the same memory capacity can lead to a different number of chip pins requirement. Table 7.1 illustrates such an observation. It is clear from the table that increasing the number of bits per addressable location results in an increase in the number of pins needed in the integrated circuit.

Another factor pertinent to the design of the main memory subsystem is the required number of memory chips. It is important to realize that the available per chip memory capacity can be a limiting factor in designing memory subsystems.

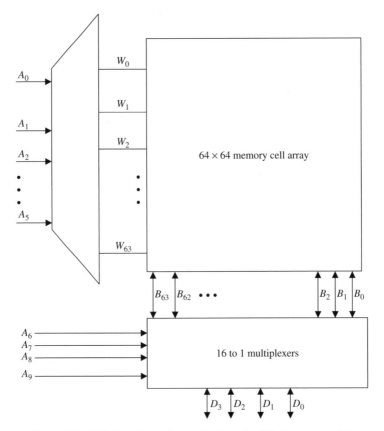

Figure 7.4   Efficient internal organization of a $1K \times 4$ memory chip

TABLE 7.1 Impact of Using Different Organizations on the Number of Pins

Organization	Number of needed address lines	Number of needed data lines
4K×1	12	1
1K×4	10	4
512×8	9	8
256×16	8	16

Consider, for example, the design of a 4M bytes main memory subsystem using 1M bit chip. The number of required chips is 32 chips. It should be noted that the number of address lines required for the 4M system is 22, while the number of data lines is 8. Figure 7.5 shows a block diagram for both the intended memory subsystem and the basic building block to be used to construct such a subsystem.

The memory subsystem can be arranged in four rows, each having eight chips. A schematic of such an arrangement is shown in Figure 7.6. In this figure, the least significant 20 address lines $A_{19} - A_0$ are used to address any of the basic building block 1M single bit chips. The high-order two address lines $A_{21} - A_{20}$ are used as inputs to a 2–4 decoder in order to generate four enable lines; each is connected to the CE line of the eight chips constituting a row.

The above discussion on main memory system design assumes the use of a six-transistor static random cell. It is possible however to use a one-transistor dynamic cell. Dynamic memory depends on storing logic values using a capacitor together with one transistor that acts as a switch. The use of dynamic memory leads to saving in chip area. However, due to the possibility of decay of the stored values

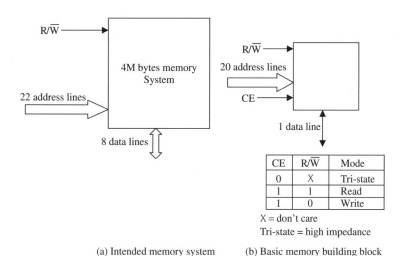

(a) Intended memory system   (b) Basic memory building block

Figure 7.5 Block diagram of a required memory system and its basic building block

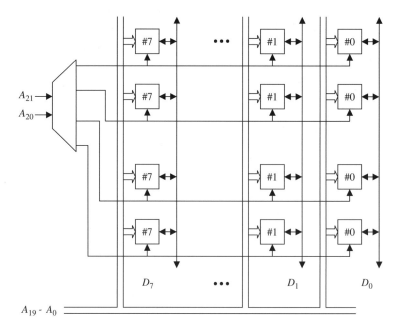

Figure 7.6 Organization of a 4M 8-bit memory using 1M 1-bit memory chips

(leakage of the stored charge on the capacitor), dynamic memory requires periodical (every few milliseconds) refreshment in order to restore the stored logic values. Figure 7.7 illustrates the dynamic memory array organization. The read/write circuitry in Figure 7.7 performs the functions of sensing the value on the bit line, amplifying it, and refreshing the value stored on the capacitor.

In order to perform a read operation, the bit line is precharged high (same as in static memory) and the word line is activated. That will cause the value stored on the capacitor to appear on the bit line, thus appearing on the data line D_i. As can be seen, a read operation is destructive; that is, the capacitor is charged to the bit line. Therefore, every read operation is followed by a write operation of the same value.

In order to perform a write operation, the intended value is placed on the bit line and the word line is activated. If the intended value is 1, then the capacitor will be charged, while if the intended value is 0, then the capacitor will be discharged. Table 7.2 summarizes the operation of the control circuitry.

TABLE 7.2 Operation of the Control Circuitry

CE	$R/\bar{W}$	Operation
0	×	None
1	1	Read
1	0	Write

× = don't care

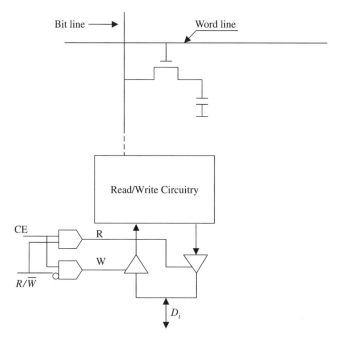

Figure 7.7 Dynamic memory array organization

As discussed before, appropriate internal organization of a memory subsystem can lead to a saving in the number of IC pins required, an important IC design factor. In order to reduce the number of pins required for a given dynamic memory subsystem, it is a normal practice (as in the case of static memory) to divide the address lines into row and column address lines. In addition, the row and column address lines are transmitted over the same pins, one after the other in a scheme known as *time-multiplexing*. This can potentially cut the number of address pins required by half. Due to time-multiplexing of address lines, it will be necessary to add two extra control lines, that is, row address strobe ($\overline{RAS}$) and column address strobe ($\overline{CAS}$). These two control lines are used to indicate to the memory chip when the row address lines are valid and when the column address lines are valid, respectively. Consider, for example, the design of a 1M×1 dynamic memory subsystem. Figure 7.8 shows a possible internal organization of the memory cell array in which the array is organized as a 1024×1024.

It should be noted that only 10 address lines are shown. These are used to multiplex both the rows and columns address lines; each is 10 lines. The rows and columns latches are used to store the row and column addresses for a duration equal to the memory cycle. In this case, a memory access will consist of a $\overline{RAS}$ and a row address, followed by a $\overline{CAS}$ and a column address.

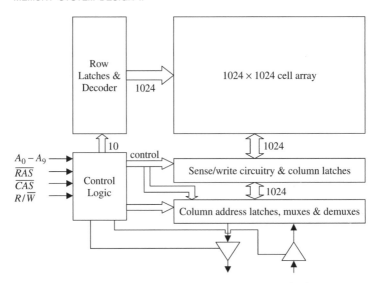

Figure 7.8   A 1024 × 1024 memory array organization

7.2. VIRTUAL MEMORY

The concept of virtual memory is in principle similar to that of the cache memory described in Section 6.2. A virtual memory system attempts to optimize the use of the main memory (the higher speed portion) with the hard disk (the lower speed portion). In effect, virtual memory is a technique for using the secondary storage to extend the apparent limited size of the physical memory beyond its actual physical size. It is usually the case that the available physical memory space will not be enough to host all the parts of a given active program. Those parts of the program that are currently active are brought to the main memory while those parts that are not active will be stored on the magnetic disk. If the segment of the program containing the word requested by the processor is not in the main memory at the time of the request, then such segment will have to be brought from the disk to the main memory. The principles employed in the virtual memory design are the same as those employed in the cache memory. The most relevant principle is that of keeping active segments in the high-speed main memory and moving inactive segments back to the hard disk.

Movement of data between the disk and the main memory takes the form of pages. A page is a collection of memory words, which can be moved from the disk to the MM when the processor requests accessing a word on that page. A typical size of a page in modern computers ranges from 2K to 16K bytes. A page fault occurs when the page containing the word required by the processor does not exist in the MM and has to be brought from the disk. The movement of pages of programs or data between the main memory and the disk is totally transparent to the application programmer. The operating system is responsible for such movement of data and programs.

It is useful to mention at this point that although based on similar principles, a significant difference exists between cache and virtual memories. A cache miss can cause a time penalty that is 5 to 10 times as costly as a cache hit. A page fault, on the other hand can be 1000 times as costly as a page hit. It is therefore unreasonable to have the processor wait on a page fault while a page is being transferred to the main memory. This is because thousands of instructions could be executed on a modern processor during page transfer.

The address issued by the processor in order to access a given word does not correspond to the physical memory space. Therefore, such address is called a *virtual (logical) address*. The memory management unit (MMU) is responsible for the translation of virtual addresses to their corresponding physical addresses. Three address translation techniques can be identified. These are *direct-mapping*, *associative-mapping*, and *set-associative-mapping*. In all these techniques, information about the main memory locations and the corresponding virtual pages are kept in a table called the *page table*. The page table is stored in the main memory. Other information kept in the page table includes a bit indicating the validity of a page, modification of a page, and the authority for accessing a page. The *valid bit* is set if the corresponding page is actually loaded into the main memory. Valid bits for all pages are reset when the computer is first powered on. The other control bit that is kept in the page table is the *dirty bit*. It is set if the corresponding page has been altered while residing in the main memory. If while residing in the main memory a given page has not been altered, then its dirty bit will be reset. This can help in deciding whether to write the contents of a page back into the disk (at the time of replacement) or just to override its contents with another page. In the following discussion, we will concentrate on the address translation techniques keeping in mind the use of the different control bits stored in the page table.

7.2.1. Direct Mapping

Figure 7.9 illustrates the address translation process according to the direct-mapping technique. In this case, the virtual address issued by the processor is divided into two fields: the virtual page number and the offset fields. If the number of bits in the virtual page number field is N, then the number of entries in the page table will be 2^N.

The virtual page number field is used to directly address an entry in the page table. If the corresponding page is valid (as indicated by the valid bit), then the contents of the specified page table entry will correspond to the physical page address. The latter is then extracted and concatenated with the offset field in order to form the physical address of the word requested by the processor. If, on the other hand, the specified entry in the page table does not contain a valid physical page number, then this represents a page fault. In this case, the MMU will have to bring the corresponding page from the hard disk, load it into the main memory, and indicate the validity of the page. The translation process is then carried out as explained before.

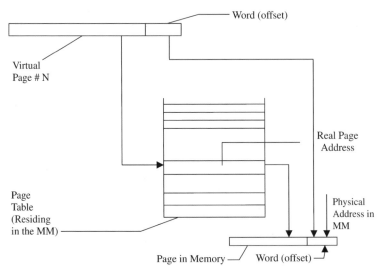

Figure 7.9 Direct-mapping virtual address translation

The main advantage of the direct-mapping technique is its simplicity measured in terms of the direct addressing of the page table entries. Its main disadvantage is the expected large size of the page table. In order to overcome the need for a large page table, the associative-mapping technique, which is explained below, is used.

7.2.2. Associative Mapping

Figure 7.10 illustrates the address translation according to the associative mapping technique. The technique is similar to direct mapping in that the virtual address issued by the processor is divided into two fields: the virtual page number and the offset fields. However, the page table used in associative mapping could be far shorter than its direct mapping counterpart. Every entry in the page table is divided into two parts: the virtual page number and the physical page number. A match is searched (associatively) between the virtual page number field of the address and the virtual page numbers stored in the page table. If a match is found, the corresponding physical page number stored in the page table is extracted and is concatenated with the offset field in order to generate the physical address of the word requested by the processor. If, on the other hand, a match could not be found, then this represents a page fault. In this case, the MMU will have to bring the corresponding page from the hard disk, load it into the main memory, and indicate the validity of the page. The translation process is then carried out as explained before.

The main advantage of the associative-mapping technique is the expected shorter page table (compared to the direct-mapping technique) required for the translation process. Its main disadvantage is the search required for matching the virtual

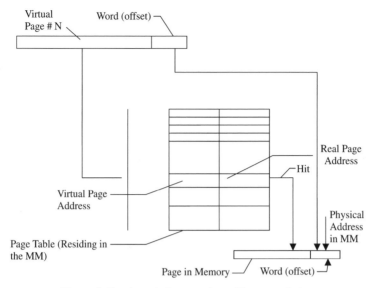

Figure 7.10 Associative mapping address translation

page number field and all virtual page numbers stored in the page table. Although such a search is done associatively, it requires the use of an added hardware overhead.

A possible compromise between the complexity of the associative mapping and the simplicity of the direct mapping is the set-associative mapping technique. This hybrid technique is explained below.

7.2.3. Set-Associative Mapping

Figure 7.11 illustrates the address translation according to the set-associative mapping. In this case, the virtual address issued by the processor is divided into three fields: the tag, the index, and the offset. The page table used in set-associative mapping is divided into sets, each consisting of a number of entries. Each entry in the page table consists of a tag and the corresponding physical page address. Similar to direct mapping, the index field is used to directly determine the set in which a search should be conducted. If the number of bits in the index field is S, then the number of sets in the page table should be 2^S. Once the set is determined, then a search (similar to associative mapping) is conducted to match the tag field with all entries in that specific set. If a match is found, then the corresponding physical page address is extracted and concatenated with the offset field in order to generate the physical address of the word requested by the processor. If, on the other hand, a match could not be found, then this represents a page fault. In this case, the MMU will have to bring the corresponding page from the hard disk, load it into the main memory, update the corresponding set and indicate the validity of the page. The translation process is then carried out as explained before.

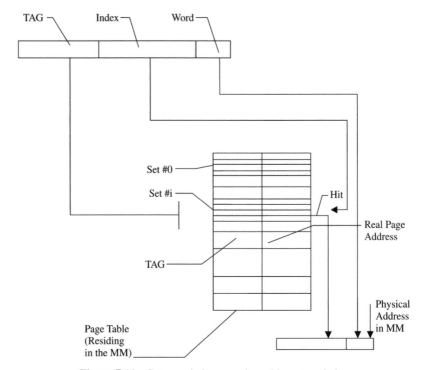

Figure 7.11 Set-associative mapping address translation

The set-associative-mapping technique strikes a compromise between the ineffi-ciency of direct mapping, in terms of the size of the page table, and excessive hard-ware overhead of associative mapping. It also enjoys the best of the two techniques: the simplicity of the direct mapping and the efficiency of the associative mapping.

It should be noted that in all the above address translation techniques extra main memory access is required for accessing the page table. This extra main memory access could potentially be saved if a copy of a small portion of the page table can be kept in the MMU. This portion consists of the page table entries that corre-spond to the most recent accessed pages. In this case, before any address translation is attempted, a search is conducted to find out whether the virtual page number (or the tag) in the virtual address field could be matched. This small portion is kept in the table look-aside buffer (TLB) cache in the MMU. This is explained below.

7.2.4. Translation Look-Aside Buffer (TLB)

In most modern computer systems a copy of a small portion of the page table is kept on the processor chip. This portion consists of the page table entries that correspond to the most recently accessed pages. This small portion is kept in the translation look-aside buffer (TLB) cache. A search in the TLB precedes that in the page table. Therefore, the virtual page field is first checked against the entries of the

TLB in the hope that a match is found. A hit in the TLB will result in the generation of the physical address of the word requested by the processor, thus saving the extra main memory access required to access the page table. It should be noted that a miss on the TLB is not equivalent to a page fault. Figure 7.12 illustrates the use of the TLB in the virtual address translation process. The typical size of a TLB is in the range of 16 to 64 entries. With this small TLB size, a hit ratio of more than 90% is always possible. Owing to its limited size, the search in the TLB is done associatively, thus reducing the required search time.

To illustrate the effectiveness of the use of a TLB, let us consider the case of using a TLB in a virtual memory system having the following specifications.

Number of entries in the TLB $= 16$	Associative search time in TLB $= 10$ ns
Main memory access time $= 50$ ns	TLB hit ratio $= 0.9$

The average access time $= 0.9(10 + 50) + 0.1(10 + 2 * 50) = 0.9 * 60 + 0.1 * 110 = 65$ ns. This is to be compared to the 100 ns access time needed in the absence of the TLB. It should be noted that for simplicity, we overlooked the existence of the cache in the above illustration.

It is clear from the above discussion that as more requests for items that do not exist in the main memory (page faults) occur, more pages would have to be brought from the hard disk to the main memory. This will eventually lead to a totally filled main memory. The arrival of any new page from the hard disk to a totally full main memory should promote the following question: Which main memory page should be removed (replaced) in order to make room for the incoming page(s)? Replacement algorithms (policies) are explained next.

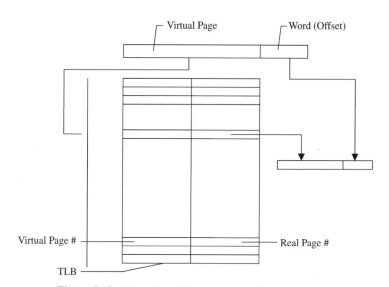

Figure 7.12   Use of the TLB in virtual address translation

It should be noted that Intel's Pentium 4 processor has a 36-bit address bus, which allows for a maximum main memory size of 64 GB. According to Intel's specifications, the virtual memory is 64 TB (65,528 GB). This increases the processor's memory access space from 2^{36} to 2^{46} bytes. This is to be compared to the PowerPC 604 which has two 12-entry, two-way set-associative translation look-aside buffers (TLBs): one for instructions and the other for data. The virtual memory space is therefore $= 2^{52} = 4$ Peta-bytes.

7.2.5. Replacement Algorithms (Policies)

Basic to the implementation of virtual memory is the concept of *demand paging*. This means that the operating system, and not the programmer, controls the swapping of pages in and out of main memory as they are required by the active processes. When a process needs a nonresident page, the operating system must decide which resident page is to be replaced by the requested page. The technique used in the virtual memory that makes this decision is called the *replacement policy*.

There exists a number of possible replacement mechanisms. The main objective in all these mechanisms is to select for removal the page that expectedly will not be referenced in the near future.

Random Replacement   According to this replacement policy, a page is selected randomly for replacement. This is the simplest replacement mechanism. It can be implemented using a pseudo-random number generator that generates numbers that correspond to all possible page frames. At the time of replacement, the random number generated will indicate the page frame that must be replaced. Although simple, this technique may not result in efficient use of the main memory, that is, a low hit ratio h. Random replacement has been used in the Intel *i860* family of RISC processor.

First-In-First-Out (FIFO) Replacement   According to this replacement policy, the page that was loaded before all the others in the main memory is selected for replacement. The basis for page replacement in this technique is the time spent by a given page residing in the main memory regardless of the pattern of usage of that page. This technique is also simple. However, it is expected to result in acceptable performance, measured in terms of the main memory hit ratio, if the page references made by the processor are in strict sequential order. To illustrate the use of the FIFO mechanism, we offer the following example.

Example   Consider the following reference string of pages made by a processor: 6, 7, 8, 9, 7, 8, 9, 10, 8, 9, 10. In particular, consider two cases: (a) the number of page frames allocated in the main memory is TWO and (b) the number of page frames allocated are THREE. Figure 7.13 illustrates a trace of the reference string for the two cases. As can be seen from the figure, when the number of page frames is TWO, there were 11 page faults (these are shown in bold in the figure). When the number of page frames is increased to THREE, the number of page

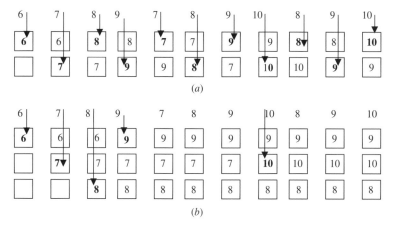

Figure 7.13 FIFO replacement technique. (a) FIFO replacement using two page frames (#PFs = 11), (b) FIFO replacement using three page frames (#PFs = 5)

faults was reduced to five. Since five pages are referenced, this is the optimum condition. The FIFO policy results in the best (minimum) page faults when the reference string is in strict order of increasing page number references.

Least Recently Used (LRU) Replacement   According to this technique, page replacement is based on the pattern of usage of a given page residing in the main memory regardless of the time spent in the main memory. The page that has not been referenced for the longest time while residing in the main memory is selected for replacement. The LRU technique matches most programs' characteristics and therefore is expected to result in the best possible performance in terms of the main memory hit ratio. It is, however, more involved compared to other techniques. To illustrate the use of the LRU mechanism, we offer the following example.

Example   Consider the following reference string of pages made by a processor: 4, 7, 5, 7, 6, 7, 10, 4, 8, 5, 8, 6, 8, 11, 4, 9, 5, 9, 6, 9, 12, 4, 7, 5, 7. Assume that the number of page frames allocated in the main memory is FOUR. Compute the number of page faults generated. The trace of the main memory contents is shown in Figure 7.14. Number of page faults = 17.

In presenting the LRU, we have a particular implementation, called *stack-based LRU*. In this implementation, the most recently accessed page is now represented by

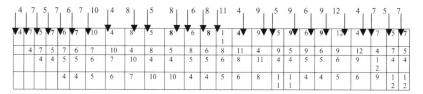

Figure 7.14   LRU replacement technique

the top page rectangle. The rectangles do not represent specific page frames as they did in the FIFO diagram. Thus, each reference generating a page fault is now on the top row. It should be noted that as more pages are allotted to the program the page references in each row do not change. Only the number of page faults changes. This will make the set of pages in memory for n page frames be a subset of the set of pages for $n + 1$ page frames. In fact, the diagram could be considered a STACK data structure with the depth of the stack representing the number of page frames. If a page is not on the stack (i.e., is found at a depth greater than the number of page frames), then a page fault occurs.

Example   Consider the case of a two-dimensional 8×8 array A. The array is stored in row-major order. For THREE page frames, compute how many page faults are generated by the following array-initialization loop. Assume that an *LRU* replacement algorithm is used and that all frames are initially empty. Assume that the page size is 16.

```
for I = 0 to 7 do
     for J = 0 to 7 do
       A[I, J] = 0;
     End for
End for
```

The arrangement of the array elements in the secondary storage is shown in Figure 7.15. The sequence of requests for the array elements in the first TWO external loop executions is as follows:

$I = 0$
    $J = 0, 1, 2, 3, 4, 5, 6, 7$
        $a_{00}, a_{01}, a_{02}, a_{03}, a_{04}, a_{05}, a_{06}, a_{07}$ The number of page faults (PFs) = 1
$I = 1$
    $J = 0, 1, 2, 3, 4, 5, 6, 7$
        $a_{10}, a_{11}, a_{12}, a_{13}, a_{14}, a_{15}, a_{16}, a_{17}$ The number of page faults (PFs) = 1

From the above analysis, it is clear that there will be one PF in every external loop execution. This makes the total number of PFs be 8. It should be noted that if the array was stored column-major, then every internal loop execution would generate eight page faults, thus causing the total number of PFs to become 64.

Clock Replacement Algorithm   This is a modified FIFO algorithm. It takes into account both the time spent by a page residing in the main memory (similar to the FIFO) and the pattern of usage of the page (similar to the LRU). The technique is therefore sometimes called the First-In-Not-Used-First-Out (FINUFO). In keeping track of both the time and the usage, the technique uses a pointer to

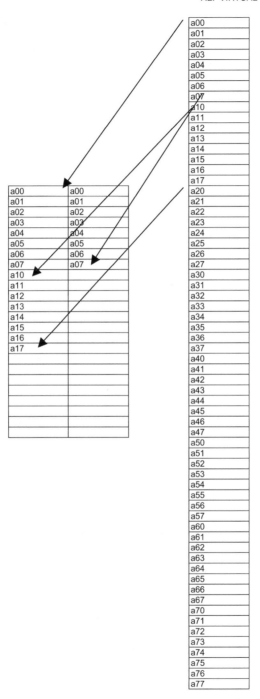

Figure 7.15   Arrangement of array elements in secondary storage and main memory built up

indicate where to place the incoming page and a used bit to indicate the usage of a given page. The technique can be explained using the following three steps.

1. If the used bit = 1, then reset bit, increment pointer and repeat.
2. If the used bit = 0, then replace corresponding page and increment pointer.
3. The used bit is SET if the page is referenced after the initial loading.

Example Consider the following page requests (Fig. 7.16) in a THREE-page frames MM system using the FINUFO technique: 2,3,2,4,6,2,5,6,1,4,6. Estimate the hit ratio. The estimated Hit Ratio = 4/11.

7.2.6. Virtual Memory Systems with Cache Memory

A typical computer system will contain a cache, a virtual memory, and a TLB. When a virtual address is received from the processor, a number of different scenarios can occur, each dependent on the availability of the requested item in the cache, the main memory, or the secondary storage. Figure 7.17 shows a general flow diagram for the different scenarios.

The first level of address translation checks for a match between the received virtual address and the virtual addresses stored in the TLB. If a match occurs (TLB hit) then the corresponding physical address is obtained. This physical address can then be used to access the cache. If a match occurs (cache hit) then the element requested by the processor can be sent from the cache to the processor. If, on the other hand, a cache miss occurs, then the block containing the targeted element is copied from the main memory into the cache (as discussed before) and the requested element is sent to the processor.

The above scenario assumes a TLB hit. If a TLB miss occurs, then the page table (PT) is searched for the existence of the page containing the targeted element in the main memory. If a PT hit occurs, then the corresponding physical address is generated (as discussed before) and a search is conducted for the block containing the requested element (as discussed above). This will require updating the TLB. If on the other hand a PT miss takes place (indicating a page fault), then the page containing the targeted element is copied from the disk into the main memory, a block is copied into the cache, and the element is sent to the processor. This last

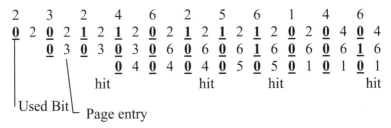

Figure 7.16 FINUFO replacement technique

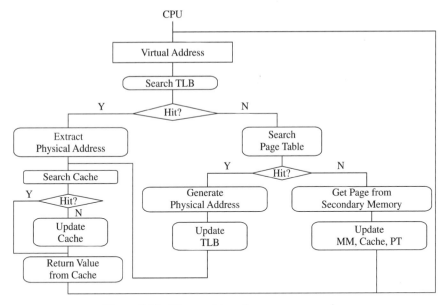

Figure 7.17   Memory hierarchy accesses scenarios

scenario will require updating the page table, the main memory, and the cache. A subsequent request of that virtual address by the processor will result in updating the TLB.

7.2.7. Segmentation

A segment is a block of contiguous locations of varying size. Segments are used by the operating system (OS) to relocate complete programs in the main and the disk memory. Segments can be shared between programs. They provide means for protection from unauthorized access and/or execution. It is not possible to enter segments from other segments unless the access has been specifically allowed. Data segments and code segments are separated. It should also not be possible to alter information in the code segment while fetching an instruction nor should it be possible to execute data in a data segment.

7.2.8. Segment Address Translation

In order to support segmentation, the address issued by the processor should consist of a segment number (base) and a displacement (or an offset) within the segment. Address translation is performed directly via a segment table. The starting address of the targeted segment is obtained by adding the segment number to the contents of the segment table pointer. One important content of the segment table is the

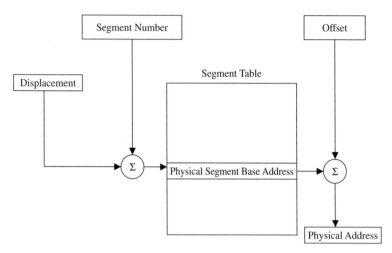

Figure 7.18 Segment address translation

physical segment base address. Adding the latter to the offset yields the required physical address. Figure 7.18 illustrates the segment address translation process.

Possible additional information included in the segment table includes:

1. Segment length
2. Memory protection (read-only, execute-only, system-only, and so on)
3. Replacement algorithm (similar to those used in the paged systems)
4. Placement algorithm (finding a suitable place in the main memory to hold the incoming segment). Examples include
   (a) First fit
   (b) Best fit
   (c) Worst fit

7.2.9. Paged Segmentation

Both segmentation and paging are combined in most systems. Each segment is divided into a number of equal sized pages. The basic unit of transfer of data between the main memory and the disk is the page, that is, at any given time, the main memory may consist of pages from various segments. In this case, the *virtual address* is divided into a *segment number*, a *page number*, and *displacement within the page*. Address translation is the same as explained above except that the physical segment base address obtained from the segment table is now added to the virtual page number in order to obtain the appropriate entry in the page table. The output of the page table is the page physical address, which when concatenated with the word field of the virtual address results in the physical address. Figure 7.19 illustrates the paged segmentation address translation.

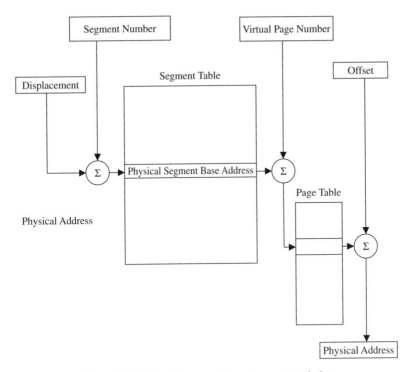

Figure 7.19   Paged segmentation address translation

7.2.10. Pentium Memory Management

In the Pentium processor, both segmentation and paging are individually available and can also be disabled. Four distinct views of the memory exist:

1. Unsegmented unpaged memory
2. Unsegmented paged memory
3. segmented unpaged memory
4. segmented paged memory

For segmentation, the 16-bit segment number (two of which are used for protection) and the 32-bit offset produce a segmented virtual address space equal to $2^{46} = 64$ terabytes. The virtual address space is divided into two parts: one half, that is, $8K \times 4$ GB, is global and shared by all processes, and the other half is local and is distinct for each process.

For paging, a two-level table lookup paging system is used. First level is a page directory with 1024 entries, that is, 1024 page groups, each with its own page table and each FOUR MB in length. Each page table contains 1024 entries; each entry corresponds to a single 4 KB page.

7.3. READ-ONLY MEMORY

Random access as well as cache memories are examples of *volatile* memories. A volatile storage is defined as one that loses its contents when power is turned off. *Nonvolatile* memory storages are those that retain the stored information if power is turned off. As there is a need for volatile storage there is also a need for nonvolatile storage. Computer system boot subroutines, microcode control, and video game cartridges are a few examples of computer software that require the use of nonvolatile storage. Read-only memory (ROM) can also be used to realize combinational logic functions.

The technology used for implementing ROM chips has evolved over the years. Early implementations of ROMs were called *mask-programmed ROMs*. In this case, a made-to-order one time ROM is programmed according to a specific encoding pattern supplied by the user. The structure of a 4×4 CMOS ROM chip is shown in Figure 7.20.

In this figure an n-type transistor is placed where a 1 is to be stored. A two-to-four address decoder is used to create four word lines; each is used to activate a row of transistors. When a 1 appears on the word line, the corresponding transistors will be turned on, thus pulling the corresponding bit line to 0. An inverter at the output of the

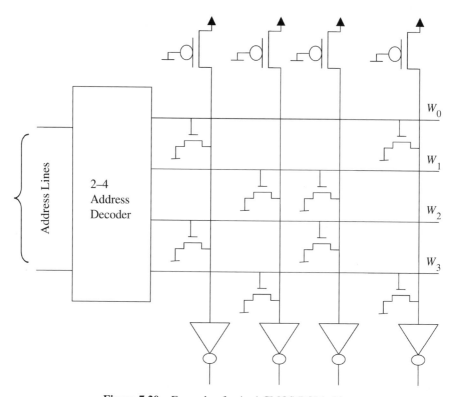

Figure 7.20   Example of a 4×4 CMOS ROM chip

TABLE 7.3   Patterns Stored at Four ROM Locations

Address lines	Word line activated	Output pattern
00	W_0	1001
01	W_1	0110
10	W_2	1010
11	W_3	0101

bit lines is used to output a 1 at the output of those pulled down bit lines. Table 7.3 shows the patterns stored at each of the four ROM locations.

Mask-programmed ROMs are primarily used to store machine microcode, desktop bootstrap loaders, and video game cartridges. Because they can be programmed only once by the manufacturer, mask-programmed ROMs are inflexible. If the user would like to program his/her ROM on site, then a different type of ROM, called the Programmable ROM (PROM) should be used. In this case, fuses, instead of transistors, are placed at the intersection of word and bit lines. The user can program the PROM by selectively blowing up the appropriate fuses. This can be done by allowing a high current to flow in those particular fuses, thus causing them to blow up. This process is known as "burning the ROM."

Although it allows for some added flexibility, PROM is still restricted by the fact that it can only be programmed once (by the user). A third type of ROM, called Erasable PROM (EPROM), is reprogrammable; that is, it allows stored data to be erased and new data to be stored. In order to provide such flexibility, EPROMs are constructed using a special type of transistors. These transistors are able to assume one of two statuses, normal or disabled. A disabled transistor acts like a switch that is turned off all the time. A normal transistor can be programmed to become open all the time by inducing a certain amount of charge to be trapped under its gate. A disabled transistor can become normal again by removing the induced charge. This requires exposing those transistors to ultraviolet light. Exposing the EPROM chip to such ultraviolet light will lead to the erasure of the entire chip contents. This is considered a major drawback of EPROMs. Both PROMs and EPROMs are used in prototyping, of moderate size systems.

Flash EPROMs (FEPROMs) have emerged as strong contenders to EPROMs. This is because FEPROMs are more compact, faster, and removable compared to EPROMs. The erasure time of a FEPROM is far faster than that of an EPROM.

A different type of ROM, which overcomes the drawback of the EPROM, is the Electrically EPROM or EEPROM. In this case, the erasure of the EPROM can be done electrically and, moreover, selectively; that is, only the contents of selective cells can be erased, leaving the other cells' contents untouched. Both FEPROMs and EEPROMs are used in applications requiring occasional updating of information, such as Programmable TVs, VCR, and automotives.

Table 7.4 summarizes the main characteristics of the different types of ROM discussed above.

TABLE 7.4   Characteristics of Different ROM Implementations

ROM type	Cost	Programmability	Typical applications
Mask-programmed ROM	Truly inexpensive	Once at manufacture	Microcode
PROM	Inexpensive	Once on site	Prototyping
EPROM	Moderate	Many times	Prototyping
FEPROM	Expensive	Many times	VCR & TVs
EEPROM	Truly expensive	Many times	VCR & TVs

7.4. SUMMARY

The discussion in this chapter has been a continuation of that conducted in Chapter 6. In particular, this chapter has been dedicated to cover the design aspects that relate to the internal and external organization of the main memory. The design of a static RAM cell was introduced with emphasis on the read and write operations. Our discussion on virtual memory started with the issues related to address translation. Three address translation techniques were discussed and compared. These are the direct, associative, and the set-associative techniques. The use of a TLB to improve the average access time was explained. Three replacement techniques were introduced. These are the FIFO, LRU, and clock replacement. Segmented paged systems were also introduced. Our discussion on virtual memory ended with an explanation of the virtual memory aspects of the Pentium IV processor. Toward the end of the chapter, we have touched on a number of implementations for ROMs.

EXERCISES

1. Consider the case of a computer system employing both a cache and a paged virtual memory as shown below (Fig. 7.21). One can analyze this system through identifying FIVE combinations of accesses. What are these combinations? Determine the probability and the access time in each case assuming the following information. Compute also the overall average access time.

TLB address translation and search	25 ns
Cache search time to determine whether address in cache	25 ns
Cache access time	25 ns
Main memory access time	250 ns
Hard disk access time	100 ms
TLB hit ratio	0.9
Cache hit ratio	0.95
Main memory hit ratio	0.8

2. A 64×64 array of words (elements) is to be "normalized" as follows. For each row, the largest element is found and all elements of the row are divided by

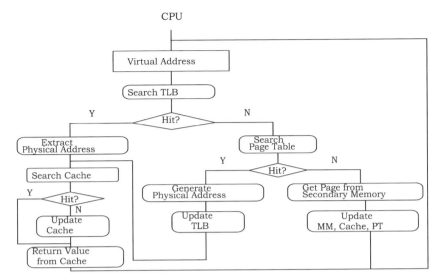

Figure 7.21   Computer system with cache and paged virtual memory

this maximum value. Assume that each page in the virtual memory consists of 64 words, and that 2K words of the main memory are allocated for storing data during this computation. Suppose that it takes 100 ms to load a page from the disk into the main memory when a page fault occurs.

(a) Write a simple piece of code (in a notational form) that can perform the above job.

(b) How many page faults would occur if the elements of the array are stored in column order in the virtual memory?

(c) How many page faults would occur if the elements of the array are stored in row order in the virtual memory?

(d) Estimate the total time needed to perform this normalization for both arrangements (b) and (c).

3. Design a 64M×8-bit memory using a number of 16M×1-bit static RAM chips. Assume that each individual chip has a chip select ($\overline{CS}$) line and a read/write ($R/\overline{W}$) line. Compute the number of chips required and show a complete connection diagram of the designed memory.

4. Consider the following stream of page requests: 1,2,3,4,5,1,2,3,4,5,1,2,3,4,5. Assume that the main memory consists of FOUR page frames. Show a trace of the status of the page frames in the MM and estimate the hit ratio assuming each of the following page replacement algorithms.

(a) FIFO

(b) LRU

(c) FINUFO

5. Consider the case of a two-dimensional 20×20 array A. The array is stored column-major. For FIVE main memory page frames, compute how many

page faults are generated by the following array-initialization loop. Assume that *LRU* replacement algorithm is used and that all frames are initially empty. Assume also that the page size is 40 elements.

```
for I = 1 to 20 do
for J = 1 to 20 do
A[I, J] = 0;
```

6. In this problem you are asked to pick a real-life computer memory system that uses both caching and virtual memory schemes. Your job is to apply all the knowledge that you have gained in this chapter concerning "Memory System Design and Analysis" in describing and analyzing your selected system. Examples that you may pick include but are not limited to Intel Pentium 4, The PowerPC, Alpha AXP 21064, and so on. Use examples and illustrations to support your analysis and be as specific as possible. Remember that the emphasis should be on the analysis and the basic design issues involved. You can use any reference material but make sure that your include it in your reference list.

REFERENCES AND FURTHER READING

S. D. Burd, *Systems Architecture*, 3rd ed., Thomson Learning Ltd, Boston, 2001.

H. Cragon, *Memory Systems and Pipelined Processors*, Jones and Bartlett: Sudbury, MA, 1996.

V. C. Hamacher, Z. G. Vranesic, and S. G. Zaky, *Computer Organization*, 5th ed., McGraw-Hill, NY, 2002.

J. L. Hennessy, and Patterson, D. A., *Computer Architecture*: *A Quantitative Approach*, Morgan Kaufmann, San Francisco, CA, 1996.

V. P. Heuring, and H. F. Jordan, *Computer Systems Design and Architecture*, Addison-Wesley, NJ, USA, 1997.

D. A. Patterson, and J. L. Hennessy, *Computer Organization & Design*: *The Hardware/Software Interface*, Morgan Kaufmann, San Mateo, CA, 1994.

H. S. Stone, *High-Performance Computer Architecture*, Addison-Wesley, Amsterdam, Netherlands, 1987.

B. Wilkinson, *Computer Architecture: Design and Performance*, Prentice-Hall, Hertfordshire, UK, 1996.

Websites

http://www.sysopt.com

http://www.intel.com

http://www.AcerHardware.com

http://www.pmc-sierra.com/products/details/rm7000a

http://physinfo.ulb.ac.be/divers_html/PowerPC_Programming_Info/into_to_ppc/ppc2_hardware.html

CHAPTER 8

Input–Output Design and Organization

Having considered the fundamental concepts related to instruction set design, assembly language programming, processor design, and memory design, we now turn our attention to the issues related to input–output (I/O) design and organization. It should be emphasized at the outset that I/O plays a crucial role in any modern computer system. Therefore, a clear understanding and appreciation of the fundamentals of I/O operations, devices, and interfaces are of great importance.

Input–output (I/O) devices vary substantially in their characteristics. One distinguishing factor among input devices (and also among output devices) is their data processing rate, defined as the average number of characters that can be processed by a device per second. For example, while the data processing rate of an input device such as the keyboard is about 10 characters (bytes)/second, a scanner can send data at a rate of about 200,000 characters/second. Similarly, while a laser printer can output data at a rate of about 100,000 characters/second, a graphic display can output data at a rate of about 30,000,000 characters/second.

Striking a character on the keyboard of a computer will cause a character (in the form of an ASCII code) to be sent to the computer. The amount of time passed before the next character is sent to the computer will depend on the skill of the user and even sometimes on his/her speed of thinking. It is often the case that the user knows what he/she wants to input, but sometimes they need to think before touching the next button on the keyboard. Therefore, input from a keyboard is slow and burst in nature and it will be a waste of time for the computer to spend its valuable time waiting for input from slow input devices. A mechanism is therefore needed whereby a device will have to interrupt the processor asking for attention whenever it is ready. This is called *interrupt-driven* communication between the computer and I/O devices (see Section 8.3).

Consider the case of a disk. A typical disk should be capable of transferring data at rates exceeding several million bytes/second. It would be a waste of time to transfer data byte by byte or even word by word. Therefore, it is always the case that data is transferred in the form of blocks, that is, entire programs. It is also necessary to provide a mechanism that allows a disk to transfer this huge volume of data without the intervention of the CPU. This will allow the CPU to perform other

Fundamentals of Computer Organization and Architecture, by M. Abd-El-Barr and H. El-Rewini
ISBN 0-471-46741-3   Copyright © 2005 John Wiley & Sons, Inc.

useful operation(s) while a huge amount of data is being transferred between the disk and the memory. This is the essence of the *direct memory access* (DMA) mechanism discussed in Section 8.4.

We begin our discussion by offering some basic concepts in Section 8.1.

8.1. BASIC CONCEPTS

Figure 8.1 shows a simple arrangement for connecting the processor and the memory in a given computer system to an input device, for example, a keyboard and an output device such as a graphic display. A single bus consisting of the required address, data, and control lines is used to connect the system's components in Figure 8.1.

The way in which the processor and the memory exchange data has been explained in Chapters 6 and 7. We are here concerned with the way the processor and the I/O devices exchange data. It has been indicated in the introduction part that there exists a big difference in the rate at which a processor can process information and those of input and output devices. One simple way to accommodate this speed difference is to have the input device, for example, a keyboard, deposit the character struck by the user in a register (*input register*), which indicates the availability of that character to the processor. When the input character has been taken by the processor, this will be indicated to the input device in order to proceed and input the next character, and so on. Similarly, when the processor has a character to output (display), it deposits it in a specific register dedicated for communication with the graphic display (*output register*). When the character has been taken by the graphic display, this will be indicated to the processor such that it can proceed and output the next character, and so on. This simple way of communication between the processor and I/O devices, called *I/O protocol*, requires the availability of the input and output registers. In a typical computer system, there is a number of input registers, each belonging to a specific input device. There is also a number of output registers,

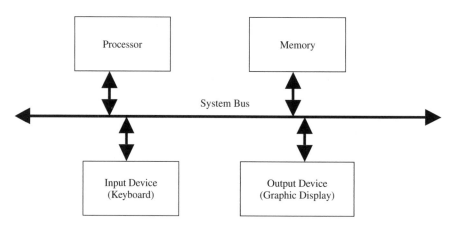

Figure 8.1 A single bus system

each belonging to a specific output device. In addition, a mechanism according to which the processor can address those input and output registers must be adopted. More than one arrangement exists to satisfy the abovementioned requirements. Among these, two particular methods are explained below.

In the first arrangement, I/O devices are assigned particular addresses, isolated from the address space assigned to the memory. The execution of an *input instruction* at an input device address will cause the character stored in the *input register* of that device to be transferred to a specific register in the CPU. Similarly, the execution of an *output instruction* at an output device address will cause the character stored in a specific register in the CPU to be transferred to the *output register* of that output device. This arrangement, called *shared I/O*, is shown schematically in Figure 8.2. In this case, the address and data lines from the CPU can be shared between the memory and the I/O devices. A separate control line will have to be used. This is because of the need for executing input and output instructions. In a typical computer system, there exists more than one input and more than one output device. Therefore, there is a need to have *address decoder circuitry* for device identification. There is also a need for *status registers* for each input and output device. The status of an input device, whether it is ready to send data to the processor, should be stored in the status register of that device. Similarly, the status of an output device, whether it is ready to receive data from the processor, should be stored in the status register of that device. Input (output) registers, status registers, and address decoder circuitry represent the main components of an I/O interface (module).

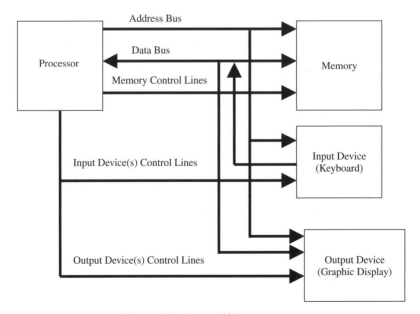

Figure 8.2 Shared I/O arrangement

The main advantage of the shared I/O arrangement is the separation between the memory address space and that of the I/O devices. Its main disadvantage is the need to have special *input* and *output instructions* in the processor instruction set. The shared I/O arrangement is mostly adopted by Intel.

The second possible I/O arrangement is to deal with *input* and *output registers* as if they are regular memory locations. In this case, a *read* operation from the address corresponding to the *input register* of an input device, for example, *Read Device 6*, is equivalent to performing an *input operation* from the input register in Device #6. Similarly, a *write* operation to the address corresponding to the *output register* of an output device, for example, *Write Device 9*, is equivalent to performing an *output operation* into the output register in Device #9. This arrangement is called *memory-mapped I/O*. It is shown in Figure 8.3.

The main advantage of the memory-mapped I/O is the use of the read and write instructions of the processor to perform the input and output operations, respectively. It eliminates the need for introducing special I/O instructions. The main disadvantage of the memory-mapped I/O is the need to reserve a certain part of the memory address space for addressing I/O devices, that is, a reduction in the available memory address space. The memory-mapped I/O has been mostly adopted by Motorola.

8.2. PROGRAMMED I/O

In this section, we present the main hardware components required for communications between the processor and I/O devices. The way according to which such

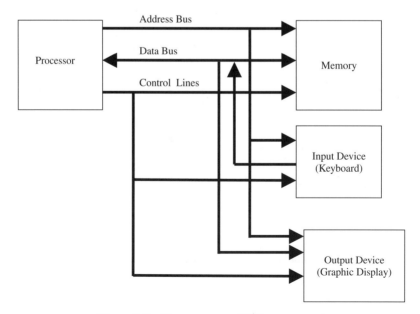

Figure 8.3 Memory-mapped I/O arrangement

communications take place (protocol) is also indicated. This protocol has to be programmed in the form of routines that run under the control of the CPU. Consider, for example, an input operation from *Device 6* (could be the keyboard) in the case of *shared* I/O arrangement. Let us also assume that there are eight different I/O devices connected to the processor in this case (see Fig. 8.4).

The following protocol steps (program) have to be followed:

1. The processor executes an input instruction from device 6, for example, *INPUT 6*. The effect of executing this instruction is to send the device number to the address decoder circuitry in each input device in order to identify the specific input device to be involved. In this case, the output of the decoder in Device #6 will be enabled, while the outputs of all other decoders will be disabled.
2. The buffers (in the figure we assumed that there are eight such buffers) holding the data in the specified input device (Device #6) will be enabled by the output of the address decoder circuitry.
3. The data output of the enabled buffers will be available on the data bus.

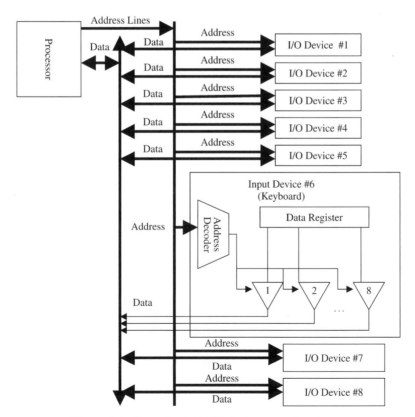

Figure 8.4   Example eight-I/O device connection to a processor

4. The instruction decoding will gate the data available on the data bus into the input of a particular register in the CPU, normally the *accumulator*.

Output operations can be performed in a way similar to the input operation explained above. The only difference will be the direction of data transfer, which will be from a specific CPU register to the output register in the specified output device. I/O operations performed in this manner are called *programmed I/O*. They are performed under the CPU control. A complete instruction fetch, decode, and execute cycle will have to be executed for every input and every output operation. Programmed I/O is useful in cases whereby one character at a time is to be transferred, for example, keyboard and character mode printers. Although simple, programmed I/O is slow.

One point that was overlooked in the above description of the programmed I/O is how to handle the substantial speed difference between I/O devices and the processor. A mechanism should be adopted in order to ensure that a character sent to the output register of an output device, such as a screen, is not overwritten by the processor (due to the processor's high speed) before it is displayed and that a character available in the input register of a keyboard is read only once by the processor. This brings up the issue of the status of the input and output devices. A mechanism that can be implemented requires the availability of a *Status Bit* (B_{in}) in the interface of each input device and *Status Bit* (B_{in}) in the interface of each output device. Whenever an input device such as a keyboard has a character available in its input register, it indicates that by setting $B_{in} = 1$. A program in the processor can be used to continuously monitor B_{in}. When the program sees that $B_{in} = 1$, it will interpret that to mean a character is available in the input register of that device. Reading such character will require executing the protocol explained above. Whenever the character is read, then the program can reset $B_{in} = 0$, thus avoiding multiple read of the same character. In a similar manner, the processor can deposit a character in the output register of an output device such as a screen only when $B_{out} = 0$. It is only after the screen has displayed the character that it sets $B_{out} = 1$, indicating to the program that monitors B_{out} that the screen is ready to receive the next character. The process of checking the status of I/O devices in order to determine their readiness for receiving and/or sending characters, is called *software I/O polling*. A *hardware I/O polling* scheme is shown in Figure 8.5.

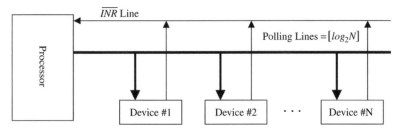

Figure 8.5 Hardware polling scheme

In the figure, each of the N I/O devices has access to the interrupt line $\overline{INR}$. Upon recognizing the arrival of a request (called Interrupt Request) on $\overline{INR}$, the processor polls the devices to determine the requesting device. This is done through the $\lceil Log_2 N \rceil$ polling lines. The priority of the requesting device will determine the order in which addresses are put on the polling lines. The address of the highest priority device is put first, followed by the next priority, and so on until the least priority device.

In addition to the I/O polling, two other mechanisms can be used to carry out I/O operations. These are *interrupt-driven I/O* and *direct memory access* (DMA). These are discussed in the next two sections.

8.3. INTERRUPT-DRIVEN I/O

It is often necessary to have the normal flow of a program interrupted, for example, to react to abnormal events, such as power failure. An interrupt can also be used to acknowledge the completion of a particular course of action, such as a printer indicating to the computer that it has completed printing the character(s) in its input register and that it is ready to receive other character(s). An interrupt can also be used in time-sharing systems to allocate CPU time among different programs. The instruction sets of modern CPUs often include instruction(s) that mimic the actions of the hardware interrupts.

When the CPU is interrupted, it is required to discontinue its current activity, attend to the interrupting condition (serve the interrupt), and then resume its activity from wherever it stopped. Discontinuity of the processor's current activity requires finishing executing the current instruction, saving the processor status (mostly in the form of pushing register values onto a stack), and transferring control (jump) to what is called the *interrupt service routine* (ISR). The service offered to an interrupt will depend on the source of the interrupt. For example, if the interrupt is due to power failure, then the action taken will be to save the values of all processor registers and pointers such that resumption of correct operation can be guaranteed upon power return. In the case of an I/O interrupt, serving an interrupt means to perform the required data transfer. Upon finishing serving an interrupt, the processor should restore the original status by popping the relevant values from the stack. Once the processor returns to the normal state, it can enable sources of interrupt again.

One important point that was overlooked in the above scenario is the issue of serving *multiple interrupts*, for example, the occurrence of yet another interrupt while the processor is currently serving an interrupt. Response to the new interrupt will depend upon the priority of the newly arrived interrupt with respect to that of the interrupt being currently served. If the newly arrived interrupt has priority less than or equal to that of the currently served one, then it can wait until the processor finishes serving the current interrupt. If, on the other hand, the newly arrived interrupt has priority higher than that of the currently served interrupt, for example, power failure interrupt occurring while serving an I/O interrupt, then the processor will have to push its status onto the stack and serve the higher priority interrupt. Correct handling of multiple interrupts in terms of storing and restoring the correct processor status is guaranteed due to the way the push and pop operations are performed. For example, to serve the first interrupt, STATUS 1 will be pushed onto the stack. Upon receiving the second interrupt, STATUS 2 will be pushed onto the stack. Upon serving the second interrupt, STATUS 2 will be popped out of the stack and upon serving the first interrupt, STATUS 1 will be popped out of the stack.

It is possible to have the interrupting device identify itself to the processor by sending a code following the interrupt request. The code sent by a given I/O device can represent its I/O address or the memory address location of the start of the ISR for that device. This scheme is called *vectored interrupt*.

8.3.1. Interrupt Hardware

In the above discussion, we have assumed that the processor has recognized the occurrence of an interrupt before proceeding to serve it. Computers are provided with *interrupt hardware* capability in the form of specialized *interrupt lines* to the processor. These lines are used to send interrupt signals to the processor. In the case of I/O, there exists more than one I/O device. The processor should be provided with a mechanism that enables it to handle simultaneous interrupt requests and to recognize the interrupting device. Two basic schemes can be implemented to achieve this task. The first scheme is called *daisy chain bus arbitration* (DCBA) and the second is called *independent source bus arbitration* (ISBA).

According to the DCBA (see Fig. 8.6a), I/O devices present their interrupt requests to the interrupt request line $\overline{INR}$ (similar to the polling arrangement). Upon recognizing the arrival of an interrupt request, the processor, through a daisy chained *grant line* (GL), sends its grant to the requesting device to start communication with the processor. The GL goes through all devices starting from the first device nearer to the processor and going to the next device and so on until it reaches the last device (Device #N). If Device #1 has put a request, then it will hold the grant signal and start communication with the processor. If, on the other hand, Device #1 has no interrupt request, it will pass the grant signal to device #2, which will repeat the same procedure, and so on. In the case of multiple requests, the DCBA arrangement gives highest priority to the device physically nearer to the processor. The furthest device from the processor has the lowest priority.

According to the ISBA (see Fig. 8.6b), each I/O device has its own interrupt request line, through which it can send its interrupt request, independent of the other devices. Similarly, each I/O device has its own grant line, through which it receives the grant signal for its request such that it can start communicating with the processor. I/O device priority in the ISBA does not depend on the device location. A priority arbitration circuitry is needed in order to deal with simultaneous interrupt requests.

8.3.2. Interrupt in Operating Systems

When an interrupt occurs, the operating system gains control. The operating system saves the state of the interrupted process, analyzes the interrupt, and passes control to the appropriate routine to handle the interrupt. There are several

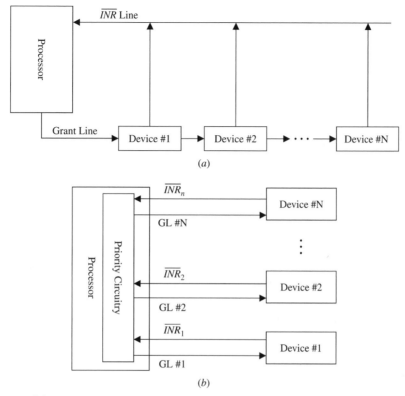

Figure 8.6 Interrupt hardware schemes. (*a*) Daisy chain interrupt arrangement (*b*) Independent interrupt arrangement

types of interrupts, including I/O interrupts. An I/O interrupt notifies the operating system that an I/O device has completed or suspended its operation and needs some service from the CPU. To process an interrupt, the context of the current process must be saved and the interrupt handling routine must be invoked. This process is called *context switching*. A process context has two parts: processor context and memory context. The processor context is the state of the CPU's registers including program counter (PC), program status words (PSWs), and other registers. The memory context is the state of the program's memory including the program and data. The interrupt handler is a routine that processes each different type of interrupt.

The operating system must provide programs with save area for their contexts. It also must provide an organized way for allocating and deallocating memory for the interrupted process. When the interrupt handling routine finishes processing the interrupt, the CPU is dispatched to either the interrupted process, or to the highest priority ready process. This will depend on whether the interrupted process is preemptive or nonpreemptive. If the process is nonpreemptive, it gets the CPU again. First the context must be restored, then control is returned to the interrupts process.

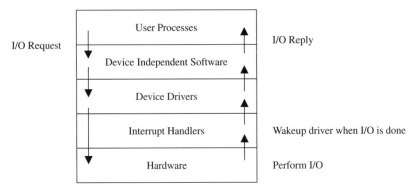

Figure 8.7 Layered I/O software

Figure 8.7 shows the layers of software involved in I/O operations. First, the program issues an I/O request via an I/O call. The request is passed through to the I/O device. When the device completes the I/O, an interrupt is sent and the interrupt handler is invoked. Eventually, control is relinquished back to the process that initiated the I/O.

Example 1: 80×86 Interrupt Architecture The 80×86 processors have just two hardware interrupt pins. These are labeled INTR and NMI. NMI is a nonmaskable interrupt, which means it cannot be blocked and the processor must respond to it. The NMI input is usually reserved for critical system functions. The INTR input is a maskable interrupt request line between the CPU and the programmable interrupt controller (8259A PIC). Interrupts on INTR can be enabled and disabled using the instructions STI (set interrupt flag) and CLI (clear interrupt flag), respectively.

Interrupt handlers are called interrupt service routines (ISR). The address of each interrupt service routine is stored in four consecutive memory locations in the interrupt vector table (IVT). The IVT stores pointers to ISR for each type of interrupt. When an interrupt occurs, an 8-bit type number is supplied to the processor, which identifies the appropriate entry in this table.

When an interrupt is generated by a device, it goes to the PIC. Multiple interrupts may be generated simultaneously. However, they are all buffered by the PIC. The PIC decides which one of these interrupts should be forwarded to the CPU. To inform the CPU that an outstanding interrupt is waiting to be processed, the PIC sends an interrupt request (INTR) to the CPU, which then, at the appropriate time, responds with an interrupt acknowledgment (INTA). At this time, PIC will put an 8-bit interrupt type number associated with the device on the bus so that the CPU can identify which interrupt handler to invoke. In the case when several interrupts are pending, PIC will send next interrupt request to the CPU only after it receives an end of interrupt command from the current ISR. Figure 8.8 shows the simple protocol that is used to determine which ISR is to be invoked.

In the computer designs that used a single PIC (PC and XT), eight different interrupt requests are allowed (IRQ0–IRQ7). Table 8.1 shows a list of standard interrupt type numbers for typical devices. When AT was designed, a second PIC was added,

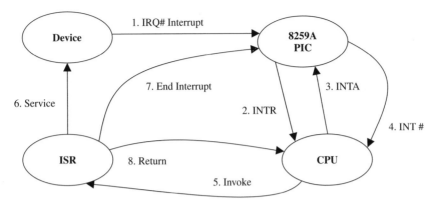

Figure 8.8   Interrupt handling in 80×86

increasing the number of interrupt inputs to 15. Figure 8.9 shows two PICS wired in cascade. One PIC is designated as master and the other becomes the slave. As shown in the figure, all slave interrupts are input via IRQ1 of the master. In general, eight different slaves can be accommodated by a single PIC.

Example 2: ARM Interrupt Architecture   ARM stands for Advanced RISC Machines. ARM is a 16/32-bit architecture that is used for portable devices because of its low power consumption and reasonable performance. Interrupt requests to the ARM core are collected and controlled by the interrupt controller, which is called ATIC. The interrupt controller provides an interface to the core and can collect up to 64 interrupt requests.

The usual sequence of events for interrupts is as follows. Interrupts would be enabled at the source (such as a peripheral), then enabled in the interrupt controller, and finally, enabled to the core. When an interrupt occurs at the source, its signal is routed to the interrupt controller then to the ARM core. In the interrupt controller, the interrupt can be enabled or disabled to the core and can be assigned a priority

TABLE 8.1   Standard IBM-PC Interrupt Type Numbers for Typical Devices

Device	IRQ no.	Interrupt type number
Programmable interval timer	0	08H
Keyboard	1	09H
Cascading to the second PICs	2	Reserved
Serial communication port (COM2)	3	0BH
Serial communication port (COM1)	4	0CH
Fixed disk controller	5	0DH
Floppy disk controller	6	0EH
Parallel printer controller	7	0FH

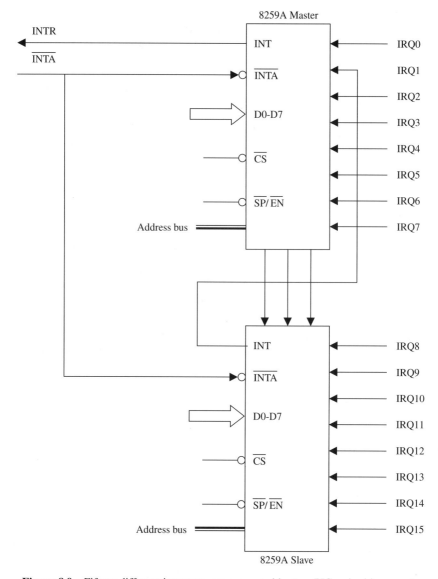

Figure 8.9 Fifteen different interrupts are supported by two PICs wired in cascade

level. Once the interrupt request reaches the core, it will halt the core from its normal processing routines to allow the interrupt request to be serviced.

Among the different interrupt requests that the ARM core can handle are IRQ and FIQ requests. The IRQ (normal interrupt request) is used for general-purpose interrupt handling. It has a lower priority than an FIQ (fast interrupt request) and is masked out when an FIQ sequence is entered. The FIQ is used to support high-speed data transfer or channel processes.

TABLE 8.2   Interrupt Vector Table

Exception type	Mode	Address
Reset	Supervisor	0×00000000
Undefined instructions	Undefined	0×00000004
Software interrupts (SWI)	Supervisor	0×00000008
Prefetch abort	Abort	$0 \times 0000000C$
Data abort	Abort	0×00000010
IRQ (Normal interrupt)	IRQ	0×00000018
FIQ (Fast interrupt)	FIQ	$0 \times 0000001C$

Similar to the 80×86, the addresses of the interrupt handlers are stored in a vector table, which is shown in Table 8.2. For example, when an IRQ is detected by the core, it accesses address 0×18 of the vector table and executes the instruction loaded in that address. Normally, the instruction found at 0×18 of the vector table is of the form: *LDR PC, IRQ_Handler* (load the address of the IRQ interrupt handler in the PC). When an FIQ is detected by the core, it accesses address $0 \times 1C$ of the vector table and executes the instruction loaded in that address. Normally, the instruction found at $0 \times 1C$ of the vector table is of the form: *LDR PC, FIQ_Handler.*

When an interrupt occurs, the following happens inside the core:

1. The CPSR (current program state register) is copied to the SPSR (saved program status register) of the mode being entered.
2. The CPSR bits are set as appropriate to the mode being entered, the core is set to ARM state, and the relevant interrupt disable flags are set.
3. The appropriate set of banked registers are banked in.
4. The return address is stored in the link register (of the relevant mode).
5. The PC is set to the relevant vector address.

For example, when an IRQ interrupt is detected, the ARM core enables SPSR_irq as the CPSR, enters the IRQ mode by setting the mode bits in the CSPR to 10010, disables Normal interrupts by setting the I bit in the CPSR, saves the address of the next instruction R14_irq, and loads 0×18 into the PC. At address 0×18, an instruction will load the address of the interrupt handler into the PC. Similarly, when an FIQ interrupt is detected, the ARM core enables SPSR_fiq as the CPSR, enters the FIQ mode by setting the mode bits in the CSPR to 10001, disables Normal and Fast interrupts by setting the F and I bits in the CPSR, saves the address of the next instruction R14_fiq, and loads $0 \times 1C$ into the PC. At address $0 \times 1C$, an instruction will load the address of the interrupt handler into the PC.

MC9328MX1/MXL AITC   The MC9328MX1/MXL AITC contains twenty-six 32-bit registers, which are described in Table 8.3. Using these registers, the AITC allows the selection of whether a pending interrupt source will create a Normal interrupt (IRQ) or a Fast interrupt (FIQ) to the core. This is accomplished via the

TABLE 8.3 The AITC Registers

Register	Description
INTCNTL	Configures specific control functions of the AITC.
NIMASK	Controls the Normal interrupt mask level. All Normal interrupt priority levels at or below what is programmed in the NIMASK register will be masked. Normal interrupt priorities are programmed via the NIPRIORITY[7 : 0] registers.
INTENNUM	Provides hardware accelerated enabling of interrupts. This is done by programming this register with the interrupt source that is desired to be enabled. Doing so will immediately enable (set) this interrupt source bit in the INTENABLEH/L register.
INTDISNUM	Provides hardware accelerated disabling of interrupts. This is done by programming this register with the interrupt source that is desired to be disabled. Doing so will immediately disable (clear) this interrupt source bit in the INTENABLEH/L register.
INTENABLEH	Used to enable pending interrupt source bits [63–32] to the core.
INTENABLEL	Used to enable pending interrupt source bits [31–0] to the core.
INTTYPEH	Used to select whether an enabled and pending interrupt source bit [63–32] will create a Normal interrupt or Fast interrupt to the core.
INTTYPEL	Used to select whether an enabled and pending interrupt source bit [31–0] will create a Normal interrupt or Fast interrupt to the core.
NIPRIORITY[7 : 0]	Provides software prioritization of Normal interrupts.
NIVECSR	Provides the priority of the highest pending Normal interrupt and provides the source number of the highest pending Normal interrupt.
FIVECSR	Provides the source number of the highest pending Fast interrupt.
INTSRCH	Reflects the status of interrupt request inputs (sources 63–32) into the interrupt controller.
INTSCRL	Reflects the status of interrupt request inputs (sources 31–0) into the interrupt controller.
INTFRCH	Allows for software generation of interrupts for interrupt sources 63 through 32.
INTFRCL	Allows for software generation of interrupts for interrupt sources 31 through 0.
NIPNDH	Reflects the source number(s) of pending Normal interrupt requests, for interrupt sources 63 through 32.
NIPNDL	Reflects the source number(s) of pending Normal interrupt requests, for interrupt sources 31 through 0.
FIPNDH	Reflects the source number(s) of pending Fast interrupt requests, for interrupt sources 63 through 32.
FIPNDL	Reflects the source number(s) of pending Fast interrupt requests, for interrupt sources 31 through 0.

INTTYPEH and INTTYPEL registers. Each bit in these registers corresponds to an interrupt source available in the system. Setting a bit will select its corresponding interrupt source as a Fast interrupt, whereas clearing this bit will select its corresponding bit as a Normal interrupt. In the INTTYPEL register, bit 0 corresponds to interrupt source 0, bit 1 corresponds to interrupt source 1, and so on up to bit 31, which corresponds to interrupt source 31. In the INTTYPEH register, bit 0 corresponds to interrupt source 32, bit 1 corresponds to interrupt source 33, and so on up to bit 31, which corresponds to interrupt source 63.

After determining the type of the pending interrupt, the next step is to enable the interrupt. This can be done via the INTENABLEH and INTENABLEL registers. To enable a pending interrupt to the core, its corresponding interrupt source bit in the INTENABLEH or INTENABLEL must be set. Likewise, to disable the interrupt, clear this bit. In the INTENABLEL register, bit 0 corresponds to interrupt source 0, bit 1 corresponds to interrupt source 1, and so on up to bit 31, which corresponds to interrupt source 31. In the INTENABLEH register, bit 0 corresponds to interrupt source 32, bit 1 corresponds to interrupt source 33, and so on up to bit 31, which corresponds to interrupt source 63. For example, to select interrupt source bit 15 as a Normal interrupt, clear bit 15 in the INTTYPEL register. Then, to enable this interrupt, set bit 15 in the INTENABLEL register. Likewise, to select interrupt source bit 45 as a Fast interrupt, set bit 13 in the INTTYPEH register. Then, to enable this interrupt, set bit 13 in the INTENABLEH. The AITC also allows the programmer to prioritize the pending Normal interrupt sources to one of 16 different priority levels. This can be done in the NIPRIORITY[7:0] registers.

8.4. DIRECT MEMORY ACCESS (DMA)

The main idea of direct memory access (DMA) is to enable peripheral devices to cut out the "middle man" role of the CPU in data transfer. It allows peripheral devices to transfer data directly from and to memory without the intervention of the CPU. Having peripheral devices access memory directly would allow the CPU to do other work, which would lead to improved performance, especially in the cases of large transfers.

The DMA controller is a piece of hardware that controls one or more peripheral devices. It allows devices to transfer data to or from the system's memory without the help of the processor. In a typical DMA transfer, some event notifies the *DMA controller* that data needs to be transferred to or from memory. Both the DMA and CPU use memory bus and only one or the other can use the memory at the same time. The DMA controller then sends a request to the CPU asking its permission to use the bus. The CPU returns an acknowledgment to the DMA controller granting it bus access. The DMA can now take control of the bus to independently conduct memory transfer. When the transfer is complete the DMA relinquishes its control of the bus to the CPU. Processors that support DMA provide one or more input signals that the bus requester can assert to gain control of the bus and one or more output signals that the CPU asserts to indicate it has relinquished the bus. Figure 8.10 shows how the DMA controller shares the CPU's memory bus.

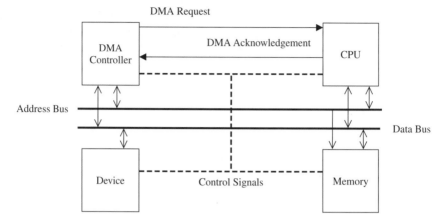

Figure 8.10   DMA controller shares the CPU's memory bus

Direct memory access controllers require initialization by the CPU. Typical setup parameters include the address of the source area, the address of the destination area, the length of the block, and whether the DMA controller should generate a processor interrupt once the block transfer is complete. A DMA controller has an address register, a word count register, and a control register. The address register contains an address that specifies the memory location of the data to be transferred. It is typically possible to have the DMA controller automatically increment the address register after each word transfer, so that the next transfer will be from the next memory location. The word count register holds the number of words to be transferred. The word count is decremented by one after each word transfer. The control register specifies the transfer mode.

Direct memory access data transfer can be performed in burst mode or single-cycle mode. In burst mode, the DMA controller keeps control of the bus until all the data has been transferred to (from) memory from (to) the peripheral device. This mode of transfer is needed for fast devices where data transfer cannot be stopped until the entire transfer is done. In single-cycle mode (cycle stealing), the DMA controller relinquishes the bus after each transfer of one data word. This minimizes the amount of time that the DMA controller keeps the CPU from controlling the bus, but it requires that the bus request/acknowledge sequence be performed for every single transfer. This overhead can result in a degradation of the performance. The single-cycle mode is preferred if the system cannot tolerate more than a few cycles of added interrupt latency or if the peripheral devices can buffer very large amounts of data, causing the DMA controller to tie up the bus for an excessive amount of time.

The following steps summarize the DMA operations:

1. DMA controller initiates data transfer.
2. Data is moved (increasing the address in memory, and reducing the count of words to be moved).

3. When word count reaches zero, the DMA informs the CPU of the termination by means of an interrupt.
4. The CPU regains access to the memory bus.

A DMA controller may have multiple channels. Each channel has associated with it an address register and a count register. To initiate a data transfer the device driver sets up the DMA channel's address and count registers together with the direction of the data transfer, read or write. While the transfer is taking place, the CPU is free to do other things. When the transfer is complete, the CPU is interrupted.

Direct memory access channels cannot be shared between device drivers. A device driver must be able to determine which DMA channel to use. Some devices have a fixed DMA channel, while others are more flexible, where the device driver can simply pick a free DMA channel to use.

Linux tracks the usage of the DMA channels using a vector of dma_chan data structures (one per DMA channel). The dma_chan data structure contains just two fields, a pointer to a string describing the owner of the DMA channel and a flag indicating if the DMA channel is allocated or not.

8.5. BUSES

A bus in computer terminology represents a physical connection used to carry a signal from one point to another. The signal carried by a bus may represent address, data, control signal, or power. Typically, a bus consists of a number of connections running together. Each connection is called a *bus line*. A bus line is normally identified by a number. Related groups of bus lines are usually identified by a name. For example, the group of bus lines 1 to 16 in a given computer system may be used to carry the address of memory locations, and therefore are identified as *address lines*. Depending on the signal carried, there exist at least four types of buses: *address*, *data*, *control*, and *power* buses. Data buses carry data, control buses carry control signals, and power buses carry the power-supply/ground voltage. The *size* (number of lines) of the address, data, and control bus varies from one system to another. Consider, for example, the bus connecting a CPU and memory in a given system, called the *CPU bus*. The size of the memory in that system is 512M-word and each word is 32 bits. In such system, the size of the address bus should be $\log_2(512 \times 2^{20}) = 29$ lines, the size of the data bus should be 32 lines, and at least one control line ($\bar{R}/W$) should exist in that system.

In addition to carrying control signals, a control bus can carry timing signals. These are signals used to determine the exact timing for data transfer to and from a bus; that is, they determine when a given computer system component, such as the processor, memory, or I/O devices, can place data on the bus and when they can receive data from the bus. A bus can be *synchronous* if data transfer over the bus is controlled by a *bus clock*. The clock acts as the timing reference for all bus signals. A bus is *asynchronous* if data transfer over the bus is based on the availability of the data and not on a clock signal. Data is transferred over an asynchronous bus using a technique called *handshaking*. The operations of synchronous and asynchronous buses are explained below.

To understand the difference between synchronous and asynchronous, let us consider the case when a master such as a CPU or DMA is the source of data to be transferred to a slave such as an I/O device. The following is a sequence of events involving the master and slave:

1. Master: send request to use the bus
2. Master: request is granted and bus is allocated to master
3. Master: place address/data on bus
4. Slave: slave is selected
5. Master: signal data transfer
6. Slave: take data
7. Master: free the bus

8.5.1. Synchronous Buses

In synchronous buses, the steps of data transfer take place at fixed clock cycles. Everything is synchronized to bus clock and clock signals are made available to both master and slave. The bus clock is a square wave signal. A cycle starts at one rising edge of the clock and ends at the next rising edge, which is the beginning of the next cycle. A transfer may take multiple bus cycles depending on the speed parameters of the bus and the two ends of the transfer.

One scenario would be that on the first clock cycle, the master puts an address on the address bus, puts data on the data bus, and asserts the appropriate control lines. Slave recognizes its address on the address bus on the first cycle and reads the new value from the bus in the second cycle.

Synchronous buses are simple and easily implemented. However, when connecting devices with varying speeds to a synchronous bus, the slowest device will determine the speed of the bus. Also, the synchronous bus length could be limited to avoid clock-skewing problems.

8.5.2. Asynchronous Buses

There are no fixed clock cycles in asynchronous buses. Handshaking is used instead. Figure 8.11 shows the handshaking protocol. The master asserts the data-ready line

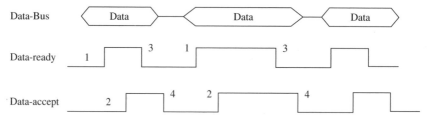

Figure 8.11   Asynchronous bus timing using handshaking protocol

(point 1 in the figure) until it sees a data-accept signal. When the slave sees a data-ready signal, it will assert the data-accept line (point 2 in the figure). The rising of the data-accept line will trigger the falling of the data-ready line and the removal of data from the bus. The falling of the data-ready line (point 3 in the figure) will trigger the falling of the data-accept line (point 4 in the figure). This handshaking, which is called fully interlocked, is repeated until the data is completely transferred. Asynchronous bus is appropriate for different speed devices.

8.5.3. Bus Arbitration

Bus arbitration is needed to resolve conflicts when two or more devices want to become the bus master at the same time. In short, arbitration is the process of selecting the next bus master from among multiple candidates. Conflicts can be resolved based on fairness or priority in a centralized or distributed mechanisms.

Centralized Arbitration In centralized arbitration schemes, a single arbiter is used to select the next master. A simple form of centralized arbitration uses a bus request line, a bus grant line, and a bus busy line. Each of these lines is shared by potential masters, which are daisy-chained in a cascade. Figure 8.12 shows this simple centralized arbitration scheme.

In the figure, each of the potential masters can submit a bus request at any time. A fixed priority is set among the masters from left to right. When a bus request is received at the central bus arbiter, it issues a bus grant by asserting the bus grant line. When the potential master that is closest to the arbiter (potential master 1) sees the bus grant signal, it checks to see if it had made a bus request. If yes, it takes over the bus and stops propagation of the bus grant signal any further. If it has not made a request, it will simple turn the bus grant signal to the next master to the right (potential master 2), and so on. When the transaction is complete, the busy line is deasserted.

Instead of using shared request and grant lines, multiple bus request and bus grant lines can be used. In one scheme, each master will have its own independent request and grant line as shown in Figure 8.13. The central arbiter can employ any priority-based or fairness-based tiebreaker. Another scheme allows the masters to have multiple priority levels. For each priority level, there is a bus request and a bus grant line. Within each priority level, daisy chain is used. In this scheme, each device is attached to the daisy chain of one priority level. If the arbiter receives multiple

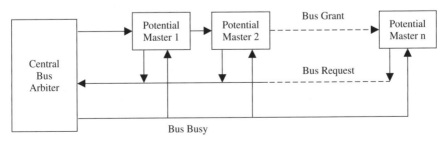

Figure 8.12 Centralized arbiter in a daisy-chain scheme

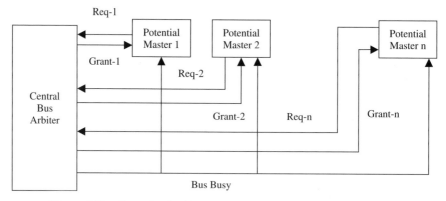

Figure 8.13 Centralized arbiter with independent request and grant lines

bus requests from different levels, it grants the bus to the level with the highest priority. Daisy chaining is used among the devices of that level. Figure 8.14 shows an example of four devices included in two priority levels. Potential master 1 and potential master 3 are daisy-chained in level 1 and potential master 2 and potential master 4 are daisy-chained in level 2.

Decentralized Arbitration   In decentralized arbitration schemes, priority-based arbitration is usually used in a distributed fashion. Each potential master has a unique arbitration number, which is used in resolving conflicts when multiple requests are submitted. For example, a conflict can always be resolved in favor of the device with the highest arbitration number. The question now is how to determine which device has the highest arbitration number? One method is that a requesting device would make its unique arbitration number available to all other devices. Each device compares that number with its own arbitration number. The device with the smaller number is always dismissed. Eventually, the requester with the highest arbitration number will survive and be granted bus access.

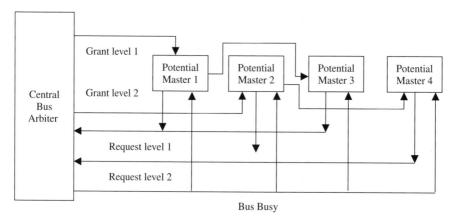

Figure 8.14 Centralized arbiter with two priority levels (four devices)

8.6. INPUT–OUTPUT INTERFACES

An interface is a data path between two separate devices in a computer system. Interface to buses can be classified based on the number of bits that are transmitted at a given time to serial versus parallel ports. In a serial port, only 1 bit of data is transferred at a time. Mice and modems are usually connected to serial ports. A parallel port allows more than 1 bit of data to be processed at once. Printers are the most common peripheral devices connected to parallel ports. Table 8.4 shows a summary of the variety of buses and interfaces used in personal computers.

TABLE 8.4 Descriptions of Buses and Interfaces Used in Personal Computers

Bus/Interface	Description
PS/2	A type of port (or interface) that can be used to connect mice and keyboards to the computer. The PS/2 port is sometimes called the mouse port.
Industry standard architecture (ISA)	ISA was originally an 8-bit bus and later expanded to a 16-bit bus in 1984. In 1993, Intel and Microsoft introduced a plug and play ISA bus that allowed the computer to automatically detect and set up computer ISA peripherals such as a modem or sound card.
Extended industry standard architecture (EISA)	EISA is an enhanced form of ISA, which allows for 32-bit data transfers, while maintaining support for 8- and 16-bit expansion boards. However, its bus speed, like ISA, is only 8 MHz. EISA is not widely used, due to its high cost and complicated nature.
Micro channel architecture (MCA)	MCA was introduced by IBM in 1987. It offered several additional features over the ISA such as a 32-bit bus, automatically configured cards and bus mastering for greater efficiency. It is slightly superior to EISA, but not many expansion boards were ever made to fit MCA specifications.
VESA (Video electronics standards association) local bus (VLB)	The VESA, a nonprofit organization founded by NEC, released the VLB in 1992. It is a 32-bit bus that had direct access to the system memory at the speed of the processor, commonly the 486 CPU (33/40 MHz). VLB 2.0 was later released in 1994 and had a 64-bit bus and a bus speed of 50 MHz.
Peripheral component interconnect (PCI)	PCI was introduced by Intel in 1992, revised in 1993 to version 2.0, and later revised in 1995 to PCI 2.1. It is a 32-bit bus that is also available as a 64-bit bus today. Many modern expansion boards are connected to PCI slots.
Advanced graphic port (AGP)	AGP was introduced by Intel in 1997. AGP is a 32-bit bus designed for the high demands of 3D graphics. AGP has a direct line to memory, which allows 3D elements to be stored in the system memory instead of the video memory. AGP is geared towards data-intensive graphics cards, such as 3D accelerators; its design allows for data throughput at rates of 266 MB/s.

(*continued*)

TABLE 8.4 *Continued*

Bus/Interface	Description
Universal serial bus (USB)	USB is an external bus developed by Intel, Compaq, DEC, IBM, Microsoft, NEC and Northern Telcom. It was released in 1996 with the Intel 430HX Triton II Mother Board. USB has the capability of transferring 12 Mbps, supporting up to 127 devices. Many devices can be connected to USB ports, which support plug and play.
FireWire (IEEE 1394)	FireWire is a type of external bus, which supports very fast transfer rates: 400 Mbps. Because of this, FireWire is suitable for connecting video devices, such as VCRs, to the computer.
Small computer system interface (SCSI)	SCSI is a type of parallel interface that is commonly used for mass storage devices. SCSI can transfer data at rates of 4 MB/s; in addition, there are several varieties of SCSI that support higher speeds: Fast SCSI (10 MB/s), Ultra SCSI and Fast Wide SCSI (20 MB/s), as well as Ultra Wide SCSI (40 MB/s).
Integrated drive electronics (IDE)	IDE is a commonly used interface for hard disk drives and CD-ROM drives. It is less expensive than SCSI, but offers slightly less in terms of performance.
Enhanced integrated drive electronics (EIDE)	EIDE is an improved version of IDE, which offers better performance than standard SCSI. It offers transfer rates between 4 and 16.6 MB/s.
PCI-X	PCI-X is a high performance bus that is designed to meet the increased I/O demands of technologies such as Fibre Channel, Gigabit Ethernet, and Ultra3 SCSI.
Communication and network riser (CNR)	CNR was introduced by Intel in 2000. It is a specification that supports audio, modem USB and local area networking interfaces of core logic chipsets.

8.7. SUMMARY

One of the major features in a computer system is its ability to exchange data with other devices and to allow the user to interact with the system. This chapter focused on the I/O system and the way the processor and the I/O devices exchange data in a computer system. The chapter described three ways of organizing I/O: programmed I/O, interrupt-driven I/O, and DMA. In programmed I/O, the CPU handles the transfers, which take place between registers and the devices. In interrupt-driven I/O, CPU handles data transfers and an I/O module is running concurrently. In DMA, data are transferred between memory and I/O devices without intervention of the CPU. We also studied two methods for synchronization: polling and interrupts. In polling, the processor polls the device while waiting for I/O to complete. Clearly processor cycles are wasted in this method. Using interrupts, processors are free to switch to other tasks during I/O. Devices assert interrupts when I/O is complete. Interrupts incurs some delay penalty. Two examples of interrupt handling were covered: 80×86 family and ARM. The chapter also covered buses and interfaces. A wide variety of interfaces and buses used in personal computers are summarized.

EXERCISES

1. Conduct an Internet search on I/O devices and prepare a table categorizing the different devices into separate categories, for example input, output, character-based, block-based, and so on. For every entry in the table, indicate its speed, interface, and category.

2. What are the advantages and disadvantages of isolated versus memory mapped I/O.

3. Show how data transfer from disk to memory is conducted under each of the following I/O schemes: programmed I/O, interrupt-driven I/O, and DMA. Show the steps taken in each case.

4. If an interrupt requires 50 ms of overhead time, and polling requires 5 ms per device, describe different situations where each seems better than the other.

5. What entities in a computer system does a device driver communicate with? What are the functions of a device driver? List all operations.

6. What types of operations is DMA used to accelerate?

7. A DMA module is transferring data to memory using cycle stealing from a device that transmits data at rate of 19,200 bits per second. The speed of the CPU is 3 MIPS. By how much would the DMA module affect the performance of the CPU.

8. Describe the scenarios in which a synchronous bus would outperform an asynchronous bus and vice versa.

9. Discuss the advantages and disadvantages of the different bus arbitration policies covered in the chapter. Prepare a contract table that compares the arbitration techniques from both the implementation and operational aspects.

REFERENCES AND FURTHER READING

I. Englander, *The Architecture of Computer Hardware and System Software*, John Wiley, New York, 1996.

C. Hamacher, Z. Vranesic, and S. Zaky, *Computer Organization*, 5th ed., McGraw-Hill, New York, 2002.

V. Heuring, and H. Jordan, *Computer Systems Design and Architecture*, Addison Wesley, NJ, USA, 1997.

S. Shiva, *Computer Design and Architecture*, Harper Collins, MA, USA, 1991.

A. Tanenbaum, *Structured Computer Organization*, 4th ed., Prentice Hall, NJ, USA, 1999.

J. Uffenbeck, *The 80×86 Family, Design, Programming, and Interfacing*, 3rd ed., Prentice Hall, Essex, UK, 2002.

Websites

PCI Local Bus Specifications, www.pcisig.com/developers

SCSI-3 Architecture Model (SAM), www.ansi.org

Universal Serial Bus Specification, www.usb.org/developers

www.arm.com

www.motorola.com/semiconductors

CHAPTER 9

Pipelining Design Techniques

There exist two basic techniques to increase the instruction execution rate of a processor. These are to increase the clock rate, thus decreasing the instruction execution time, or alternatively to increase the number of instructions that can be executed simultaneously. Pipelining and instruction-level parallelism are examples of the latter technique. Pipelining owes its origin to car assembly lines. The idea is to have more than one instruction being processed by the processor at the same time. Similar to the assembly line, the success of a pipeline depends upon dividing the execution of an instruction among a number of subunits (stages), each performing part of the required operations. A possible division is to consider instruction fetch (F), instruction decode (D), operand fetch (F), instruction execution (E), and store of results (S) as the subtasks needed for the execution of an instruction. In this case, it is possible to have up to five instructions in the pipeline at the same time, thus reducing instruction execution latency. In this Chapter, we discuss the basic concepts involved in designing instruction pipelines. Performance measures of a pipeline are introduced. The main issues contributing to instruction pipeline hazards are discussed and some possible solutions are introduced. In addition, we introduce the concept of arithmetic pipelining together with the problems involved in designing such a pipeline. Our coverage concludes with a review of a recent pipeline processor.

9.1. GENERAL CONCEPTS

Pipelining refers to the technique in which a given task is divided into a number of subtasks that need to be performed in sequence. Each subtask is performed by a given functional unit. The units are connected in a serial fashion and all of them operate simultaneously. The use of pipelining improves the performance compared to the traditional sequential execution of tasks. Figure 9.1 shows an illustration of the basic difference between executing four subtasks of a given instruction (in this case fetching F, decoding D, execution E, and writing the results W) using pipelining and sequential processing.

Fundamentals of Computer Organization and Architecture, by M. Abd-El-Barr and H. El-Rewini
ISBN 0-471-46741-3 Copyright © 2005 John Wiley & Sons, Inc.

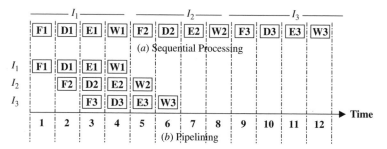

Figure 9.1 Pipelining versus sequential processing

It is clear from the figure that the total time required to process three instructions (I_1, I_2, I_3) is only six time units if four-stage pipelining is used as compared to 12 time units if sequential processing is used. A possible saving of up to 50% in the execution time of these three instructions is obtained. In order to formulate some performance measures for the goodness of a pipeline in processing a series of tasks, a space time chart (called the Gantt's chart) is used. The chart shows the succession of the subtasks in the pipe with respect to time. Figure 9.2 shows a Gantt's chart. In this chart, the vertical axis represents the subunits (four in this case) and the horizontal axis represents time (measured in terms of the time unit required for each unit to perform its task). In developing the Gantt's chart, we assume that the time (T) taken by each subunit to perform its task is the same; we call this the *unit time*.

As can be seen from the figure, 13 time units are needed to finish executing 10 instructions (I_1 to I_{10}). This is to be compared to 40 time units if sequential processing is used (ten instructions each requiring four time units).

In the following analysis, we provide three performance measures for the goodness of a pipeline. These are the *Speed-up S(n)*, *Throughput U(n)*, and *Efficiency E(n)*. It should be noted that in this analysis we assume that the unit time $T = t$ units.

1. *Speed-up S(n)* Consider the execution of m tasks (instructions) using n-stages (units) pipeline. As can be seen, $n + m - 1$ time units are required

	1	2	3	4	5	6	7	8	9	10	11	12	13
U_4				I_1	I_2	I_3	I_4	I_5	I_6	I_7	I_8	I_9	I_{10}
U_3			I_1	I_2	I_3	I_4	I_5	I_6	I_7	I_8	I_9	I_{10}	
U_2		I_1	I_2	I_3	I_4	I_5	I_6	I_7	I_8	I_9	I_{10}		
U_1	I_1	I_2	I_3	I_4	I_5	I_6	I_7	I_8	I_9	I_{10}			

Figure 9.2 The space–time chart (Gantt chart)

to complete m tasks.

$$Speed\text{-}up\ S(n) = \frac{\text{Time using sequential processing}}{\text{Time using pipeline processing}} = \frac{m \times n \times t}{(n+m-1) \times t}$$

$$= \frac{m \times n}{n+m-1}$$

$$\lim_{m \to \infty} S(n) = n \quad \text{(i.e., } n\text{-fold increase in speed is theoretically possible)}$$

2. *Throughput $U(n)$*

$$\textit{Throughput}\ U(n) = \text{no. of tasks executed per unit time} = \frac{m}{(n+m-1) \times t}$$

$$\lim_{m \to \infty} U(n) = 1 \text{ assuming that } t = 1 \text{ unit time}$$

3. *Efficiency $E(n)$*

$$\textit{Efficiency}\ E(n) = \text{Ratio of the actual speed-up to the maximum speed-up}$$

$$= \frac{Speed\text{-}up}{n} = \frac{m}{n+m-1}$$

$$\lim_{m \to \infty} E(n) = 1$$

9.2. INSTRUCTION PIPELINE

The simple analysis made in Section 9.1 ignores an important aspect that can affect the performance of a pipeline, that is, *pipeline stall*. A pipeline operation is said to have been stalled if one unit (stage) requires more time to perform its function, thus forcing other stages to become idle. Consider, for example, the case of an instruction fetch that incurs a *cache miss*. Assume also that a cache miss requires *three extra time units*. Figure 9.3 illustrates the effect of having instruction I_2 incurring a cache miss (assuming the execution of ten instructions I_1 to I_{10}).

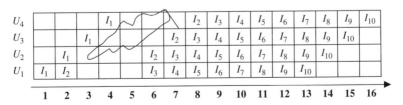

Figure 9.3   Effect of a cache miss on the pipeline

The figure shows that due to the extra time units needed for instruction I_2 to be fetched, the pipeline stalls, that is, fetching of instruction I_3 and subsequent instructions are delayed. Such situations create what is known as pipeline *bubble* (or pipeline *hazards*). The creation of a pipeline bubble leads to wasted unit times, thus leading to an overall increase in the number of time units needed to finish executing a given number of instructions. The number of time units needed to execute the 10 instructions shown in Figure 9.3 is now 16 time units, compared to 13 time units if there were no cache misses.

Pipeline hazards can take place for a number of other reasons. Among these are instruction dependency and data dependency. These are explained below.

9.2.1. Pipeline "Stall" Due to Instruction Dependency

Correct operation of a pipeline requires that operation performed by a stage MUST NOT depend on the operation(s) performed by other stage(s). Instruction dependency refers to the case whereby fetching of an instruction depends on the results of executing a previous instruction. Instruction dependency manifests itself in the execution of a conditional branch instruction. Consider, for example, the case of a "branch if negative" instruction. In this case, the next instruction to fetch will not be known until the result of executing that "branch if negative" instruction is known. In the following discussion, we will assume that the instruction following a conditional branch instruction is not fetched until the result of executing the branch instruction is known (stored). The following example shows the effect of instruction dependency on a pipeline.

Example 1   Consider the execution of ten instructions I_1-I_{10} on a pipeline consisting of four pipeline stages: *IF* (instruction fetch), *ID* (instruction decode), *IE* (instruction execute), and *IS* (instruction results store). Assume that the instruction I_4 is a conditional branch instruction and that when it is executed, the branch is not taken, that is, the branch condition(s) is(are) not satisfied. Assume also that when the branch instruction is fetched, the pipeline stalls until the result of executing the branch instruction is stored. Show the succession of instructions in the pipeline; that is, show the Gantt's chart. Figure 9.4 shows the required Gantt's chart. The bubble created due to the pipeline stall is clearly shown in the figure.

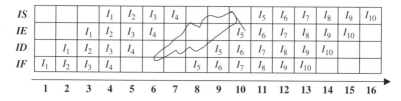

Figure 9.4   Instruction dependency effect on a pipeline

9.2.2. Pipeline "Stall" Due to Data Dependency

Data dependency in a pipeline occurs when a source operand of instruction I_i depends on the results of executing a preceding instruction, I_j, $i > j$. It should be noted that although instruction I_i can be fetched, its operand(s) may not be available until the results of instruction I_j are stored. The following example shows the effect of data dependency on a pipeline.

Example 2 Consider the execution of the following piece of code:

•

ADD	R_1, R_2, R_3;	$R_3 \leftarrow R_1 + R_2$
SL	R_3;	$R_3 \leftarrow SL(R_3)$
SUB	R_5, R_6, R_4;	$R_4 \leftarrow R_5 - R_6$

•

In this piece of code, the first instruction, call it I_i, adds the contents of two registers R_1 and R_2 and stores the result in register R_3. The second instruction, call it I_{i+1}, shifts the contents of R_3 one bit position to the left and stores the result back into R_3. The third instruction, call it I_{i+2}, stores the result of subtracting the content of R_6 from the content of R_5 in register R_4. In order to show the effect of such data dependency, we will assume that the pipeline consists of five stages, IF, ID, OF, IE, and IS. In this case, the OF stage represents the operand fetch stage. The functions of the remaining four stages remain the same as explained before. Figure 9.5 shows the Gantt's chart for this piece of code. As shown in the figure, although instruction I_{i+1} has been successfully decoded during time unit $k + 2$, this instruction cannot proceed to the OF unit during time unit $k + 3$. This is because the operand to be fetched by I_{i+1} during time unit $k+3$ should be the content of register R_3, which has been modified by execution of instruction I_i. However, the modified value of R_3 will not be available until the end of time unit $k + 4$. This will require instruction I_{i+1} to wait (at the output of the ID unit) until $k + 5$. Notice that instruction I_{i+2} will

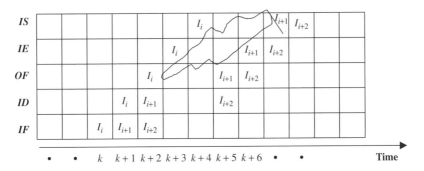

Figure 9.5   The write-after-write data dependency

have also to wait (at the output of the *IF* unit) until such time that instruction I_{i+1} proceeds to the *ID*. The net result is that pipeline stall takes place due to the data dependency that exists between instruction I_i and instruction I_{i+1}.

The data dependency presented in the above example resulted because register R_3 is the destination for both instructions I_i and I_{i+1}. This is called a write-after-write data dependency. Taking into consideration that any register can be written into (or read from), then a total of four different possibilities exist, including the write-after-write case. The other three cases are read-after-write, write-after-read, and read-after-read. Among the four cases, the read-after-read case should not lead to pipeline stall. This is because a register read operation does not change the content of the register. Among the remaining three cases, the write-after-write (see the above example) and the read-after-write lead to pipeline stall. The following piece of code illustrates the read-after-write case:

●

ADD $R_1, R_2, R_3;$ $R_3 \leftarrow R_1 + R_2$
SUB $R_3, 1, R_4;$ $R_4 \leftarrow R_3 - 1$

●

In this case, the first instruction modifies the content of register R_3 (through a write operation) while the second instruction uses the modified contents of R_3 (through a read operation) to load a value into register R_4. While these two instructions are proceeding within a pipeline, care should be taken so that the value of register R_3 read in the second instruction is the updated value resulting from execution of the previous instruction. Figure 9.6 shows the Gantt's chart for this case assuming that the first instruction is called I_i and the second instruction is called I_{i+1}.

It is clear that the operand of the second instruction cannot be fetched during time unit $k+3$ and that it has to be delayed until time unit $k+5$. This is because the modified value of the content of register R_3 will not be available until time slot $k+5$.

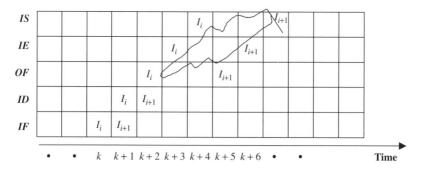

Figure 9.6   The read-after-write data dependency

Fetching the operand of the second instruction during time slot $k + 3$ will lead to incorrect results.

Example 3   Consider the execution of the following sequence of instructions on a five-stage pipeline consisting of *IF*, *ID*, *OF*, *IE*, and *IS*. It is required to show the succession of these instructions in the pipeline.

$I_1 \rightarrow$	Load	$-1, R1;$	$R1 \leftarrow -1;$
$I_2 \rightarrow$	Load	$5, R2;$	$R2 \leftarrow 5;$
$I_3 \rightarrow$	Sub	$R2, 1, R2$	$R2 \leftarrow R2 - 1;$
$I_4 \rightarrow$	Add	$R1, R2, R3;$	$R3 \leftarrow R1 + R2;$
$I_5 \rightarrow$	Add	$R4, R5, R6;$	$R6 \leftarrow R4 + R5;$
$I_6 \rightarrow$	SL	$R3$	$R3 \leftarrow SL\ (R3)$
$I_7 \rightarrow$	Add	$R6, R4, R7;$	$R7 \leftarrow R4 + R6;$

In this example, the following data dependencies are observed:

Instructions	Type of data dependency
I_3 and I_2	Read-after-write and write-after-write (W-W)
I_4 and I_1	Read-after-write (R-W)
I_4 and I_3	Read-after-write (R-W)
I_6 and I_4	Read-after-write and write-after-write (W-W)
I_7 and I_5	Read-after-write (R-W)

Figure 9.7 illustrates the progression of these instructions in the pipeline taking into consideration the data dependencies mentioned above. The assumption made in constructing the Gantt's chart in Figure 9.7 is that fetching an operand by an instruction that depends on the results of a previous instruction execution is delayed until such operand is available, that is, the result is stored. A total of 16 time units are required to execute the given seven instructions taking into consideration the data dependencies among the different instructions.

	1	2	3	4	5	6	7	8	9	10	11	12	13	14	15	16
IS					I_1	I_2			I_3			I_4	I_5		I_6	I_7
IE				I_1	I_2			I_3			I_4	I_5		I_6	I_7	
OF			I_1	I_2			I_3			I_4	I_5		I_6	I_7		
ID		I_1	I_2	I_3			I_4			I_5	I_6		I_7			
IF	I_1	I_2	I_3	I_4			I_5			I_6	I_7					

Figure 9.7   Gantt's chart for Example 3

Based on the results obtained above, we can compute the speed-up and the throughput for executing the piece of code given in Example 3 as:

$$\textit{Speed-up } S(5) = \frac{\text{Time using sequential processing}}{\text{Time using pipeline processing}} = \frac{7 \times 5}{16} = 2.19$$

$$\textit{Throughput } U(5) = \text{No. of tasks executed per unit time} = \frac{7}{16} = 0.44$$

The discussion on pipeline stall due to instruction and data dependencies should reveal three main points about the problems associated with having such dependencies. These are:

1. Both instruction and data dependencies lead to added delay in the pipeline.
2. Instruction dependency can lead to the fetching of the wrong instruction.
3. Data dependency can lead to the fetching of the wrong operand.

There exist a number of methods to deal with the problems resulting from instruction and data dependencies. Some of these methods try to prevent the fetching of the wrong instruction or the wrong operand while others try to reduce the delay incurred in the pipeline due to the existence of instruction or data dependency. A number of these methods are introduced below.

Methods Used to Prevent Fetching the Wrong Instruction or Operand

Use of NOP *(No Operation)*   This method can be used in order to prevent the fetching of the wrong instruction, in case of instruction dependency, or fetching the wrong operand, in case of data dependency. Recall Example 1. In that example, the execution of a sequence of ten instructions $I_1 - I_{10}$ on a pipeline consisting of four pipeline stages: *IF, ID, IE,* and *IS* were considered. In order to show the execution of these instructions in the pipeline, we have assumed that when the branch instruction is fetched, the pipeline stalls until the result of executing the branch instruction is stored. This assumption was needed in order to prevent fetching the wrong instruction after fetching the branch instruction. In real-life situations, a mechanism is needed to guarantee fetching the appropriate instruction at the appropriate time. Insertion of "*NOP*" instructions will help carrying out this task. A "*NOP*" is an instruction that has no effect on the status of the processor.

Example 4   Consider the execution of ten instructions $I_1 - I_{10}$ on a pipeline consisting of four pipeline stages: *IF, ID, IE,* and *IS*. Assume that instruction I_4 is a conditional branch instruction and that when it is executed, the branch is not taken; that is, the branch condition is not satisfied.

	1	2	3	4	5	6	7	8	9	10	11	12	13	14	15	16
IS				I_1	I_2	I_3	I_4	Nop	Nop	Nop	I_5	I_6	I_7	I_8	I_9	I_{10}
IE			I_1	I_2	I_3	I_4	Nop	Nop	Nop	I_5	I_6	I_7	I_8	I_9	I_{10}	
ID		I_1	I_2	I_3	I_4	Nop	Nop	Nop	I_5	I_6	I_7	I_8	I_9	I_{10}		
IF	I_1	I_2	I_3	I_4	Nop	Nop	Nop	I_5	I_6	I_7	I_8	I_9	I_{10}			

Figure 9.8   The use of *NOP* instructions

In order to execute this set of instructions while preventing the fetching of the wrong instruction, we assume that a specified number of *NOP* instructions have been inserted such that they follow instruction I_4 in the sequence and they precede instruction I_5. Figure 9.8 shows the Gantt's chart illustrating the execution of the new sequence of instructions (after inserting the *NOP* instructions). The figure shows that the insertion of THREE *NOP* instructions after instruction I_4 will guarantee that the correct instruction to fetch after I_4, in this case I_5, will only be fetched during time slot number 8 at which the result of executing I_4 would have been stored and the condition for the branch would have been known.

It should be noted that the number of *NOP* instructions needed is equal to $(n - 1)$, where n is the number of pipeline stages.

Example 4 illustrates the use of *NOP* instructions to prevent fetching the wrong instruction in the case of instruction dependency. A similar approach can be used to prevent fetching the wrong operand in the case of data dependency. Consider the execution of the following piece of code on a five-stage pipeline (*IF, ID, OF, IE, IS*).

$$ADD \quad R_1, R_2, R_3; \qquad R_3 \leftarrow R_1 + R_2$$
$$SUB \quad R_3, 1, R_4; \qquad R_4 \leftarrow R_3 - 1$$
$$MOV \quad R_5, R_6; \qquad R_6 \leftarrow R_5$$

Note the data dependency in the form of read-after-write (R-W) between the first two instructions. Fetching the operand for the second instruction, that is, fetching the content of R_3, cannot proceed until the result of the first instruction has been stored. In order to achieve that, *NOP* instructions can be inserted between the first two instructions as shown below.

$$ADD \quad R_1, R_2, R_3; \qquad R_3 \leftarrow R_1 + R_2$$
$$NOP$$
$$NOP$$
$$SUB \quad R_3, 1, R_4; \qquad R_4 \leftarrow R_3 - 1$$
$$MOV \quad R_5, R_6; \qquad R_6 \leftarrow R_5$$

Execution of the modified sequence of instructions is shown in Figure 9.9. The figure shows that the use of *NOP* guarantees that during time unit #6 instruction

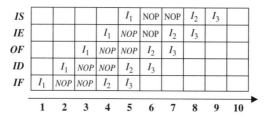

Figure 9.9 Use of *NOP* in data dependency

I_2 will fetch the correct value of R_3. This is the value stored as a result of executing instruction I_1 during time unit #5.

Methods Used to Reduce Pipeline Stall Due to Instruction Dependency

Unconditional Branch Instructions   In order to be able to reduce the pipeline stall due to unconditional branches, it is necessary to identify the unconditional branches as early as possible and before fetching the wrong instruction. It may also be possible to reduce the stall by reordering the instruction sequence. These methods are explained below.

REORDERING OF INSTRUCTIONS   In this case, the sequence of instructions are reordered such that correct instructions are brought to the pipeline while guaranteeing the correctness of the final results produced by the reordered set of instructions. Consider, for example, the execution of the following group of instructions $I_1, I_2, I_3, I_4,$ $I_5, \cdot, I_j, I_{j+1}, \cdot, \cdot$ on a pipeline consisting of three pipeline stages: *IF*, *IE*, and *IS*. In this group of instructions, I_4 is an unconditional branch instruction whereby the target instruction is I_j. Execution of this group of instructions in the same sequence as given will lead to the incorrect fetching of instruction I_5 after fetching instruction I_4. However, consider execution of the reordered sequence $I_1, I_4, I_2, I_3,$ $I_5, \cdot, I_j, I_{j+1}, \cdot, \cdot$. Execution of this reordered sequence using the three-stage pipeline is shown in Figure 9.10.

The figure shows that the reordering of the instructions causes instruction I_j to be fetched during time unit #5, that is, after instruction I_4 has been executed. Reordering of instructions can be done using a "smart" compiler that can scan the sequence of code and decide on the appropriate reordering of instructions that will lead to

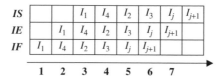

Figure 9.10 Instruction reordering

producing the correct final results while minimizing the number of time units lost due to the instruction dependency. One important condition that must be satisfied in order for the reordering of the instruction method to produce correct results is that the set of instructions that are swapped with the branch instruction hold no data and/or instruction dependency relationship among them.

USE OF DEDICATED HARDWARE IN THE FETCH UNIT   In this case, the fetch unit is assumed to have associated with it a dedicated hardware unit capable of recognizing unconditional branch instructions and computing the branch target address as quickly as possible. Consider, for example, the execution of the same sequence of instructions as illustrated above. Assume also that the fetch unit has a dedicated hardware unit capable of recognizing unconditional branch instructions and computing the branch address using no additional time units. Figure 9.11 shows the Gantt's chart for this sequence of instructions. The figure shows that the correct sequence of instructions is executed while incurring no extra unit times.

The assumption of needing no additional time units to recognize branch instructions and computing the target branch address is unrealistic. In typical cases, the added hardware unit to the fetch unit will require additional time unit(s) to carry out its task of recognizing branch instructions and computing target branch addresses. During the extra time units needed by the hardware unit, if other instructions can be executed, then the number of extra time units needed may be reduced and indeed may be eliminated altogether. This is the essence of the method shown below.

PRECOMPUTING OF BRANCHES AND REORDERING OF INSTRUCTIONS   This method can be considered as a combination of the two methods discussed in the previous two sections above. In this case, the dedicated hardware (used to recognize branch instructions and computing the target branch address) executes its task concurrently with the execution of other instructions. Consider, for example, the same sequence of instructions given above. Assume also that the dedicated hardware unit requires one time unit to carry out its task. In this case, reordering of the instructions to become $I_1, I_2, I_4, I_3, I_5 \cdot, \cdot, I_j, I_{j+1}, \cdot, \cdot$ should produce the correct results while causing no additional lost time units. This is illustrated using the Gantt's chart in Figure 9.12. Notice that time unit #4 is used by the dedicated

IS			I_1	I_2	I_3	I_4	I_j	I_{j+1}	
IE		I_1	I_2	I_3	I_4	I_j	I_{j+1}		
IF	I_1	I_2	I_3	I_4	I_j	I_{j+1}			
	1	2	3	4	5	6	7		

Figure 9.11   Use of additional hardware unit for branch instruction recognition

Figure 9.12 Branch folding

hardware unit to compute the target branch address concurrently with the fetching of instruction I_3.

It should be noted that the success of this method depends on the availability of instructions to be executed concurrently while the dedicated hardware unit is computing the target branch address. In the case presented above, it was assumed that reordering of instructions can provide those instructions that can be executed concurrently with the target branch computation. However, if such reordering is not possible, then the use of an instruction queue together with prefetching of instructions can help provide the needed conditions. This is explained below.

INSTRUCTION PREFETCHING   This method requires that instructions can be fetched and stored in an instruction queue before they are needed. The method also calls for the fetch unit to have the required hardware needed to recognize branch instructions and compute the target branch address. If a pipeline stalls due to data dependency causing no new instructions to be fetched into the pipeline, then the fetch unit can use such time to continue fetching instructions and add them to the instruction queue. On the other hand, if a delay in the fetching of instructions occurs, for example, due to instruction dependency, then those prefetched instructions in the instruction queue can be used to provide the pipeline with new instructions, thus eliminating some of the otherwise lost time units due to instruction dependency. Providing the appropriate instruction from the instruction queue to the pipeline is usually done using what is called a "dispatch unit." The technique of prefetching of instructions and executing them during a pipeline stall due to instruction dependency is called "branch folding."

Conditional Branch Instructions   The techniques discussed above in the context of unconditional branch instructions may not work in the case of conditional branch instructions. This is because in conditional branching the target branch address will not be known until the execution of the branch instruction has been completed. Therefore, a number of techniques can be used to minimize the number of lost time units due to instruction dependency represented by conditional branching.

DELAYED BRANCH   Delayed branch refers to the case whereby it is possible to fill the location(s) following a conditional branch instruction, called the *branch delay slot(s)*, with useful instruction(s) that can be executed until the target branch address is known. Consider, for example, the execution of the following program loop on a pipeline consisting of two stages: Fetch (F) and Execute (E).

$I_1 \rightarrow$	*Again*:	*Load* 5, R_1;	$R_1 \leftarrow 5$;
$I_2 \rightarrow$		*Sub* R_2;	$R_2 \leftarrow R_2 - 1$;
$I_3 \rightarrow$		*Bnn Again*;	Branch to Again if result is Not Negative;
$I_4 \rightarrow$		*Add* R_4, R_5, R_3;	$R_3 \leftarrow R_4 + R_5$;

It should be noted that at the end of the first loop, either instruction I_1 or instruction I_4 will have to be fetched depending on the result of executing instruction I_3. The way with which such a situation has been dealt will delay fetching of the next instruction until the result of executing instruction I_3 is known. This will lead to incurring extra delay in the pipeline. However, this extra delay may be avoided if the sequence of instructions has been reordered to become as follows.

Again:	*Sub* R_2;	$R_2 \leftarrow R_2 - 1$;
	Load 5, R_1;	$R_1 \leftarrow 5$;
	Bnn Again;	Branch to Again if result is Not Negative;
	Add R_4, R_5, R_3;	$R_3 \leftarrow R_4 + R_5$;

Figure 9.13 shows the Gantt's chart for executing the modified piece of code for the case $R_2 = 3$ before entering the loop.

The figure indicates that branching takes place one instruction later than the actual place where the branch instruction appears in the original instruction sequence, hence the name "*delayed branch*." It is also clear from Figure 9.13 that by reordering the sequence of instructions, it was possible to fill the branch delay time slot with a useful instruction, thus eliminating any extra delay in the pipeline. It has been shown in a number of studies that "smart" compilers were able to make use of one branch delay time slot in more than 80% of the cases. The use of branch delay time slots has led to the improvement of both the speed-up and the throughput of those processors using "smart" compilers.

PREDICTION OF THE NEXT INSTRUCTION TO FETCH   This method tries to reduce the time unit(s) that can potentially be lost due to instruction dependency by predicting the next instruction to fetch after fetching a conditional branch instruction. The basis is that if the branch outcomes are random, then it would be possible to save about 50% of the otherwise lost time. A simple way to carry out such a technique is to

E		I_2	I_1	I_3	I_2	I_1	I_3	I_2	I_1	I_3	I_2	I_1	I_3	I_4
F	I_2	I_1	I_3	I_2	I_1	I_3	I_2	I_1	I_3	I_2	I_1	I_3	I_4	
	1	2	3	4	5	6	7	8	9	10	11	12	13	14

Figure 9.13   Delayed branch

assume that whenever a conditional branch is encountered, the system predicts that the branch will not be taken (or alternatively will be taken). In this way, fetching of instructions in sequential address order will continue (or fetching of instructions starting from the target branch instruction will continue). At the completion of the branch instruction execution, the results will be known and a decision will have to be made as to whether the instructions that were executed assuming that the branch will not be taken (or taken) were the intended correct instruction sequence or not. The outcome of this decision is one of two possibilities. If the prediction was correct, then execution can continue with no wasted time units. If, on the other hand, the wrong prediction has been made, then care must be taken such that the status of the machine, measured in terms of memory and register contents, should be restored as if no *speculative execution* took place.

Prediction based on the above scheme will lead to the same branch prediction decision every time a given instruction is encountered, hence the name *static branch prediction*. It is the simplest branch prediction scheme and is done during compilation time.

Another technique that can be used in branch prediction is dynamic branch prediction. In this case, prediction is done at run time, rather than at compile time. When a branch is encountered, then a record is checked to find out whether that same branch has been encountered before and if so, what was the decision made at that time; that is, was the branch taken or not taken. A run time decision is then made whether to take or not to take the branch. In making such a decision, a two-state algorithm, "likely to be taken" (LTK) or "likely not to be taken" (LNK), can be followed. If the current state is LTK and if the branch is taken, then the algorithm will maintain the LTK state; otherwise it will switch to the LNK. If, on the other hand, the current state is LNK and the branch is not taken, then the algorithm will maintain the LNK state; otherwise it will switch to the LTK state. This simple algorithm should work fine, particularly if the branch is going backwards, for example during the execution of a loop. It will, however, lead to misprediction when control reaches the last pass through the loop. A more robust algorithm that uses four states has been used by the ARM 11 microarchitecture (see below).

It is interesting to notice that a combination of dynamic and static branch prediction techniques can lead to performance improvement. An attempt to use a dynamic branch prediction is first made, and if it is not possible, then the system can resort to the static prediction technique.

Consider, for example, the ARM 11 microarchitecture (the first implementation of the ARMv6 instruction set architecture). This architecture uses a dynamic/static branch prediction combination. A record in the form of a 64-entry, four-state branch target address cache (BTAC) is used to help the dynamic branch prediction finding whether a given branch has been encountered before. If the branch has been encountered, the record will also show whether it was most frequently taken or most frequently not taken. If the BTAC shows that a branch has been encountered before, then a prediction is made based on the previous outcome. The four states are: strongly taken, weakly taken, strongly not taken, and weakly not taken.

In the case that a record cannot be found for a branch, then a static branch prediction procedure is used. The static branch prediction procedure investigates the branch to find out whether it is going backwards or forwards. A branch going backwards is assumed to be part of a loop and the branch is assumed to be taken. A branch going forwards is not taken. The ARM 11 employs an eight-stage pipeline. Every correctly predicted branch is found to lead to a typical saving of five processor clock cycles. Around 80% of branches are found to be correctly predicted using the dynamic/static combination in the ARM 11 architecture. The pipeline features of the ARM 11 are introduced in the next subsection.

A branch prediction technique based on the use of a 16K-entry branch history record is employed in the UltraSPARC III RISC processor, a 14-stage pipeline. However, the impact of a misprediction, in terms of the number of cycles lost due to a branch misprediction is reduced by using the following approach. On predictions that a branch will be taken and while the branch target instructions are being fetched, the "fall-through" instructions are prepared for issue in parallel through the use of a four-entry branch miss queue (BMQ). This reduces the misprediction penalty to two cycles. The UltraSPARC III has achieved 95% success in branch prediction. The pipeline features of the UltraSPARC III are introduced in the next subsection.

Methods Used to Reduce Pipeline Stall Due to Data Dependency

Hardware Operand Forwarding Hardware operand forwarding allows the result of one ALU operation to be available to another ALU operation in the cycle that immediately follows. Consider the following two instructions.

$$ADD \quad R_1, R_2, R_3; \quad R_3 \leftarrow R_1 + R_2$$
$$SUB \quad R_3, 1, R_4; \quad R_4 \leftarrow R_3 - 1$$

It is easy to notice that there exists a read-after-write data dependency between these two instructions. Correct execution of this sequence on a five-stage pipeline (*IF*, *ID*, *OF*, *IE*, *IS*) will cause a stall of the second instruction after decoding it and until the result of the first instruction is stored in R_3. Only at that time, the operand of the second instruction, that is, the new value stored in R_3, can be fetched by the second instruction. However, if it is possible to have the result of the first instruction forwarded to the ALU during the same time unit as it is being stored in R_3, then it will be possible to reduce the stall time. This is illustrated in Figure 9.14.

The assumption that the operand of the second instruction be forwarded immediately after it is available and while it is being stored in R_3 requires a modification in the data path such that an added feedback path is created to allow for such operand forwarding. This modification is shown using dotted lines in Figure 9.15. It should be noted that the needed modification to achieve hardware operand forwarding is expensive and requires careful issuing of control signals. It should also be noted that if it is possible to perform both instruction decoding and operand fetching during the same time unit, then there will be no lost time units.

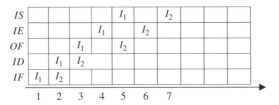

Figure 9.14 Hardware forwarding

Software Operand Forwarding Operand forwarding can alternatively be performed in software by the compiler. In this case, the compiler should be "smart" enough to make the result(s) of performing some instructions quickly available, as operand(s), for subsequent instruction(s). This desirable feature requires the compiler to perform data dependency analysis in order to determine the operand(s) that can possibly be made available (forwarded) to subsequent instructions, thus reducing the stall time. This data dependency analysis requires the recognition of basically three forms. These are explained below using simple examples.

STORE-FETCH This case represents data dependency in which the result of an instruction is stored in memory followed by a request for a fetch of the same result by a subsequent instruction. Consider the following sequence of two instructions:

$$Store \quad R_2, (R_3); \quad M[R_3] \leftarrow R_2$$
$$Load \quad (R_3), R_4; \quad R_4 \leftarrow M[R_3]$$

In this sequence, the operand needed by the second instruction (the contents of memory location whose address is stored in register R_3) is already available in register R_2 and therefore can be immediately (forwarded) moved into register R_4.

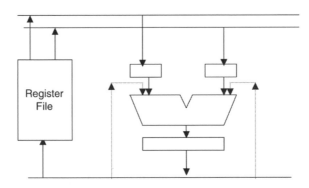

Figure 9.15 Hardware forwarding

When it recognizes such data dependency, a "smart" compiler can replace the above sequence by the following sequence:

Store $R_2, (R_3)$; $M[R_3] \leftarrow R_2$
Move R_2, R_4; $R_4 \leftarrow R_2$

FETCH-FETCH   This case represents data dependency in which the data stored by an instruction is also needed as an operand by a subsequent instruction. Consider the following instruction sequence:

Load $(R_3), R_2$; $R_2 \leftarrow M[R_3]$
Load $(R_3), R_4$; $R_4 \leftarrow M[R_3]$

In this sequence, the operand needed by the first instruction (the contents of memory location whose address is stored in register R_3) is also needed as an operand for the second instruction. Therefore, this operand can be immediately (forwarded) moved into register R_4. When it recognizes such data dependency, a "smart" compiler can replace the above sequence by the following sequence.

Load $(R_3), R_2$; $R_2 \leftarrow M[R_3]$
Move R_2, R_4; $R_4 \leftarrow R_2$

STORE-STORE   This is the case in which the data stored by an instruction is overwritten by a subsequent instruction. Consider the following instruction sequence:

Store $R_2, (R_3)$; $M[R_3] \leftarrow R_2$
Store $R_4, (R_3)$; $M[R_3] \leftarrow R_4$

In this sequence, the results written during the first instruction (the content of register R_2 is written into memory location whose address is stored in register R_3) is overwritten during the second instruction by the contents of register R_4. Assuming that these two instructions are executed in sequence and that the result written by the first instruction will not be needed by an I/O operation, for example, a DMA, then the sequence of these two instructions can be replaced by the following single instruction.

Store $R_4, (R_3)$; $M[R_3] \leftarrow R_4$

9.3. EXAMPLE PIPELINE PROCESSORS

In this section, we briefly present two pipeline processors that use a variety of the pipeline techniques presented in this chapter. Our focus in this coverage is on the pipeline features of these architectures. The two processors are the ARM 1026EJ-S and the UltraSPARC III.

9.3.1. ARM 1026EJ-S Processor   This processor is part of a family of RISC processors designed by Advanced RISC Machine (ARM) Company. The series is designed to suit high-performance, low-cost, and low-power embedded applications. The ARM 022EJ-S integer core has multiple execution units, thus allowing a number of instructions to exist in the same pipeline stage. It also allows the execution of simultaneous instructions. The ARM 1026EJ-S can deliver a peak throughput of one instruction per cycle. The integer core consists of the following units:

1. Prefetch unit: This unit is responsible for instruction fetch. It also predicts the outcome of branches whenever possible.
2. Integer unit: This unit is responsible for decoding of instructions coming out of the prefetch unit. This unit contains a barrel shifter, ALU, and a multiplier. It executes instructions such as *MOV*, *ADD*, and *MUL*. The integer unit helps the load/store unit to execute load and store instructions. It also helps in executing some coprocessor instructions.
3. Load/Store unit: This unit can load or store two registers (64 bits) per cycle.

ARM 1022EJ-S is a pipeline processor whose ALU consists of six stages. These are:

1. Fetch stage: for instruction cache access and branch prediction for instructions that have already been fetched.
2. Issue stage: for initial instruction decoding.
3. Decode stage: for final instruction decode, register read for ALU operations, forwarding, and initial interlock resolution.
4. Execute stage: for data access address calculation, data processing shift, shift and saturate, ALU operations, first stage multiplication, flag setting, condition code check, branch mispredict detection, and store data register read.
5. Memory stage: for data cache access, second stage multiplication, and saturations.
6. Write stage: for register write and instruction retirement.

In this arrangement, the Fetch stage uses a first-in-first-out (FIFO) buffer that can hold up to three instructions. The Issue and Decode stages can contain a predicted branch in parallel with one other instruction. The Execute, Memory, and Write stages can simultaneously contain any of the following.

1. A predicted branch
2. An ALU or multiply instruction
3. Ongoing multiply load or store multiple instructions
4. Ongoing multicycle coprocessor instructions

The prefetch unit operates in the Fetch stage and can fetch 64 bits every cycle from an instruction-side cache. It can, however, issue one 32-bit instruction per cycle to the integer unit. Pending instructions are placed in the prefetch buffer by the prefetch unit. While an instruction is in the prefetch buffer, the branch prediction logic can decode it to see if it is a predictable branch. The prefetch buffer can hold up to three instructions and enable the prefetch unit to:

1. Detect branch instructions ahead of the fetch stage
2. Predict those branches that are likely to be taken
3. Remove those branches that are not likely to be taken

If the branch is predicted to be taken, then the instruction address is redirected to the branch target address. If, however, the branch is predicted not to be taken, then the next instruction is fetched. In case there is not enough time to completely remove a branch, the fetch address is redirected anyway, thus reducing branch penalty.

The integer unit executes unpredictable branches. To quickly obtain the required address, a dedicated fast branch adder is used. This is done in order to avoid passing through the barrel shift.

The prefetch buffer is flushed in the following cases:

1. Entry into an exception processing sequence
2. A load to the program counter (PC)
3. An arithmetic manipulation of the PC
4. Execution of an unpredicted branch
5. Detection of an erroneously predicted branch

A taken predicted branch is the only case that does not lead to automatic flush of the prefetch buffer. Mispredicted branches and unpredicted taken branches lead to a three-cycle penalty.

9.3.2. UltraSPARC III Processor

The UltraSPARC III is based on the SUN SPARC-V9 RISC architectural specifications. A number of features characterize the SPARC-V9. Among these are the following:

1. Few and simple instruction formats. All instructions are 32-bit. Memory access is done exclusively using Load and Store instructions.
2. Few addressing modes. Memory addressing has only two modes, the Register + Register and the Register + Immediate modes.
3. Triadic register operands. Most instructions operate on two register operands or one register and a constant operand. The results in both cases are stored in a third register.
4. Large window register file.

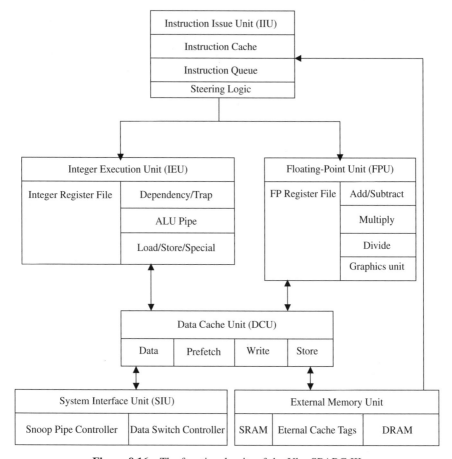

Figure 9.16 The functional units of the UltraSPARC III

The UltraSPARC III processor uses six independent units (see Fig. 9.16). These are:

1. The Instruction Issue Unit (IIU). This unit predicts the program flows, fetches the predicted path from memory and directs the fetched instructions to the execution pipeline. Instructions are forwarded to either the IEU or the FPU. The IIU incorporates a four-way associative instruction cache, an address translation buffer, and a 16K-entry branch predictor.
2. The Integer Execute Unit (IEU). This unit executes all integer instructions, including the integer loading and storing, the integer arithmetic, the logic, and the branch instructions. The IEU is capable of executing up to four integer instructions concurrently during a cycle time.

3. The Data Cache Unit (DCU). This unit contains three different level-one (L1) data caches and a data address translation buffer. The data caches are: a demand fetch (a four-way associative 64KB with 32-byte block size), a prefetch cache (a four-way associative 2KB with 64-byte block size), and a write cache (a four-way associative 2KB with 64-byte block size).

4. The Floating-Point Unit (FPU). This unit executes all floating-point and graphical instructions.

5. The External Memory Unit (EMU). This unit controls access to the two off-chip memory modules. The two off-chip modules are the level-two (L2) data cache and the main memory.

6. The System Interface Unit (SIU). This unit provides a communication interface between the microprocessor and the system external to it, such as the main memory, I/O devices, and other processors in a multiprocessing configuration.

The UltraSPARC III has a 14-stage instruction pipeline. These are:

1. Address Generation Unit (A). This unit generates instruction fetch addresses.

2. Instruction Prefetch Unit (P). This unit fetches the second cycle of instructions from the cache and accesses the first cycle of branch prediction.

3. Instruction Fetch Unit (F). This unit fetches the second cycle of instructions from the cache and accesses the second cycle of branch prediction. The F unit also performs the virtual to physical address translation.

4. Branch Target Calculation Unit (B). This unit computes the target address of branches and decodes the first cycle of instructions.

5. Instruction Decode Unit (I). This unit decodes the second cycle of instructions and directs them to the queue.

6. Instruction Steer Unit (J). This unit directs instructions to the appropriate execution unit. Integer instructions are directed to the integer execution unit while floating-point and graphical instructions are directed to the floating-point unit.

7. Register File Read Unit (R). This unit reads the operands of the integer register file.

8. Integer Execution Unit (E). This unit executes the integer instructions.

9. Date Cache Access Unit (C). This unit accesses the second cycle of date cache, forwards load data for word and double word loads and executes the first cycle of floating-point instructions.

10. Memory Bypass Unit (M). This unit loads data alignment for half word and bytes loads and executes the second cycle of floating-point instructions.

11. Working Register File Write Unit (W). This unit performs writes to the integer register file and executes the third cycle of floating-point instructions.

12. Pipe Extend Unit (X). This unit extends the integer pipeline for precise floating-point traps and executes the fourth cycle of floating-point instructions.

13. Trap Unit (T). This unit reports traps upon their occurrences.

14. Done Unit (D). This unit writes the architectural register file.

Two main techniques are employed in the UltraSPARC III in dealing with branches. These are explained below:

Branch Prediction   The UltraSPARC III uses a branch prediction technique that combines the static and the dynamic branch prediction techniques explained before. In this case, branch prediction takes place in the IIU unit. It uses a branch prediction table and a hardware implementation of a dynamic prediction algorithm.

BRANCH PREDICTION TABLE   The branch prediction table (BPT) is a hardware implementation of a table of a two-bit finite state machine (FSM). It is a saturated up–down counter. When a branch is encountered, the branch target address and/ or the branch history are used to find the table index of the location where the prediction for the branch is found. The branch condition is predicted to be taken if it corresponds to one of two FSM states: strong not taken or weak not taken. The branch condition is predicted to be taken if it corresponds to one of two FSM states: weak taken or strong taken. The counter is incremented each time a branch is taken; otherwise it is decremented, hence the name up–down counter. If a counter reaches the strong taken state (11-state), it stays there as long as the branch is taken and if it reaches the strong not taken (00-state), it stays there as long as the branch is not taken, hence the name saturation. The BPT in the UltraSPARC III consists of 16K-entry (16K 2-bit saturation up–down counters).

GLOBAL SHARE DYNAMIC PREDICTION ALGORITHM   The global share (*gshare*) algorithm uses two levels of branch-history information to dynamically predict the direction of branches. The first level registers the history of the last k branches faced. This represents the global branching behavior. This level is implemented by providing a global branch history register. This is basically a shift register that enters a 1 for every taken branch and a 0 for every untaken branch. The second level of branch history information registers the branching of the last s occurrences of the specific pattern of the k branches. This information is kept in the branch prediction table. The *gshare* algorithm works by taking the lower bits of the branch target address and *XORing* them with the history register to get the index that should be used with the prediction table.

The UltraSPARC III uses a modified version of the *gshare* algorithm. This modification requires that the predictor be pipelined over two stages, that is, if the original *gshare* algorithm were used, the predictor would be indexed by an old copy of the program counter (PC). With the modified *gshare* algorithm, each time the predictor is accessed, eight counters are read out and the three low-order bits of the PC register are used to select one of them at the B pipeline stage.

Instruction Buffer (Queues)   The UltraSPARC III instruction issue unit (IIU) incorporates two instruction buffering queues: the branch instruction queue (BIQ) and the branch miss queue (BMQ). These are introduced below.

BRANCH INSTRUCTION QUEUE (BIQ)   This is a 20-entry queue that allows the fetch and the execution unit to operate independently. The fetch unit predicts the execution path and continuously fills the BIQ. When a taken branch is encountered, two fetch cycles are lost to fill the BIQ.

BRANCH MISS QUEUE (BMQ)   During the lost two cycles, the sequential instructions that have been already accessed are buffered into a four-entry BMQ. If it is then found that the branch has been mispredicted, the instructions from the BMQ are directed to the execution unit directly.

9.4. INSTRUCTION-LEVEL PARALLELISM

Contrary to pipeline techniques, instruction-level parallelism (ILP) is based on the idea of *multiple issue processors* (MIP). An MIP has multiple pipelined datapaths for instruction execution. Each of these pipelines can issue and execute one instruction per cycle. Figure 9.17 shows the case of a processor having three pipes. For comparison purposes, we also show in the same figure the sequential and the single pipeline case. It is clear from the figure that while the limit on the number of cycles per instruction in the case of a single pipeline is CPI = 1, the MIP can achieve CPI < 1.

In order to make full use of ILP, an analysis should be made to identify the instruction and data dependencies that exist in a given program. This analysis should lead to the appropriate scheduling of the group of instructions that can be issued simultaneously while retaining the program correctness. Static scheduling results in the use of very long instruction word (VLIW) architectures, while dynamic scheduling results in the use of superscalar architectures.

In VLIW, an instruction represents a bundle of many operations to be issued simultaneously. The compiler is responsible for checking all dependencies and making the appropriate groupings/scheduling of operations. This is in contrast with superscalar architectures, which rely entirely on the hardware for scheduling of instructions.

Superscalar Architectures   A scalar machine is able to perform only one arithmetic operation at once. A superscalar architecture (SPA) is able to fetch, decode, execute, and store results of several instructions at the same time. It does so by transforming a static and sequential instruction stream into a dynamic and parallel one, in order to execute a number of instructions simultaneously. Upon completion, the SPA reinforces the original sequential instruction stream such that instructions can be completed in the original order.

In an SPA instruction, processing consists of the fetch, decode, issue, and commit stages. During the fetch stage, multiple instructions are fetched simultaneously.

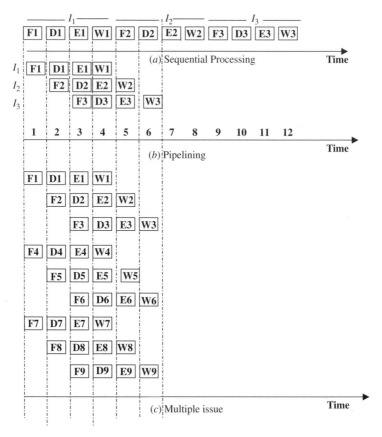

Figure 9.17 Multiple issue versus pipelining versus sequential processing

Branch prediction and speculative execution are also performed during the fetch stage. This is done in order to keep on fetching instructions beyond branch and jump instructions.

Decoding is done in two steps. Predecoding is performed between the main memory and the cache and is responsible for identifying branch instructions. Actual decoding is used to determine the following for each instruction: (1) the operation to be performed; (2) the location of the operands; and (3) the location where the results are to be stored. During the issue stage, those instructions among the dispatched ones that can start execution are identified. During the commit stage, generated values/results are written into their destination registers.

The most crucial step in processing instructions in SPAs is the dependency analysis. The complexity of such analysis grows quadratically with the instruction word size. This puts a limit on the degree of parallelism that can be achieved with SPAs such that a degree of parallelism higher than four will be impractical. Beyond this limit, the dependence analysis and scheduling must be done by the compiler. This is the basis for the VLIW approach.

Very Long Instruction Word (VLIW) In this approach, the compiler performs dependency analysis and determines the appropriate groupings/scheduling of operations. Operations that can be performed simultaneously are grouped into a very long instruction word (VLIW). Therefore, the instruction word is made long enough in order to accommodate the maximum possible degree of parallelism. For example, the IBM DAISY machine has an instruction word that is eight operation long, called 8-issue machine.

In VLIW, resource binding can be done by devoting each field of an instruction word to one and only one functional unit. However, this arrangement will lead to a limit on the mix of instructions that can be issued per cycle. A more flexible approach is to allow a given instruction field to be occupied by different kinds of operations. For example, the Philips TriMedia machine, a 5-issue machine, has 27 functional units mapped to a 5-issue slot. In the IBM DAISY, every instruction implements a multiway path selection scheme. In this case, the first 72 bits of the VLIW is called the *header* and contain information on the tree form, condition tests, and branch targets. The header is followed by eight 23-bit parcels, each encoding an operation. In order to solve the problem of providing operands to a large number of functional units, the IBM DAISY keeps eight identical copies of the same register file, one for each of the eight functional units.

9.5. ARITHMETIC PIPELINE

The principles used in instruction pipelining can be used in order to improve the performance of computers in performing arithmetic operations such as add, subtract, and multiply. In this case, these principles will be used to realize the arithmetic circuits inside the ALU. In this section, we will elaborate on the use of arithmetic pipeline as a means to speed up arithmetic operations. We will start with fixed-point arithmetic operations and then discuss floating-point operations.

9.5.1. Fixed-Point Arithmetic Pipelines

The basic fixed point arithmetic operation performed inside the ALU is the addition of two n-bit operands $A = a_{n-1}a_{n-2} \cdots a_2 a_1 a_0$ and $B = b_{n-1}b_{n-2} \cdots b_2 b_1 b_0$. Addition of these two operands can be performed using a number of techniques. These techniques differ in basically two attributes: degree of complexity and achieved speed. These two attributes are somewhat contradictory; that is, a simple realization may lead to a slower circuit while a complex realization may lead to a faster circuit. Consider, for example, the carry ripple through (CRTA) and a carry look-ahead (CLAA) adders. The CRTA is simple, but slower, while the CLAA is complex, but faster.

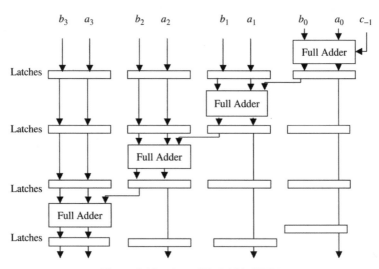

Figure 9.18   A modified 4-bit CRTA

It is possible to modify the CRTA in such a way that a number of pairs of operands are operated upon, that is, pipelined, inside the adder, thus improving the overall speed of addition in the CRTA. Figure 9.18 shows an example of a modified 4-bit CRTA. In this case, the two operands A and B are presented to the CRTA through the use of synchronizing elements, such as clocked latches. These latches will guarantee that the movement of the partial carry values within the CRTA are synchronized at the input of the subsequent stages of the adder with the higher order operand bits. For example, the arrival of the first carry out (c_0) and the second pair of bits (a_1 and b_1) is synchronized at the input of the second full adder (counting from low order bits to high order bits) using a latch.

Although the operation of the modified CRTA remains in principle the same; that is, the carry ripples through the adder, the provision of latches allows for the possibility of presenting multiple sets of pairs of operands to the adder at the same time. Consider, for example, the case of adding M pairs of operands, whereby the operands of each pair are n-bit. The time needed to perform the addition of these M pairs using a nonpipelined CRTA is given by $T_{np} = M \times n \times T_a$, where T_a is the time needed to perform single bit addition. This is to be compared to the time needed to perform the same computation using a pipelined CTRA which is given by $T_{pp} = (n + M - 1) \times T_a$. For example, if $M = 16$ and $n = 64$ bits, then we have $T_{np} = 1024 \times T_a$ and $T_{pp} = 79 \times T_a$, thus resulting in a speed-up of about 13. In the extreme case whereby it is possible to present unlimited number of pairs of operands (M) to the CRTA at the same time, the speed up will reach 64, the number of bits in each operand.

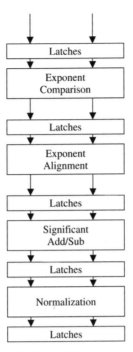

Figure 9.19   A schematic for a pipeline FP adder

9.5.2. Floating-Point Arithmetic Pipelines

Using a similar approach, it is possible to pipeline floating-point (FP) addition/subtraction. In this case, the pipeline will have to be organized around the operations needed to perform FP addition. The main operations needed in FP addition are exponent comparison (EC), exponent alignment (EA), addition (AD), and normalization (NZ). Therefore, a possible pipeline organization is to have a four-stage pipeline,

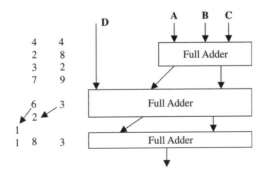

Figure 9.20   Carry-save addition

$$P = A*B$$
$$= A*(B_7*2^7 + B_6*2^6 + B_5*2^5 + ... + B_0*2^0)$$
$$= \sum_{i=0}^{7} A*B_i*2^i$$
$$= \sum_{i=0}^{7} S_i$$

$S_i = A*B_i*2^i$ represents a 16-bit partial product.

Figure 9.21 A carry-save based multiplication of two 8-bit operands M and Q

each performing an operation from EC, EA, AD, and NZ. Figure 9.19 shows a schematic for a pipeline FP adder. It is possible to have multiple sets of FP operands proceeding inside the adder at the same time, thus reducing the overall time needed for FP addition. Synchronizing latches are needed, as before, in order to synchronize the operands at the input of a given stage in the FP adder.

9.5.3. Pipelined Multiplication Using Carry-Save Addition

As indicated before, one of the main problems with addition is the fact that the carry has to ripple through from one stage to the next. Carry rippling through stages can be eliminated using a method called carry-save addition. Consider the case of adding 44, 28, 32, and 79. A possible way to add these without having the carry ripple through is illustrated in Figure 9.20. The idea is to delay the addition of the carry resulting in the intermediate stages until the last step in the addition. Only at the last stage is a carry-ripple stage employed.

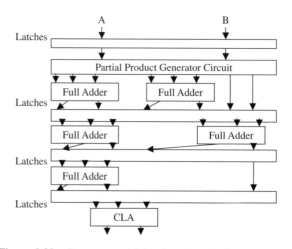

Figure 9.22 Carry-save addition-based multiplication scheme

Carry-save addition can be used to realize a pipelined multiplication building block. Consider, for example, the multiplication of two n-bit operands A and B. The multiplication operation can be transformed into an addition as shown in Figure 9.21. The figure illustrates the case of multiplying two 8-bit operands A and B. A carry-save based multiplication scheme using the principle shown in Figure 9.21 is shown in Figure 9.22. The scheme is based on the idea of producing the set of partial products needed and then adding them up using a carry-save addition scheme.

9.6. SUMMARY

In this chapter, we have considered the basic principles involved in designing pipeline architectures. Our coverage started with a discussion on a number of metrics that can be used to assess the goodness of a pipeline. We then moved to present a general discussion on the main problems that need to be considered in designing a pipelined architecture. In particular we considered two main problems: instruction and data dependency. The effect of these two problems on the performance of a pipeline has been elaborated. Some possible techniques that can be used to reduce the effect of the instruction and data dependency have been introduced and illustrated. Two examples of recent pipeline architectures, the ARM 11 microarchitecture, and the UltraSPARC III Processor, have been presented. Our discussion in the chapter ended up with an introduction of some of the ideas that can be used in realizing pipeline arithmetic architectures.

EXERCISES

1. Consider the execution of 500 instructions on a five-stage pipeline machine. Compute the speed-up due to the use of pipelining given that the probability of an instruction being a branch is $p = 0.3$? What must be the value of p and the expected number of branch instructions such that a speed-up of at least 4 is possible? What must be the value of p such that a speed-up of at least 5 is possible? Assume that each stage takes one cycle to perform its task.

2. Assume that a RISC machine executes one instruction per clock cycle if no branches are executed. Delayed branch is used with three delay clock cycles. Consider the execution of 1000 instructions, 30% of which are branch instructions, on such a machine in two cases. The first case is the use of a novice compiler that is not able to reduce the extra clock cycles wasted due to branch instructions. In the second case, a smart compiler that is able to utilize 85% of the extra clock cycles is used. Compute the average number of instructions per cycle in each case. Compute also the percentage of performance gain due to the use of the smart compiler.

3. A computer system has a four-stage pipeline consisting of an instruction fetch unit (F), an instruction decode unit (D), an instruction execution unit (E), and a write unit (W). Compute the speed-up time $P(4)$, throughput $U(4)$, and the efficiency $\zeta(4)$ of the pipeline in executing a code segment consisting of 20 instructions, given that branch instructions occur as follows: $I_3, I_9, I_{10}, I_{15}, I_{20}$. Assume that when a branch instruction is fetched, the pipeline *stalls* until the next instruction to fetch is known. Determine the time required to execute those same 20 instructions using two-way interleaved memory if the functions performed by the F, E, and W units require the use of the memory. What is the average number of cycles per instruction in both cases? Use the following space–time chart to compute the number of time units.

4. Consider the integer multiplication of two 16-bit numbers M and Q to produce a product P. Show that this operation can be represented as

$$P = \sum_{i=0}^{15} P_i$$

where $P_i = M * Q_i * 2^i$ represents a 32-bit partial product.

Design a pipeline unit to perform the above operation using the minimum number of carry-save adders and one carry-look-ahead adder. Show also the design of a pipeline for performing floating-point addition/subtraction. Give numerical examples to support your design.

5. A computer system has a three-stage pipeline consisting of a Fetch unit (F), a Decode unit (D), and an Execute (E) unit. Determine (using the space–time chart) the time required to execute 20 sequential instructions using two-way interleaved memory if all three units require the use of the memory simultaneously.

6. What is the average instruction processing time of a five-stage instruction pipeline for 36 instructions if conditional branch instructions occur as follows: $I_5, I_7, I_{10}, I_{25}, I_{27}$. Use both the space–time chart and the analytical model.

7. A computer has a five-stage instruction pipeline of one cycle each. The five stages are: Instruction Fetch (IF), Instruction Decode (ID), Operand Fetch (OF), Instruction Execution (IE), and Operand Store (OS). Consider the following code sequence, which is to be run on this computer.

	Load -1, $R1$;	$R1 \leftarrow -1$;
	Load 5, $R2$;	$R2 \leftarrow 5$;
Again:	Sub $R2$, 1, $R2$	$R2 \leftarrow R2 - 1$;
	Add $R1$, $R2$, $R3$;	$R3 \leftarrow R1 + R2$;
	Bnn Again;	branch to Again if result is <u>N</u>ot <u>N</u>egative;
	Add $R4$, $R5$, $R6$;	$R6 \leftarrow R4 + R5$;
	Add $R6$, $R4$, $R7$;	$R7 \leftarrow R4 + R6$;

a. Analyze the execution of the above piece of code in order to calculate the number of cycles needed to execute the above code without pipelining, assuming that each instruction requires exactly 5 cycles to execute.

b. Calculate (using the Gantt's chart) the number of cycles needed to execute the above code if the pipeline described above is used. Assume that there is no forwarding hardware and that when branch instructions are fetched, the pipeline will "stall" until the target address is calculated and the branch decision is made. Ignore any data dependency.

c. Repeat (b) above if data dependency is considered with the remaining conditions the same.

d. Calculate the percentage of improvement due to the use of pipeline in each of the above cases (b) and (c).

REFERENCES AND FURTHER READING

An Overview of UltraSPARC III Cu, Version 1.1 September 2003, A White Paper, Sun Microsystems, 1–18.

D. Brash, The ARM Architecture Version 6 (ARMv6), ARM Ltd., January 2002, White Paper, 1–15.

A. Clements, *The Principles of Computer Hardware*, 3rd ed., Oxford University Press, New York, 2000.

D. Cormie, The ARTM11 Microarchitecture, ARM Ltd., April 2002, A White Paper, 1–9.

K. Ebcioglu, J. Fritts and S. Kosonocky, An eight-issue tree VLIW processor for dynamic binary translation, *IEEE Proc.*, ICCD, (1998).

M. Flynn, *Computer Architecture: Pipelined and Parallel Processor Design*, Jones and Bartlett Publisher, New York, 1995.

S. Furber, *ARM System-on-Chip Architecture*, Addison-Wesley, MA, USA, 2000.

G. Goldman and P. Tirumalai, UltraSPARC-III: The advancement of Ultra Computing, *Proc. IEEE COMPCON'97*, p. 417.

C. Hamacher, Z. Vranesic, S. Zaky, *Computer Organization*, 5th ed., McGraw-Hill, New York, 2002.

V. Heuring and H. Jordan, *Computer Systems Design and Architecture*, Prentice-Hall, New Jersey, 1997.

S. Hily and A. Seznec, Branch prediction and simultaneous multireading, *Proc. IEEE PACT'96*, p. 170.

J. Hoogerbrugge and L. Augusteijn, Instruction scheduling for TriMedia, *J. Instruction-Level Parallelism* (1999).

W.-M. Hwu, Introduction to predicted execution, *IEEE Comput.*, Vol. 31, No. 1, 49–50 (1998).

D. Jaggar, ARM architecture and systems, *IEEE Micro*, 17(4), 9–11 (1997).

G. Lauthbatch and T. Horel, UltraSPARC-III: Designing third generation 64-bit performance, *IEEE Micro*, May–June, 73–85 (1999).

R. Nair, Optimal 2-bit branch predictors, *IEEE Trans. Comput.*, 698, 1995.

R. Oehler and R. Groves, IBM RISC system/6000 processor architecture, *IBM J. Res. Dev.*, 34; 23–36 (1990).

B. Rau and J. Fisher, Instruction-level parallel processing: history, overview and perspective, *J. Supercomput.*, 7; 9–50 (1993).

A. Scott, K. Burkhart, A. Kumar, R. Blumberg and G. Ranson, Four-way superscalar PA-RISC processors, *Hewlett-Packard J.*, August (1997).

J. Smith and G. Sohi, The microarchitecture of superscalar processors, *Proc. IEEE*, Vol. 83, No. 12, 1609–1624 (1995).

M. Tremblay, Increasing work, pushing the clock, *IEEE Comput.*, Vol. 31, No. 1, 40–41 (1998).

B. Wilkinson, *Computer Architecture: Design and Performance*, 2nd ed., Prentice-Hall, Hertfordshire, UK, 1996.

Websites

http://www.ar.com
http://www.arm.com/support/White_Papers
http://www.sun.com/ultrasparc

CHAPTER 10

Reduced Instruction Set Computers (RISCs)

This chapter is dedicated to a study of reduced instruction set computers (RISCs). These machines represent a noticeable shift in computer architecture paradigm. This paradigm promotes simplicity rather than complexity. The RISC approach is substantiated by a number of studies indicating that assignment statements, conditional branching, and procedure calls/return represent more than 90% and that complex operations such as long division represent only about 2% of the operations performed in a typical set of benchmark programs. These studies showed also that among all operations, procedure calls/return are the most time-consuming. Based on such results, the RISC approach calls for enhancing architectures with the resources needed to make the execution of the most frequent and the most time-consuming operations most efficient. The seed for the RISC approach started as early as the mid-1970s. Its real-life manifestation appeared in the Berkeley RISC-I and the Stanford MIPS machines, which were introduced in the mid-1980s. Today, RISC-based machines are reality and they are characterized by a number of common features such as simple and reduced instruction set, fixed instruction format, one instruction per machine cycle, pipeline instruction fetch/execute units, ample number of general purpose registers (or alternatively optimized compiler code generation), Load/Store memory operations, and hardwired control unit design. Our coverage in this chapter starts with a discussion on the evolution of RISC architectures. We then provide a brief discussion on some of the performance studies that led to the adoption of the RISC paradigm. Overlapped Register Windows, an essential concept in the RISC development, is then discussed. Toward the end of the chapter we provide details on a number of RISC-based architectures, such as the Berkeley RISC, the Stanford MIPS, the Compaq Alpha, and the SUN UltraSparc.

10.1. RISC/CISC EVOLUTION CYCLE

The term RISCs stands for Reduced Instruction Set Computers. It was originally introduced as a notion to mean architectures that can execute as fast as one

Fundamentals of Computer Organization and Architecture, by M. Abd-El-Barr and H. El-Rewini
ISBN 0-471-46741-3   Copyright © 2005 John Wiley & Sons, Inc.

instruction per clock cycle. RISC started as a notion in the mid-1970s and has eventually led to the development of the first RISC machine, the IBM 801 minicomputer. The launching of the RISC notion announces the start of a new paradigm in the design of computer architectures. This paradigm promotes simplicity in computer architecture design. In particular, it calls for going back to basics rather than providing extra hardware support for high-level languages. This paradigm shift relates to what is known as the *semantic gap*, a measure of the difference between the operations provided in the high-level languages (HLLs) and those provided in computer architectures.

It is recognized that the wider the semantic gap, the larger the number of undesirable consequences. These include (a) execution inefficiency, (b) excessive machine program size, and (c) increased compiler complexity. Because of these expected consequences, the conventional response of computer architects has been to add layers of complexity to newer architectures. These include increasing the number and complexity of instructions together with increasing the number of addressing modes. The architectures resulting from the adoption of this "add more complexity" are now known as Complex Instruction Set Computers (CISCs). However, it soon became apparent that a complex instruction set has a number of disadvantages. These include a complex instruction decoding scheme, an increased size of the control unit, and increased logic delays. These drawbacks prompted a team of computer architects to adopt the principle of "less is actually more." A number of studies were then conducted to investigate the impact of complexity on performance. These are discussed below.

10.2. RISCs DESIGN PRINCIPLES

A computer with the minimum number of instructions has the disadvantage that a large number of instructions will have to be executed in realizing even a simple function. This will result in a speed disadvantage. On the other hand, a computer with an inflated number of instructions has the disadvantage of complex decoding and hence a speed disadvantage. It is then natural to believe that a computer with a carefully selected reduced set of instructions should strike a balance between the above two design alternatives. The question then becomes what constitutes a carefully selected reduced set of instructions? In order to arrive at an answer to this question, it is necessary to conduct in-depth studies on a number of aspects of computation. These aspects should include (a) operations that are most frequently performed during execution of typical (benchmark) programs, (b) operations that are most time consuming, and (c) the type of operands that are most frequently used.

A number of early studies were conducted in order to find out the typical breakdown of operations that are performed in executing benchmark programs. The estimated distribution of operations is shown in Table 10.1.

A careful look at the estimated percentage of operations performed reveals that assignment statements, conditional branches, and procedure calls constitute about 90% of the total operations performed, while other operations, however complex they may be, make up the remaining 10%.

TABLE 10.1   Estimated Distribution of Operations

Operations	Estimated percentage
Assignment statements	35
Loops	5
Procedure calls	15
Conditional branches	40
Unconditional branches	3
Others	2

In addition to the above findings, studies on time–performance characteristics of operations revealed that among all operations, procedure calls/return are the most time-consuming. With regards to the type of operands used during typical computation, it was noticed that the majority of references (no less than 60%) are made to simple scalar variables and that no less than 80% of scalars are local variables (to procedures).

The above observations about typical program behavior have led to the following conclusions:

1. Simple movement of data (represented by assignment statements), rather than complex operations, are substantial and should be optimized.

2. Conditional branches are predominant and therefore careful attention should be paid to the sequencing of instructions. This is particularly true when it is known that pipelining is indispensable to use.

3. Procedure calls/return are the most time-consuming operations and therefore a mechanism should be devised to make the communication of parameters among the calling and the called procedures cause the least number of instructions to execute.

4. A prime candidate for optimization is the mechanism for storing and accessing local scalar variables.

The above conclusions have led to the argument that instead of bringing the instruction set architecture closer to HLLs, it should be more appropriate to rather optimize the performance of the most time-consuming features of typical HLL programs. This is obviously a call for making the architecture simpler rather than complex. Remember that complex operations such as long division represent only a small portion (less than 2%) of the operations performed during a typical computation. One then should ask the question: how can we achieve that? The answer is by (a) keeping the most frequently accessed operands in CPU registers and (b) minimizing the register-to-memory operations.

The above two principles can be achieved using the following mechanisms:

1. Use a large number of registers to optimize operand referencing and reduce the processor memory traffic.

2. Optimize the design of instruction pipelines such that minimum compiler code generation can be achieved (see Chapter 8).
3. Use a simplified instruction set and leave out those complex and unnecessary instructions.

The following two approaches were identified to implement the above three mechanisms.

1. Software approach.   Use the compiler to maximize register usage by allocating registers to those variables that are used the most in a given time period (this is the philosophy adopted in the Stanford MIPs machine).
2. Hardware approach.   Use ample CPU registers so that more variables can be held in registers for larger periods of time (this is the philosophy adopted in the Berkeley RISC machine). The hardware approach necessitates the use of a new register organization, called *overlapped register window*. This is explained below.

10.3. OVERLAPPED REGISTER WINDOWS

The main idea behind the use of register windows is to minimize memory accesses. In order to achieve that, a large number of CPU registers are needed. For example, the number of CPU general-purpose registers available in the original SPARC machine (one of the earliest RISCs) was 120. However, it is desirable to have only a subset of these registers visible at any given time and to have them addressed as if they were the only set of registers available. Therefore, CPU registers are divided into multiple small sets, each assigned to a different procedure. A procedure call will automatically switch the CPU to use a different fixed-size window of registers. In order to minimize the actual movement of parameters among the calling and the called procedures, each set of registers is divided into three subsets: parameter registers, local registers, and temporary registers. When a procedure call is made, a new overlapping window will be created such that the temporary registers of the caller are physically the same as the parameter registers of the called procedure. This overlap allows parameters to be passed among procedure without actual movement of data (Fig. 10.1).

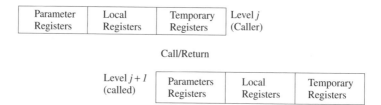

Figure 10.1   Register window overlapping

TABLE 10.2 **Different Register Windows Characteristics**

Architecture	Number of windows	Number of registers per window
Berkeley RISC-I	8	16
Pyramids	16	32
SPARC	32	32

In addition, a set of a fixed number of CPU registers are identified as global registers and are available to all procedures. For example, references to registers 0 through 7 in the *SPARC* architecture refer to unique global registers, and references to registers 8 through 31 indicate registers in the current window. The current window is pointed to using what is normally called the *current window pointer* (CWP). Upon having all windows filled, the register window wraps around, thus acting like a "circular buffer." Table 10.2 shows the number of windows and the window size for a number of architectures.

It should be noted that a study was conducted in 1985 to find out the impact of using register window on the performance of the Berkeley RISC. In this study, two versions of the machine were studied. The first is designed with register windows and the second was a hypothetical Berkeley RISC implemented without windows. The results of the study indicated a decrease by a factor of 2 to 4 (depending on specific benchmark) in the memory traffic due to the use of register windows.

10.4. RISCs VERSUS CISCs

The choice of RISC versus CISC depends totally on the factors that must be considered by a computer designer. These factors include size, complexity, and speed. A RISC architecture has to execute more instructions to perform the same function performed by a CISC architecture. To compensate for this drawback, RISC architectures must use the chip area saved by not using complex instruction decoders in providing a large number of CPU registers, additional execution units, and instruction caches. The use of these resources leads to a reduction in the traffic between the processor and the memory. On the other hand, a CISC architecture with a richer and more complex instructions, will require a smaller number of instructions than its RISC counterpart. However, a CISC architecture requires a complex decoding scheme and hence is subject to logic delays. It is therefore reasonable to consider that the RISC and CISC paradigms differ primarily in the strategy used to trade off different design factors.

There is very little reason to believe that an idea that improves performance for a RISC architecture will fail to do the same thing in a CISC architecture and vice versa. For example, one key issue in RISC development is the use of optimizing the compiler to reduce the complexity of the hardware and to optimize the use of CPU registers. These same ideas should be applicable to CISC compilers. Increasing

TABLE 10.3   RISC Versus CISC Performance

Application	MIPS CPI (RISC)	VAX CPI (CISC)	CPI ratio	Instruction ratio
Spice 2G6	1.80	8.02	4.44	2.48
Matrix300	3.06	13.81	4.51	2.37
Nasa 7	3.01	14.95	4.97	2.10
Espresso	1.06	5.40	5.09	1.70

the number of CPU registers could very much improve the performance of a CISC machine. This could be the reason behind not finding a pure commercially available RISC (or CISC) machine. It is not unusual to see a RISC machine with complex floating-point instructions (see the details of the SPARC architecture in the next section). It is equally expected to see CISC machines making use of the register windows RISC idea. In fact there have been studies indicating that a CISC machine such as the Motorola 680xx with a register window will achieve a 2 to 4 times decrease in the memory traffic. This is the same factor that can be achieved by a RISC architecture, such as the Berkeley RISC, due to the use of a register window.

It should, however, be noted that most processor developers (except for Intel and its associates) have opted for RISC processors. Computer system manufacturers such as Sun Microsystems are using RISC processors in their products. However, for compatibility with the PC-based market, such companies are still producing CISC-based products.

Tables 10.3 and 10.4 show a limited comparison between an example RISC and CISC machine in terms of performance and characteristics, respectively.

An elaborate comparison among a number of commercially available RISC and CISC machines is shown in Table 10.5.

It is worth mentioning at this point that the following set of common characteristics among RISC machines is observed:

1. Fixed-length instructions
2. Limited number of instructions (128 or less)
3. Limited set of simple addressing modes (minimum of two: indexed and PC-relative)
4. All operations are performed on registers; no memory operations
5. Only two memory operations: Load and Store

TABLE 10.4   RISC Versus CISC Characteristics

Characteristic	VAX-11 (CISC)	Berkeley RISC-1 (RISC)
Number of instructions	303	31
Instruction size (bits)	16-456	32
Addressing modes	22	3
No. general purpose registers	16	138

TABLE 10.5   Summary of Features of a Number of RISC and a CISC

	Motorola 88110	Alpha AXP 21264	Pentium	Power PC 601
Company	Motorola	Compaq (DEC)	Intel	IBM
Architecture	RISC	RISC	CISC	RISC
# Registers(I)	32	80	64	32
Cache I/D	8/8 KB	64/64 KB	8/8 KB	32
# Registers (GP/FP)	32/32	31/31	8/8	32/32
# Inst/cycle	2	1	2	3
# Pipelines (I/FP)	NS	4/2	5/8	4/6
Multiprocessing Support	No	Yes	Yes	Yes

6. Pipelined instruction execution
7. Large number of general-purpose registers or the use of advanced compiler technology to optimize register usage
8. One instruction per clock cycle
9. Hardwired control unit design rather than microprogramming

10.5. PIONEER (UNIVERSITY) RISC MACHINES

In this section, we present brief descriptions of the main architectural features of two pioneer university-introduced RISC machines. The first machine is the Berkeley RISC and the second is the Stanford MIPS machine. These machines are presented as a means to show how original RISC machines look and also to make the reader appreciate the advances made in RISC machines development since their inception.

10.5.1. The Berkeley RISC

There are two Berkeley RISC machines: RISC-I and RISC-II. Unless otherwise mentioned, we refer to RISC-I in our discussion. RISC is a 32-bit LOAD/STORE architecture. There are 138 32-bit registers R_0–R_{137} available to the users. The first ten registers R_0–R_9 are global registers (seen by all procedures). Register R_0 is used to synthesize addressing modes and operations that are not directly available on the machine. Registers R_{10}–R_{137} are divided into an overlapping register window scheme with 32 registers visible at any instant. A 5-bit variable, called *current window pointer* (CWP) is used to point to the current register set.

All RISC instructions occupy a full word (32 bits). The RISC instruction set is divided into four categories. These are ALU (a total of 12 instructions), Load/Store (a total of 16 instructions), Branch & Call (a total of seven instructions), and special instructions (a total of four instructions). Some examples of the RISC instructions are:

1. ALU: *ADD R_s, S, R_d*; $R_d \leftarrow R_s + S$
2. Load/Store: *LDXW (R_x)S, R_d*; $R_d \leftarrow M[R_x + S]$

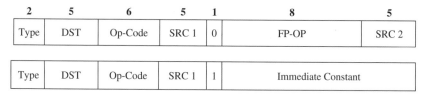

Figure 10.2 Three operand instructions formats used in RISC

3. Branch & Call: *JMPX COND*, (R$_x$)S; PC ← R$_x$ + S; where *COND* is a condition
4. Special Instructions: *GETPSW R$_d$; R$_d$ ← PSW*

All arithmetic and logical instructions have three operands and have the form *Destination* : = *source1 op source2* (Fig. 10.2). The LOAD and STORE instructions may use either of the indicated formats with DST being the register to be loaded or stored. The low order 19 bits of the instructions are used to determine the effective address.

Instructions load and store 8-, 16-, 32-, and 64-bit quantities into 32-bit registers. Two methods are provided for calling procedures. The CALL instruction uses a 30-bit PC relative offset (Fig. 10.3).

The JMP instruction uses any of the instruction formats used for arithmetic and logical operations and allows the return address to be put in any register.

RISC uses a three-address instruction format with the availability of some two- and one-address instructions. There are only two addressing modes. These are indexed mode and PC relative modes. The indexed mode can be used to synthesize three other modes. These are base-absolute (direct), register indirect, and indexed for linear byte array modes. RISC uses a static two-stage pipeline: fetch and execute.

The floating-point unit (FPU) contains thirty-two 32-bit registers to hold 32 single precision (32-bit) floating-point operands, 16 double-precision (64-bit) operands, or eight extended-precision (128-bit) operands. The FPU can execute about 20 floating-point instructions most of them in single-, double-, or extended-precision using the first instruction format used for arithmetic. In addition to instructions for loading and storing FPUs registers, the CPU can also test FPUs registers and branch conditionally on results. RISC employs a conventional MMU supporting a single paged 32-bit address space. The RISC four-bus organization is shown in Figure 10.4.

10.5.2. Stanford MIPS (Microprocessor Without Interlock Pipe Stages)

MIPS is a 32-bit pipelined LOAD/STORE machine. It uses a five-stage pipeline consisting of Instruction Fetch (*IF*), Instruction Decode (*ID*), Operand Decode

Figure 10.3 Procedure call instruction in RISC

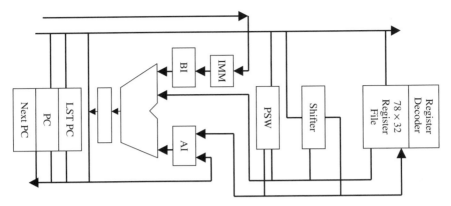

Figure 10.4 RISC four-bus organization

(*OD*), Operand Store/Execution (*OS/EX*), and Operand Fetch (*OF*). The first three stages perform respectively instruction fetch, instruction decode, and operand fetch. The OS/EX stage sends operand to memory in the case of a store instruction or use the ALU in case of instruction execution. The OF stage receives the operand in case of a load instruction. MIPS uses a mechanism called *pipeline interlock* in order to prevent an instruction from continuing until the needed operand is available.

Unlike the Berkeley RISC, MIPS has a single set of sixteen 32-bit general-purpose registers. The MIPS compiler optimizes the use of registers in whatever way is best for the program currently being compiled. In addition to the 16 general-purpose registers, MIPS provided four additional registers in order to hold the four previous PC values (to support backtracking and restart in case of a fault). A fifth register is used to hold the future PC value (to support branch instructions).

Four addressing modes are used in MIPS. These are *immediate*, *indexed*, *based with offset*, and *base shifted*. Four instruction groups were identified in MIPS. These are *ALU*, *Load/Store*, *Control*, and *Special* instructions. A total of 13 ALU instructions were provided. These include all register-to-register two- or three-operand formats (Fig. 10.5). A total of 10 LOAD/STORE instructions were provided. They use 16 or 32 bits. In the latter case, indexed addressing is used by adding a 16-bit signed constant to a register using the second format in Figure 10.5. A total of six control flow instructions were provided. These include

6	5	5	5	5	6
Op-Code	SRC 1	SRC 2	DST	SHIFT	Function

6	5	5	16		
Op-Code	SRC	DST	Immediate Constant		

Figure 10.5 Three-operand instructions used in MIPS

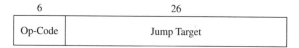

Figure 10.6 Jump instruction format used in MIPS

jumps, *relative jumps*, and *compare* instructions. Only two special flow instructions were provided. They support procedure and interrupt linkage. Some examples of MIPS instructions are:

1. ALU: *Add src$_1$, src$_2$, dst*; *dst ← src$_1$ + src$_2$*
2. Load/Store: *Ld [src$_1$ + src$_2$], dst*; *dst ← M[src$_1$ + src$_2$]*
3. Control: *Jmp dst*; *PC ← dst*
4. Special Function: *SavePC A*; *M[A] ← PC*

MIPS does not provide direct support for floating-point operations. Floating-point operations are to be done by a specialized coprocessor. Surprisingly, non-RISC instructions such as MULT and DIV were included and they use special functional units. The contents of two registers can be multiplied or divided and the 64-bit product is kept in two special registers LO and HI.

Procedure call can be made through the JUMP instruction shown in Figure 10.6. The instruction uses a 26-bit jump target address.

The MIPS virtual address is 32 bits long, thus allowing for up to four *Gwords* virtual address space. A virtual address is divided into a 20-bit virtual page number and a 12-bit offset within the page. The actual implementation of MIPS was restricted by packaging constraints allowing only 24 address pins; that is, the actual physical address space is $2^{24} = 16$ *Mwords* (32 bits each). A support for off-chip TLB for address translation is provided. The MIPS organization is shown in Figure 10.7.

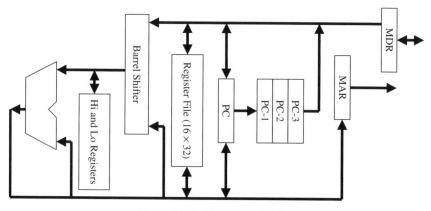

Figure 10.7 MIPS organization

10.6. EXAMPLE OF ADVANCED RISC MACHINES

In this section, we introduce two representative advanced RISC machines. Our emphasis in this coverage is on the pipeline features and the branch handling mechanisms used.

10.6.1. Compaq (Formerly DEC) Alpha 21264

Alpha 21264 (EV6) is a third generation Compaq (formerly DEC) RISC superscalar processor. It is a full 64-bit processor. The 21264 has an 80-entry integer register file and a 72-entry floating-point register file. It employs a two-level cache. The L1 data and instruction caches are 64 KB each. They are organized in a two-way set-associative manner. The L2 data cache can be 1 to 16 MB (shared by instructions and data) organized using direct-mapping. The block size is 64 bytes. The data cache can receive any combination of two loads or stores from the integer execution pipe every cycle. This is equivalent to having the 64 KB on-chip data cache delivering 16 bytes every cycle, hence twice the clock speed of the processor. The 21264 memory system can support up to 32 in-flight loads, 32 in-flight stores, and 8 in-flight (64 byte) cache block fills and 8 cache misses. It has a 64 KB, two-way set-associative cache (both instruction and data). It can also support up to two out-of-order operations (Fig. 10.8).

10.6.2. The Alpha 21264 Pipeline

The Alpha 21264 instruction pipeline is shown in Figure 10.9. It consists of SEVEN stages. These are the Fetch, Slot Assignment, Rename, Issue, Register Read, Execute, and Memory stages.

The fetch stage can fetch and execute up to four instructions per cycle. A block diagram of the fetch stage is shown in Figure 10.10. This stage uses a unique "block and set" prediction technique. According to this technique, both the locations of the next four instructions and the set (there are two sets) in which they are located, are predicted. The "block and set" prediction technique combines the speed advantages of a direct-mapped cache with the lower miss ratio of a two-way set-associative

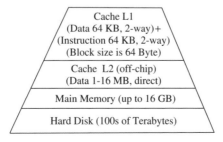

Figure 10.8 The 21264 memory hierarchy

Figure 10.9   The 21264 instruction pipeline

cache. This technique achieves more than an 85% hit ratio. The misprediction penalty is a single cycle. The 21264 uses speculative branch prediction. Branch prediction in the 21264 is a two-level scheme. It is based on the observation that branches exhibit both local and global correlation. Local correlation makes use of the branch's past behavior. Global correlation, on the other hand, makes use of the past behavior of all previous branches. The combined local/global prediction used in the 21264 correlates the branch behavior pattern with local branch history, that is, the execution of a single branch at a unique PC location, and global branch history, that is, the execution of all previous branches. The scheme dynamically selects between local and global branch history (Fig. 10.11).

The local branch predictor has two tables. The first is a 1024×10 local history table in which each entry holds a 10-bit local history of the selected branch over the last executions. The local history table is indexed by the instruction address (using the PC). The second table is a 1024×3 local prediction table in which each entry has a 3-bit saturating counter to predict the branch outcome. After branches' retirement, the 21264 updates the local history table with the true branch direction and the referenced counter. This enhances the possibility for correct prediction and is called *predictor training*.

The global branch predictor has a 4096×2 global prediction table in which each entry holds a 2-bit saturating counter. It keeps track of the global history of the last 12 branches. The global branch prediction table is indexed by a 4096×2 choice prediction table. After branches' retirement, the 21264 updates the referenced global prediction counter, enhancing the possibility for correct prediction.

Local prediction is useful in the case of an alternating taken/not-taken sequence of a given branch. In this case, the local history of the branch will eventually resolve to a pattern of ten alternating zeros and ones indicating the success, or failure, of the branch on alternate encounters. As the branch executes multiple times, it saturates the prediction counters corresponding to the local history values and hence makes the prediction correct.

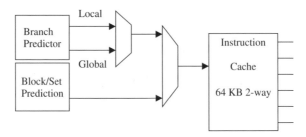

Figure 10.10   The 21264 fetch stage

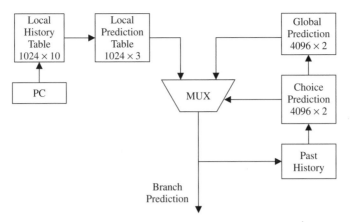

Figure 10.11   The 21264 selection branch predictor

Global prediction is useful when the outcome of a branch can be inferred from the direction of previous branches. Consider, for example, the case of repeated invocations of two branches. If the first branch that checks for a value equal to 1001 succeeds, the second branch that checks for the same value to be odd must also succeed. The global history predictor can learn this pattern with repeated invocations of these two branches.

The 2096×2 choice predictor is a table in which each entry holds a 2-bit saturating counter and is used to implement the selection (tournament) scheme. If the predictions of the local and global predictors differ, the 21264 updates the selected choice prediction entry to support the correct predictor. The 21264 updates the choice prediction table when a branch retires.

The slot assignment stage (S #2) simply assigns instructions to slots associated with the integer and the floating-point queues.

The out-of-order (OOO) issue logic in the 21264 receives four fetched instructions every cycle, renames and remaps the registers (to avoid unnecessary register dependencies), and queues the instructions until operands and/or functional units become available. It dynamically issues up to six instructions every cycle, four integer and two floating-point instructions. Register renaming means mapping instruction virtual registers to internal physical registers. There are 31 integer and 31 floating-point registers that are visible to users. These registers are renamed during execution to internal registers. It is only when instructions are finished (retired) that the internal registers are renamed back to visible registers. Register renaming eliminates write-after-write and write-after-read data dependencies. However, it preserves all the read-after-write dependencies that are necessary for correct computation.

A list of the pending instructions is maintained by the OOO queue logic. In each cycle, both the integer and the floating-point queues select those instructions that are ready to execute. This selection is made based on a scoreboard of the renamed registers. The scoreboard maintains the status of renamed registers by tracking the progress of single-cycle, multiple-cycle, and variable-cycle instructions. Upon the availability of the functional unit(s) or load data results, the scoreboard unit notifies all instructions in the queue of the availability of the required register value. Each queue selects the oldest data-ready and functional-unit-ready instructions for execution of each cycle. The 21264 integer queue statically assigns instructions to two of four pipes, either the upper or the lower pipe (Fig. 10.12).

The Alpha 21264 has four integer and two floating-point pipelines. This allows the processor to dynamically issue up to six instructions in the same cycle. The issue (or queue) stage maintains an inventory from which it can dynamically select to issue a maximum of six instructions. There is a 20-entry integer issue queue and a 15-entry floating-point issue queue. Instruction issue reordering takes place in the issue stage.

The 21264 uses two integer files, 80-entry each, to store a duplicate of register contents. Two pipes access a single file to form a cluster. The two clusters form a four-way integer instruction execution. Results are broadcasted from each cluster to the other cluster. Instructions are dynamically selected by the integer issue queue to execute on a given instruction pipe. An instruction can heuristically be selected to execute on the same cluster that produces the result. The 21264 has one 72-entry floating-point register file. The floating-point register file, together with two instruction execution pipes, form a cluster. Figure 10.12 shows the register read/execution pipes.

On a final note, we should indicate that the 21264 uses a write-invalidate cache coherence mechanism in the level 2 cache to provide support for shared-memory multiprocessing. It also supports the following cache states: modified, owned, shared, exclusive, and invalid.

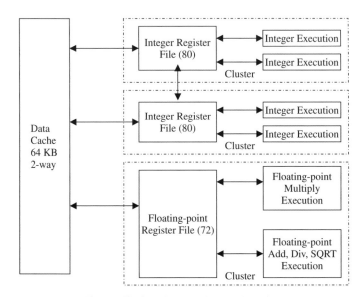

Figure 10.12   The 21264 execution pipes

10.6.3. SUN UltraSPARC III

The UltraSPARC® III is a high-performance superscalar RISC processor that implements the 64-bit SPARC®-V9 RISC architecture. There exist a number of implementations of the SPARC III processor. These include the UltraSPARC IIIi and the UltraSPARC III Cu. Our coverage in this section will be independent of any particular implementation. We will however refer to specific implementations whenever appropriate.

The UltraSPARC III is a third generation 64-bit SPARC® RISC microprocessor. It supports a 64-bit virtual address space and a 43-bit physical address space. The UltraSPARC III employs a multilevel cache architecture. For example, the Ultra-SPARC IIIi (and the UltraSPARC III Cu) architecture has a 32 KB, four-way set-associative L1 instruction cache, a 64 KB four-way set-associative L1 data cache, a 2 KB prefetch cache, and a 2 KB write cache. The UltraSPARC IIIi supports a 1 MB four-way set-associative, unified instruction/data on chip L2 cache. A cache block size of 64 bytes is used in the UltraSPARC IIIi. While the UltraSPARC III Cu architecture supports a 1, 4, or 8 MB two-way set-associative, unified instruction/data external cache. Cache block size in the UltraSPARC III Cu varies between 64 bytes (for the 1 MB cache) to 512 bytes (for the 8 MB cache) (Fig. 10.13).

The UltraSPARC III uses two instruction TLBs that can be accessed in parallel and three data TLBs that can be accessed in parallel. The two instruction TLBs are organized in a 16-entry fully associative manner to hold entries for 8 KB, 64 KB, 512 KB, and 4 MB page sizes. A 128-entry two-way set-associative TLB is used exclusively for 8 KB page sizes. The three data TLBs are organized in a 16-entry associative manner for 8 KB, 64 KB, 512 KB, and 4 MB page sizes and two 512-entry two-way set-associative TLBs that can be programmed to hold any one page size at a given time. The UltraSPARC III uses a write-allocate, write-back cache write policy.

The UltraSPARC III pipeline has been covered in Chapter 9 (pages 203–207).

On a final note, it should be mentioned that the UltraSPARC III has been designed to support a one-to-four way multiprocessing. For this purpose, it uses the *JBus*, which supports a small-scale multiprocessor system. The *JBus* is capable

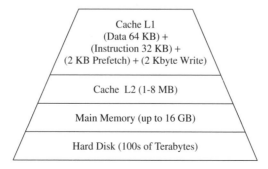

Figure 10.13 UltraSPARC III memory hierarchy

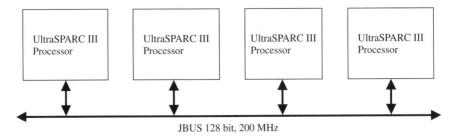

JBUS 128 bit, 200 MHz

Figure 10.14   A four-way UltraSPARC III multiprocessor configuration

of delivering the high bandwidth needed for networking and embedded systems applications. Through the *JBus*, processors can attach to a coherent shared bus with no needed glue logic (Fig. 10.14).

10.7. SUMMARY

A RISC architecture saves the extra chip area used by CISC architectures for decoding and executing complex instructions. The saved chip area is then used to provide an on-chip instruction cache that can be used to reduce instruction traffic between the processor and the memory. Common characteristics shared by most RISC designs are: limited and simple instruction set, large number of general purpose registers and/or the use of compiler technology to optimize register usage, and optimization of the instruction pipeline. An essential RISC philosophy is to keep the most frequently accessed operands in registers and minimize register-memory operations. This can be achieved using one of two approaches: Software Approach, use the compiler to maximize register usage by allocating registers to those variables that will be used the most in a given time period (this is the philosophy used in Stanford MIPs machine); or Hardware Approach, use more registers so that more variables can be held in registers for larger periods of time (this is the philosophy used in the Berkeley RISC machine). Register windows are multiple small sets of registers, each assigned to a different procedure. A procedure call automatically switches the CPU to use a different fixed-size window of registers rather than saving registers in memory at the call time. At any time, only ONE window of registers is visible and is addressed as if it were the only set of registers. Window overlapping requires that temporary registers at one level are physically the same as the parameter registers at the next level. This overlap allows parameters to be passed without the actual movement of data.

It is worthwhile mentioning that the classification of processors as entirely pure RISC or entirely pure CISC is becoming more and more inappropriate and may be irrelevant. What actually counts is how much performance gain can be achieved by including an element of a given design style. Most modern processors use a calculated combination of elements of both design styles. The decisive factor in which element(s) of each design style to include is made based on a trade-off between the required improvement in performance and the expected added cost. A number of processors are classified as RISC while employing a number of CISC features, such as integer/floating-point division instructions. Similarly, there exist processors that are classified as CISC while employing a number of RISC features, such as pipelining.

EXERCISES

1. What are the main principles used to construct a RISC machine?

2. Contrast the two approaches (the software and the hardware) used in RISC machines to minimize memory operations.

3. Explain, with examples, the concept of register window and window overlapping. Suggest a different approach to achieve the same results as those achieved using register window and window overlapping.

4. For the purpose of this problem, you are required to pick a recent RISC processor of your choice. Submit a small report (no less than 5 and no more than 10 pages in length) that summarizes the main pipelining features used and the main RISC features used. The level of your coverage should be suitable for a senior undergraduate student. Make sure that you be precise and neat in your coverage. Use simple examples whenever possible. Provide accurate and meaningful figures and tables whenever possible. You are required to cover all aspects of a pipeline processor and all aspects of a RISC machine.

5. The controversy of RISC versus CISC never ends. Suppose that you represent an advocate for the RISC approach; write at least a one-page critic of the CISC approach showing its disadvantages while showing the advantages of the RISC approach. You may want to use real-life example machine performance as a support for your support of the RISC philosophy.

6. Repeat question 5 assuming that you are an advocate for the CISC philosophy.

REFERENCES AND FURTHER READING

An Overview of UltraSPARC III Cu, Version 1.1 September 2003, A White Paper, Sun Microsystems, 1–18.

R. Colewell *et al.* Computers, complexity, and controversy, *IEEE Comput.*, 18(9), 8–19 (1985).

Z. Cvetanovic and R. Kessler, Performance analysis of the Alpha 21264-based Compaq E40 system, *Proc. 27th Annual International Symposium on Computer Architecture*, Vancouver, British Columbia, Canada, 192–202.

Exploring Alpha Power for Technical Computing. A Compaq Report on Compag High Performance Technical Computing, November 1999, pp. 1–28.

G. Goldman and P. Tirumalai, UltraSPARC-III: The advancement of ultra computing, *Proc. IEEE COMPCON'97*, p. 417.

J. Hennessy, VLSI processor architecture, *IEEE Trans. Comput.*, C-33(11), 1221–1246 (1984).

J. Hennessy and D. Patterson, *Computer Architecture: A Quantitative Approach*, Morgan Kaufmann: San Mateo, San Francisco, CA, 1996.

R. Kessler, The Alpha 21264 Microprocessor, *IEEE Micro*, Vol. 19, issue 2, 24–36 (1999).

R. Kessler, E. McLellan and D. Webb, The Alpha 21264 Microprocessor Architecture, International Conference on Computer Design, Oct. 88, pp. 96–102.

G. Lauthbatch and T. Horel, UltraSPARC-III: Designing third generation 64-bit performance, *IEEE Micro.*, 73–85 (1999).

R. Nair, Optimal 2-bit branch predictors, *IEEE Trans. Comput.*, 698 (1995).

D. Patterson, Reduced instruction set computers, *Commun. ACM*, 28(1), 8–21 (1985).

D. Patterson and R. Ditzel, The case for the reduced instruction set computer, *Comput. Architecture News*, 8(6), 25–33 (1980).

D. Patterson and C. Sequin, A VLSI RISC, *IEEE Comput.*, 15(9), 8–21 (1982).

G. Radin, The 801 minicomputer, *IBM J. Res. Develop.*, 27(3), 237–246 (1983).

R. Sherburne, M. Katevenis, D. Patterson and C. Sequin, A 32-bit NMOS processor with a large register file, *IEEE J. Solid-State Circuits*, Sc-19(5), 682–689 (1984).

A. Tanenbaum, *Structured Computer Organization*, 3rd ed., Prentice-Hall: Englewood Cliffs, New Jersey.

Websites

http://www.sun.com/processors/UltraSPARC-IIIi
http://www.sun.com/processors/whitepapers

CHAPTER 11

Introduction to Multiprocessors

Having covered the essential issues in the design and analysis of uniprocessors and pointing out the main limitations of a single-stream machine, we begin in this chapter to pursue the issue of multiple processors. Here a number of processors (two or more) are connected in a manner that allows them to share the simultaneous execution of a single task. The main argument for using multiprocessors is to create powerful computers by simply connecting many existing smaller ones. A multiprocessor is expected to reach a faster speed than the fastest uniprocessor. In addition, a multiprocessor consisting of a number of single uniprocessors is expected to be more cost-effective than building a high-performance single processor. An additional advantage of a multiprocessor consisting of n processors is that if a single processor fails, the remaining fault-free $n - 1$ processors should be able to provide continued service, albeit with degraded performance. Our coverage in this chapter starts with a section on the general concepts and terminology used. We then point to the different topologies used for interconnecting multiple processors. Different classification schemes for computer architectures are then introduced and analyzed. We then introduce a topology-based taxonomy for interconnection networks. Two memory-organization schemes for MIMD (multiple instruction multiple data) multiprocessors are also introduced. Our coverage in this chapter ends with a touch on the analysis and performance metrics for multiprocessors. It should be noted that interested readers are referred to more elaborate discussions on multiprocessors in Chapters 2 and 3 of our book on Advanced Computer Architecture and Parallel Processing (see reference list).

11.1. INTRODUCTION

A multiple processor system consists of two or more processors that are connected in a manner that allows them to share the simultaneous (parallel) execution of a given computational task. Parallel processing has been advocated as a promising approach for building high-performance computer systems. Two basic requirements are inevitable for the efficient use of the employed processors. These requirements

Fundamentals of Computer Organization and Architecture, by M. Abd-El-Barr and H. El-Rewini
ISBN 0-471-46741-3 Copyright © 2005 John Wiley & Sons, Inc.

are (1) low communication overhead among processors while executing a given task and (2) a degree of inherent parallelism in the task.

A number of communication styles exist for multiple processor networks. These can be broadly classified according to (1) the communication model (CM) or (2) the physical connection (PC). According to the CM, networks can be further classified as (1) multiple processors (single address space or shared memory computation) or (2) multiple computers (multiple address space or message passing computation). According to PC, networks can be further classified as (1) bus-based or (2) network-based multiple processors. Typical sizes of such systems are summarized in Table 11.1.

The organization and performance of a multiple processor system are greatly influenced by the interconnection network used to connect them. On the one hand, a single shared bus can be used as the interconnection network for multiple processors. On the other hand, a crossbar switch can be used as the interconnection network. While the first technique represents a simple easy-to-expand topology, it is, however, limited in performance since it does not allow more than one processor/memory transfer at any given time. The crossbar provides full processor/memory distinct connections but it is expensive. *Multistage interconnection networks* (MINs) strike a balance between the limitation of the single, shared bus system and the expense of a crossbar-based system. In a MIN more than one processor/memory connection can be established at the same time. The cost of a MIN can be considerably less than that of a crossbar, particularly for a large number of processors and/or memories. The use of multiple buses to connect multiple processors to multiple memory modules has also been suggested as a compromise between the limited single bus and the expensive crossbar. Figure 11.1 illustrates the four types of interconnection networks mentioned above. Interested readers are referred to our book on Advanced Computer Architecture and Parallel Processing (see reference list).

11.2. CLASSIFICATION OF COMPUTER ARCHITECTURES

A classification means to order a number of objects into categories, each having common features, among which certain relationship(s) exist(s). In this regard, a classification scheme for computer architectures aims at categorizing them such that those architectures that have common features fall into one category and such that different categories represent distinct groups of architectures. In addition,

TABLE 11.1 Typical Sizes of Some Multiprocessor Systems

Category	Subcategories	Number of processors
Communication model	Multiple processors	2–256
	Multiple computers	8–256
Physical connection	Bus-based	2–32
	Network-based	8–256

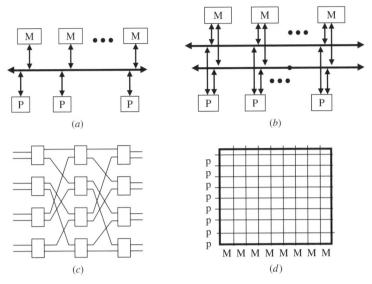

Figure 11.1 Four types of multiprocessor interconnection networks. (*a*) Single-bus system, (*b*) multi-bus system, (*c*) multi-stage interconnection network, (*d*) crossbar system

a classification scheme for computer architecture should provide a basis for information ordering and a basis for predicting the features of a given architecture.

Two broad schemes exist for computer architecture classification. The first is based on external (morphological) features of architectures and the second is based on the evolutionary features of architectures. The first scheme emphasizes the finished form of architectures, while the second scheme emphasizes the way an architecture has been derived from its predecessor and suggests speculative views on its successor. Morphological classification provides a basis for predictive power, while evolutionary classification provides a basis for better understanding of architectures. Examining the extent to which a classification scheme is satisfying its stated objective(s) could assess the pros and cons of that scheme.

A number of classification schemes have been proposed over the last three decades. These include the Flynn's classification (1966), the Kuck (1978), the Hwang and Briggs (1984), the Erlangen (1981), the Giloi (1983), the Skillicorn (1988), and the Bell (1992). A number of these are briefly discussed below.

11.2.1. Flynn's Classification

Flynn's classification scheme is based on identifying two orthogonal streams in a computer. These are the instruction and the data streams. The instruction stream is defined as the sequence of instructions performed by the computer. The data stream is defined as the data traffic exchanged between the memory and the processing unit. According to Flynn's classification, either of the instruction or data streams can be single or multiple. This leads to four distinct categories of computer architectures:

1. Single-instruction single-data streams (SISD)
2. Single-instruction multiple-data streams (SIMD)
3. Multiple-instruction single-data streams (MISD)
4. Multiple-instruction multiple-data streams (MIMD)

Figure 11.2 shows the orthogonal organization of the streams according to Flynn's classification.

Schematics for the four categories of architectures resulting from Flynn's classification are shown in Figure 11.3. Table 11.2 lists some of the commercial machines belonging to each of the four categories.

Observations on Flynn's Classification

1. Flynn's classification is among the first of its kind to be introduced and as such it must have inspired subsequent classifications.
2. The classification helped in categorizing architectures that were available and those that have been introduced later. For example, the introduction of the SIMD and MIMD machine models in the classification must have inspired architects to introduce these new machine models.
3. The classification stresses the architectural relationship at the memory-processor level. Other architectural levels are totally overlooked.
4. The classification stresses the external (morphological) features of architectures. No information is included on the revolutionary relationship of architectures that belong to the same category.
5. Owing to its pure abstractness, no practically viable machine has exemplified the MISD model introduced by the classification (at least so far). It should, however, be noted that some architects have considered pipelined machines (and perhaps systolic-array computers) as examples for MISD.
6. A very important aspect that is lacking in Flynn's classification is the issue of machine performance. Although the classification gives the impression that machines in the SIMD and the MIMD are superior to their SISD and MISD counterparts, it gives no information on the relative performance of SIMD and MIMD machines.

		Data	Stream
		Single	Multiple
Instruction	Single	SISD	SIMD
Stream	Multiple	MISD	MIMD

Figure 11.2 Flynn's classification

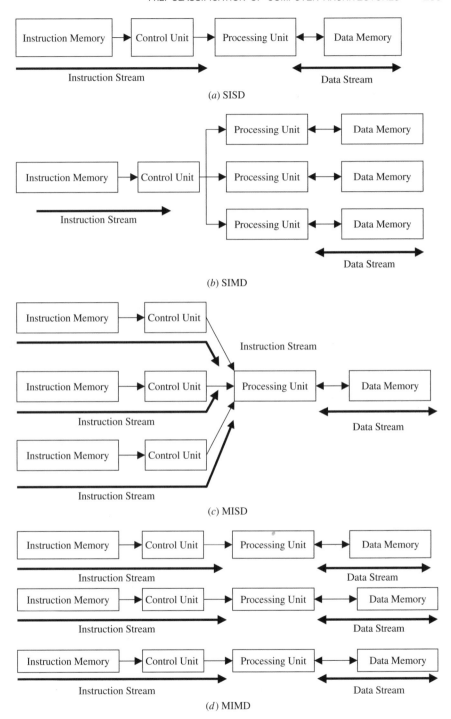

Figure 11.3 The four architecture classes resulting from Flynn's taxonomy. (*a*) SISD, (*b*) SIMD, (*c*) MISD, (*d*) MIMD

TABLE 11.2   **Example Machines and Their Flynn's Classification**

Classification category	Example machines
SISD	IBM 704, VAX 11/780, CRAY-1
SIMD	ILLIAC-IV, MPP, CM-2, STARAN
MISD	See observation 5 on page 238
MIMD	Cm*, CRAY XMP, IBM 370/168M

11.2.2. Kuck Classification Scheme

Flynn's taxonomy can be considered a general classification that has been extended by a number of computer architects. One such extension is the classification introduced by D. J. Kuck in 1978. In his classification, Kuck extended the instruction stream further to single (scalar and array) and multiple (scalar and array) streams. The data stream in Kuck's classification is called the *execution stream* and is also extended to include single (scalar and array) and multiple (scalar and array) streams. The combination of these streams results in a total of 16 categories of architectures, as shown in Table 11.3.

Our main observation is that both Flynn's and Kuck's classifications cover the entire architecture space. However, while Flynn's classification emphasizes the description of architectures at the instruction set level, the Kuck's classification emphasizes the description of architectures at the hardware level.

11.2.3. Hwang and Briggs Classification Scheme

The main new contribution of the classification due to Hwang and Briggs is the introduction of the concept of *classes*. This is a further refinement on Flynn's classification. For example, according to Hwang and Briggs, the SISD category is further refined into two subcategories: single functional unit SISD (SISD-S) and multiple

TABLE 11.3   **The 16-Architecture Categories Resulting from Kuck's Classification**

Instruction stream	Execution streams			
	Single		Multiple	
	Scalar	Array	Scalar	Array
Single				
Scalar	Uniprocessor	Uniprocessor	SIMD	
Array		ILLIAC-IV		
Multiple				
Scalar			NYU Ultracomputer	Cray X MP
Array				

functional units SISD (SISD-M). The MIMD category is further refined into loosely coupled MIMD (MIMD-L) and tightly coupled MIMD (MIMD-T). The SIMD category is further refined into word-sliced processing (SIMD-W) and bit-sliced processing (SIMD-B). Therefore, Hwang and Briggs classification added a level to the hierarchy of machine classification such that a given machine should be first classified as SISD, SIMD, MIMD, and then further classified according to its constituent descendant.

According to the Hwang and Briggs's taxonomy, it is always true to predict that an SISD-M will perform better than an SISD-S. It is, however, doubtful that such prediction can be made with respect to SIMD-W and SIMD-B. For example, it has been indicated that using the maximum degree of potential parallelism as a performance measure, then the ILLAC-IV machine (SIMD-W) is inferior to the MPP machine (SIMD-B). A final observation on the Hwang and Briggs's taxonomy is that shared memory systems (see Chapter 4 of our book on Advanced Computer Architecture and Parallel Processing, see reference list) map naturally into the MIMD-T category, while nonshared memory systems map into the MIMD-L category.

11.2.4. Erlangen Classification Scheme

In its simplest form, this classification scheme adds one more level of details to the internal structure of a computer, compared to Flynn's scheme. In particular, this scheme considers that in addition to the control (CNTL) and processing (ALU) units, a third subunit, called the *elementary logic unit* (ELU), can be used to characterize a given computer architecture. The ELU represents the circuitry required to perform the bit-level processing within the ALU. An architecture is characterized using a three-tuple system (k, d, w) such that $k =$ number of CNTLs, $d =$ number of ALU units associated with one control unit, and $w =$ number of ELUs per ALU (the width of a single data word). For example, in one of its models, the ILLAC-IV was made up of a mesh connected array of 64 64-bit ALUs controlled by a Burroughs B6700 computer. According to Erlangen, this model of the ILLAC-IV is characterized as (1, 64, 64).

Postulating that pipelining can exist at all three levels of hardware processing, the classification includes three additional parameters. These are $w' =$ the number of pipeline stages per ALU, $d' =$ the number of functional units per ALU, and $k' =$ the number of ELUs forming the control unit. Given the expected multi-unit nature of each of the three hardware processing levels, a more general six-tuple can be used to characterize an architecture as follows: $(k \times k', d \times d', w \times w')$. Figure 11.4 illustrates the Erlangen classification system.

More complex systems can still be characterized using the Erlangen system by using two additional operators, the *AND* operator, denoted by $\times$, and the *ALTERNATIVE* operator, denoted as $\vee$. For example, an architecture consisting of two computational subunits each having a six-tuple $(k_0 \times k'_0, d_0 \times d'_0, w_0 \times w'_0)$ and $(k_1 \times k'_1, d_1 \times d'_1, w_1 \times w'_1)$ is characterized using both subunits as $(k_0 \times k'_0, d_0 \times d'_0, w_0 \times w'_0) \times (k_1 \times k'_1, d_1 \times d'_1, w_1 \times w'_1)$, while an architecture that can be

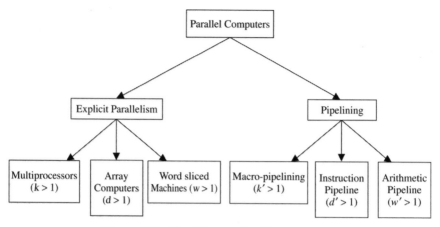

Figure 11.4 The Erlangen classification scheme

expressed using either of the two subunits is characterized as $<k_0 \times k_0', d_0 \times d_0', w_0-$ $_0 \times w_0'> \lor <k_1 \times k_1', d_1 \times d_1', w_1 \times w_1'>$.

For example, a later design of the ILLAC-IV consisted of two DEC PDP-10 as the front-end controller where data can only be accepted from one PDP-10 at a time. This version of the ILLAC-IV can be characterized as $(2, 1, 36) \times (1, 64, 64)$. Now, since the ILLAC-IV can also work in a half-word mode whereby there are 128 32-bit processors rather than the 64 64-bit processors, then an overall characterization of the ILLAC-IV is given by $(2, 1, 36) \times [(1, 64, 64) \lor (1, 128, 32)]$.

As can be seen, this classification scheme can be regarded as a hierarchical classification that puts more emphasis on the internal structure of the processing hardware. It does not provide any basis for the classification and/or grouping of computer architectures. In particular, the classification overlooks the interconnection among different units.

11.2.5. Skillicorn Classification Scheme

Owing to its inherent nature, Flynn's classification may end up grouping computer systems with similar architectural characteristics but with diverse functionality into one class. This same observation has been the main motive behind the Skillicorn classification introduced in 1988. According to this classification, an abstract von Neumann machine is modeled as shown in Figure 11.5. As can be seen, the abstract model includes two memory subdivisions, instruction memory (IM) and data memory (DM), in addition to the instruction processor (IP) and the data processor (DP). In developing the classification scheme, the following possible interconnection relationships were considered: (IP–DP), (IP–IM), (DP–DM), and (DP–IP). The interconnection scheme takes into consideration the type and number of connections among the data processors, data memories, instruction processors, and instruction memories. There may exist no, one-to-many, and many-to-many such

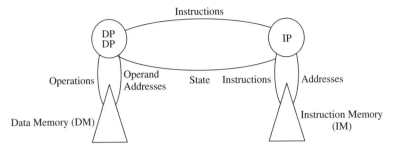

Figure 11.5 Abstract model of a simple machine

TABLE 11.4 Possible Connection Schemes

Connection type	Meaning
$1-1$	A connection between two single units
$1-n$	A connection between a single unit and n other units
$n-n$	$n(1-1)$ connections
$n \times n$	$n(1-n)$ connections

connections. Table 11.4 illustrates the different connection schemes identified by the classification.

Using the given connection schemes, Skillicorn arrived at 28 different classes. Sample classes are shown in Table 11.5. The rightmost column of the table indicates the corresponding Flynn's class. Figure 11.6 illustrates four example classes according to the classification.

Major advantages of the Skillicorn classification include (1) simplicity, (2) the proper consideration of the interconnectivity among units, (3) flexibility, and (4) the ability to represent most current computer systems. However, the classification

TABLE 11.5 Sample Connection Classes

Class	IP	DP	IP–DP	IP–IM	DP–DM	DP–DP	Description	Flynn
1	1	1	$1-1$	$1-1$	$1-1$	None	Von Neumann uniprocessor	SISD
2	1	N	$1-n$	$1-1$	$n-n$	$n \times n$	Type 1 array processors	SIMD
3	1	N	$1-n$	$1-1$	$n \times n$	None	Type 2 array processors	SIMD
4	N	N	$n-n$	$n-n$	$n-n$	$n \times n$	Loosely coupled von Neumann	MIMD
5	N	N	$n-n$	$n-n$	$n \times n$	None	Tightly coupled von Neumann	MIMD

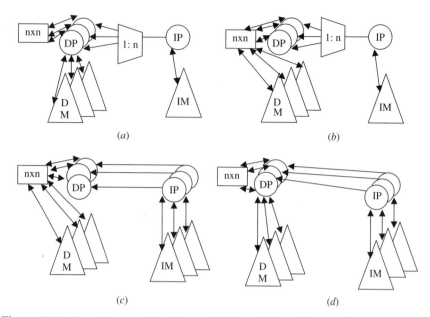

Figure 11.6 Example connection classes. (*a*) Array 1 class, (*b*) array 2 class, (*c*) tightly coupled multiprocessor, (*d*) loosely coupled multiprocessor

(1) lacks the inclusion of operational aspects such as pipelining and (2) has difficulty in predicting the relative power of machines belonging to the same class without explicit knowledge of the interconnection scheme used in that class.

Multiple processor systems can be further classified as tightly coupled versus loosely coupled. In a tightly coupled system, all processors can equally access a global memory. In addition, each processor may also have its own local or cache memory. In a loosely coupled system, the memory is divided among processors such that each processor will have its own memory attached to it. However, processors still share the same memory address space. Any processor can directly access any remote memory. Examples of tightly coupled multiple processors include the CMU *C.mmp*, Encore Computer *Multimax*, and the Sequent Corp. *Balance series*. Examples of loosely coupled multiple processors include CMU *Cm**, the BBN *Butterfly*, and the IBM *RP3*.

11.3. SIMD SCHEMES

Recall that Flynn's classification results in four basic architectures. Among those, the SIMD and the MIMD are frequently used in constructing parallel architectures. In this section, we will provide basic information on the SIMD paradigm. It is important at the outset to indicate that SIMD are mostly designed to exploit the inherent parallelism encountered in matrix (array) operations, which are required in applications such as image processing. Famous real-life machines that have been commercially constructed include the ILLIAC-IV (1972), the STARAN (1974), and the MPP (1982).

Two main SIMD configurations have been used in real-life machines. These are shown in Figure 11.7.

In the first scheme, each processor has its own local memory. Processors can communicate with each other through the interconnection network. If the interconnection network does not provide direct connection between a given pair of processors, then this pair can exchange data via an intermediate processor. The

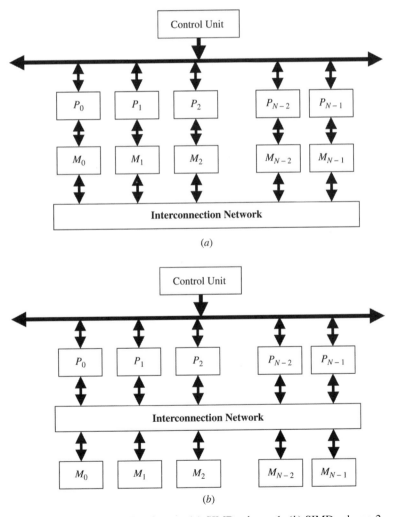

Figure 11.7 Two SIMD schemes. (*a*) SIMD scheme 1, (*b*) SIMD scheme 2

ILLIAC-IV used such an interconnection scheme. The interconnection network in the ILLIAC-IV allowed each processor to communicate directly with four neighboring processors in an 8×8 matrix pattern such that the ith processor can communicate directly with the $(i-1)$th, $(i+1)$th, $(i-8)$th, and $(i+8)$th processors.

In the second SIMD scheme, processors and memory modules communicate with each other via the interconnection network. Two processors can transfer data between each other via intermediate memory module(s) or possibly via intermediate processor(s). Assume, for example, that processor i is connected to memory modules $(i-1)$, i, and $(i+1)$. In this case, processor 1 can communicate with processor 5 via memory modules 2, 3, and 4 as intermediaries. The BSP (Burroughs' Scientific Processor) used the second SIMD scheme.

In order to illustrate the effectiveness of SIMD in handling array operations, consider, for example, the operations of adding the corresponding elements of two one-dimensional arrays A and B and storing the results in a third one-dimensional array C. Assume also that each of the three arrays has N elements. Assume also that SIMD scheme 1 is used. The N additions required can be done in one step if the elements of the three arrays are distributed such that M_0 contains the elements $A(0)$, $B(0)$, and $C(0)$, M_1 contains the elements $A(1)$, $B(1)$, and $C(1)$, ..., and M_{N-1} contains the elements $A(N-1)$, $B(N-1)$, and $C(N-1)$. In this case, all processors will execute simultaneously an add instruction of the form $C \leftarrow A + B$. After executing this single step by all processors, the elements of the resultant array C will be stored across the memory modules such that M_0 will store $C(0)$, M_1 will store $C(1)$, ..., and M_{N-1} will store $C(N-1)$.

It is customary to formally represent an SIMD machine in terms of five-tuples (N, C, I, M, F). The meaning of each argument is given below.

1. N is the number of processing elements ($N = 2^k$, $k \geq 1$).
2. C is the set of control instructions used by the control unit, for example, *do*, *for*, *step*.
3. I is the set of instructions executed by active processing units.
4. M is the subset of processing elements that are enabled.
5. F is the set of interconnection functions that determine the communication links among processing elements.

11.4. MIMD SCHEMES

MIMD machines use a collection of processors, each having its own memory, which can be used to collaborate on executing a given task. In general, MIMD systems can be categorized based on their memory organization into shared-memory and message-passing architectures. The choice between the two categories depends on the cost of communication (relative to that of the computation) and the degree of load imbalance in the application.

11.4.1. Shared Memory Organization

There has been recent growing interest in distributed shared memory systems. This is because shared memory provides an attractive conceptual model for interprocess interaction even when the underlying hardware provides no direct support. A shared memory model is one in which processors communicate by reading and writing locations in a shared memory that is equally accessible by all processors. Each processor may have registers, buffers, caches, and local memory banks as additional memory resources.

A number of basic issues in the design of shared memory systems have to be taken into consideration. These include access control, synchronization, protection, and security. Access control determines which process accesses are possible to which resources. Access control models make the required check for every access request issued by the processors to the shared memory, against the contents of the access control table. The latter contains flags that determine the legality of each access attempt. If there are access attempts to resources, then until the desired access is completed, all disallowed access attempts and illegal processes are blocked. Requests from sharing processes may change the contents of the access control table during execution. The flags of the access control with the synchronization rules determine the system's functionality. Synchronization constraints limit the time of accesses from sharing processes to shared resources. Appropriate synchronization ensures that the information flows properly and ensures system functionality. Protection is a system feature that prevents processes from making arbitrary access to resources belonging to other processes. Sharing and protection are incompatible; sharing allows access, whereas protection restricts it.

Running two copies of the same program on two processors will decrease the performance relative to that of a single processor, due to contention for shared memory. The performance degrades further as three, four, or more copies of the program execute at the same time.

A shared memory computer system consists of (1) a set of independent processors, (2) a set of memory modules, and (3) an interconnection network. The simplest shared memory system consists of one memory module (M) that can be accessed from two processors P_a and P_b (Fig. 11.8). Requests arrive at the memory module through its two ports. An arbitration unit within the memory module passes requests through to a memory controller. If the memory module is not busy and a single request arrives, then the arbitration unit passes that request to the memory controller and the request is satisfied. The module is placed in the busy state while a request is being serviced.

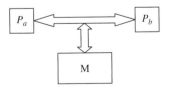

Figure 11.8   A simple shared memory scheme

If a new request arrives while the memory is busy servicing a previous request, the memory module sends a wait signal through the memory controller to the processor making the new request. In response, the requesting processor may hold its request on the line until the memory becomes free or it may repeat its request some time later. If the arbitration unit receives two requests, it selects one of them and passes it to the memory controller. Again, the denied request can be either held to be served next or it may be repeated some time later.

The arbitration unit may not be adequate to organize the use of the memory module by the two processors. The main problem will be in the sequencing of interactions between memory accesses from the two processors. Consider the following two scenarios for accessing the same memory location M(1000) by the two processors P_a and P_b (Fig. 11.9). Let us also assume that the initial value stored in memory location M(1000) is 150. Note that in both cases, the sequence of instructions performed by each processor is the same. The only difference between the two scenarios is the relative time at which the two processors update the value in M(1000). A careful examination of the two scenarios will show that the value stored in location M(1000) after the first scenario will be 151 while the stored value following the second scenario will be 152.

The above illustrative example presents the case of a nonfunctional behavior of this simple shared memory system. Such an example should demonstrate the basic requirements for the success of such systems. These requirements are:

1. A mechanism for conflict resolution among rival processors
2. A technique for specifying the sequencing constraints
3. A mechanism for enforcing the sequencing specifications

Approaches for satisfying these basic requirements are covered in Chapter 4 of our book on Advanced Computer Architecture and Parallel Processing (see reference list).

The use of different interconnection networks in a shared memory multiprocessor system leads to systems with one of the following characteristics:

1. Shared memory architecture with a uniform memory access (UMA)
2. Cache-only memory architecture (COMA)
3. Distributed shared memory architecture with nonuniform memory access (NUMA)

Cycle	Processor P_a	Processor P_b
1	a ← M(1000);	
2		b ← M(1000);
3	a ← a + 1;	
4		b ← b + 1;
5	M(1000) ← a;	
6		M(1000) ← b;

Scenario 1

Cycle	Processor P_a	Processor P_b
1	a ← M(1000);	
2	a ← a + 1;	
3	M(1000) ← a;	
4		b ← M(1000)
5		b ← b + 1;
6		M(1000) ← b;

Scenario 2

Figure 11.9 Potential shared memory problem

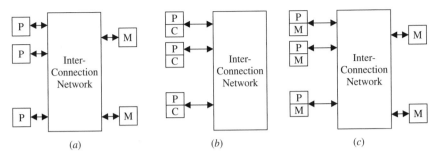

Figure 11.10 Three examples of shared-memory architectures. (*a*) UMA, (*b*) COMA, (*c*) NUMA

Figure 11.10 shows typical organization for the abovementioned three shared-memory architectures. In the UMA system, a shared memory is accessible by all processors through an interconnection network in the same way a single processor accesses its memory. Therefore, all processors have equal access time to any memory location. The interconnection network used in the UMA can be a single bus, multiple bus, a crossbar, or a multiport memory.

In the NUMA system, each processor has part of the shared memory attached. The memory has a single address space. Therefore, any processor could access any memory location directly using its real address. However, the access time to modules depends on the distance to the processor. This results in a nonuniform memory access time. A number of architectures are used to interconnect processors to memory modules in a NUMA. Among these are the tree and the hierarchical bus networks (see Chapter 2 of our book on Advanced Computer Architecture and Parallel Processing, see reference list).

Similar to the NUMA, each processor has part of the shared memory in the COMA. However, in this case the shared memory consists of cache memory. A COMA system requires that data be migrated to the processor requesting it.

11.4.2. Message-Passing Organization

Message passing represents an alternative method for communication and movement of data among multiprocessors. Local, rather than global, memories are used to communicate messages among processors. A message is defined as a block of related information that travels among processors over direct links. There exist a number of models for message passing. Examples of message-passing systems include the cosmic cube, workstation cluster, and the transputer.

The introduction of the transputer system T212 in 1983 announced the birth of the first message-passing multiprocessor. Subsequently the T414 was announced in 1985, while Inmos introduced the VISI transputer processor in 1986. Two subsequent transputer products, the T800 (1988) and T9000 (1990), have been introduced. The cosmic cube message-passing multiprocessor was designed at Caltech during the period 1981–1985. It represented the first hypercube multiprocessor system that was made to work. Wormhole routing in message passing was introduced in 1987 as an alternative to the traditional store-and-forward routing in order to reduce the size of the required buffers and to decrease the message latency. In *wormhole routing*, a packet is divided into smaller units that are called *flits* (flow control bits) such that *flits* move in a pipeline fashion with the header *flit* of the packet leading the way to the destination node. When the header flit is blocked due to network congestion, the remaining flits are blocked as well (see Chapter 5 of our book on Advanced Computer Architecture and Parallel Processing (see reference list) in Volume II for more details).

The elimination of the need for a large global memory, which is usually a reason for a slowdown of the overall system, together with its asynchronous nature, give message-passing schemes an edge over shared-memory schemes. Similar to shared-memory multiprocessors, application programs are divided into smaller parts; each can be executed by an individual processor in a concurrent manner.

A simple example of a message-passing multiprocessor architecture is shown in Figure 11.11. As can be seen from the figure, processors use local bus (internal channels) to communicate with their local memories while communicating with other processors via an interconnection networks (external channels). Processes running on a given processor use internal channels to exchange messages among themselves. Processes running on different processors use external channels to exchange messages. Such a scheme offers a great deal of flexibility in accommodating a large number of processors and being readily scalable. It should be noted that the process and the processor, which executes it, are considered as two separate entities. The size of a process is determined by the programmer and can be described by its granularity, given by:

$$Granularity = \frac{computation\ time}{communication\ time}$$

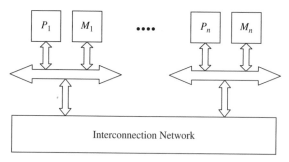

Figure 11.11 Example of a message-passing multiprocessor architecture

Three types of granularity can be distinguished. These are:

1. Coarse granularity. Each process holds a large number of sequential instructions and takes a substantial time to execute.
2. Medium granularity. Since the process communication overhead increases as the granularity decreases, medium granularity describes a middle ground whereby communication overhead is reduced in order to enable each nodal communication to take less amount of time.
3. Fine granularity. Each process contains a few numbers of sequential instructions (as few as just one instruction).

Message-passing multiprocessors use mostly medium or coarse granularity.

Message-passing multiprocessors employ static networks in local communication. In particular, hypercube networks have been receiving special attention for use in a message-passing multiprocessor. The nearest neighbor two-dimensional and three-dimensional mesh networks have the potential for being used in a message-passing system as well. Two important factors have led to the suitability of hypercube and mesh networks for use as message-passing networks. These factors are (1) the ease of VLSI implementation and (2) the suitability for two- and three-dimensional applications.

Two important design factors must be considered in designing such networks. These are (1) the link *bandwidth* and (2) the network *latency*. The link bandwidth is defined as the number of bits that can be transmitted per unit time (bits/second). The network latency is defined as the time to complete a message transfer. For example, links could be unidirectional or bidirectional and they can transfer one bit or several bits at a time. To estimate the network latency, we must first determine the path setup time, which depends on the number of nodes on the path. The actual transition time, which depends on the message size, must also be considered.

The information transfer from a given source through the network can be done in two ways:

1. Circuit-switching networks. In this type of network, there is no buffer required in each node. The path between the source and destination is first determined. All links along that path are reserved. After information transfer, reserved links are released for use by other messages. Circuit-switching networks are characterized by producing the smallest amount of delay. Inefficient link utilization is the main disadvantage of circuit-switching networks. Circuit-switching networks are, therefore, advantageously used only in the case of large message transfer.
2. Packet-switching networks. Here, messages are divided into smaller parts, called packets, before being transmitted between nodes. Each node must contain enough buffers to hold received packets before transmitting them. A complete path from source to destination may not be available at the start of transmission. As links become available, packets are moved from

a node to a node until they reach the destination node. The technique is also known as the store-and-forward packet-switching technique.

Although store-and-forward packet-switching networks eliminate the need for a complete path at the start of transmission, they tend to increase the overall network latency. This is because packets are expected to be stored in node buffers waiting for the availability of outgoing links. In order to reduce the size of the required buffers and decrease the incurred network latency, *wormhole routing* (see above) has been introduced.

Having touched on some of the machine categories based on the Flynn's classifications, we now provide an introduction into the interconnection networks used in these machines. We provide detailed coverage of multiprocessor interconnection networks in Chapter 2 of our book on Advanced Computer Architecture and Parallel Processing (see reference list).

11.5. INTERCONNECTION NETWORKS

A number of classification criteria exist for interconnection networks (INs). Among these criteria are the following.

11.5.1. Mode of Operation

According to the mode of operation, INs are classified as *synchronous* versus *asynchronous*. In synchronous mode of operation, a single global clock is used by all components in the system such that the whole system is operating in a lock-step manner. Asynchronous mode of operation, on the other hand, does not require a global clock. Handshaking signals are used instead in order to coordinate the operation of asynchronous systems. While synchronous systems tend to be slower compared to asynchronous systems, they are race and hazard-free.

11.5.2. Control Strategy

According to the control strategy, INs can be classified as *centralized* versus *decentralized*. In centralized control systems, a single central control unit is used to oversee and control the operation of the components of the system. In decentralized control, the control function is distributed among different components in the system. The function and reliability of the central control unit can become the bottleneck in a centralized control system. While the crossbar is a centralized system, the multistage interconnection networks are decentralized.

11.5.3. Switching Techniques

Interconnection networks can be classified according to the switching mechanism as *circuit* versus *packet switching* networks. In the circuit switching mechanism, a complete path has to be established prior to the start of communication between a source and a destination. The established path will remain in existence during the whole communication period. In a packet switching mechanism, communication between a source and destination takes place via messages that are divided into smaller entities, called packets. On their way to the destination, packets can be sent from one node to another in a store-and-forward manner until they reach their destination. While packet switching tends to use the network resources more efficiently, compared to circuit switching, it suffers from variable packet delays.

11.5.4. Topology

According to their topology, INs are classified as *static* versus *dynamic* networks. In dynamic networks, connections among inputs and outputs are made using switching elements. Depending on the switch settings, different interconnections can be established. In static networks, direct fixed paths exist between nodes. There are no switching elements (nodes) in static networks.

Having introduced the general criteria for classification of interconnection networks, we can now introduce a possible taxonomy for INs that is based on topology. In Figure 11.12, we provide such a taxonomy.

According to the shown taxonomy, INs are classified as either static or dynamic. Static networks can be further classified according to their interconnection patterns as one-dimension (1D), two-dimension (2D), or hypercubes (HCs). Dynamic networks, on the other hand, can be further classified according to the scheme of interconnection as bus-based versus switch-based. Bus-based INs are classified as single bus or multiple bus. Switch-based dynamic networks can be further classified according to the structure of the interconnection network as single-stage (SS), multistage (MS), or crossbar networks.

Multiprocessor interconnection networks are explained in detail in Chapter 2 of our book on Advanced Computer Architecture and Parallel Processing (see reference list).

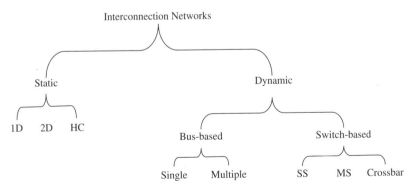

Figure 11.12   A topology-based taxonomy for interconnection networks

11.6. ANALYSIS AND PERFORMANCE METRICS

Having provided an introduction to the architecture of multiprocessors, we now provide some basic ideas about the performance issues in multiprocessors. Interested readers are referred to Chapter 3 of our book on Advanced Computer Architecture and Parallel Processing (see reference list) (Volume II) for more details.

A fundamental question that is usually asked is how much faster a given problem can be solved using multiprocessors as compared to a single processor? This question can be formulated into the speed-up factor defined below.

$S(n)$ = speed-up factor

= Increase in speed due to the use of a multiprocessor system consisting of n processors

$$= \frac{\text{Execution time using a single processor}}{\text{Execution time using } n \text{ processors}}$$

A related question is that how efficiently each of the n processors is utilized. The question can be formulated into the efficiency defined below.

$$E(n) = \text{Efficiency}$$

$$= \frac{S(n)}{n} \times 100\%$$

In executing tasks (programs) using a multiprocessor, it may be assumed that a given task can be divided into n equal subtasks each of which can be executed by one processor. Therefore, the expected speed-up will be given by the $S(n) = n$ while the efficiency $E(n) = 100\%$. The assumption that a given task can be divided into n equal subtasks, each executed by a processor, is unrealistic. In Chapter 3 of our book on Advanced Computer Architecture and Parallel Processing (see reference list) meaningful computation models will be developed and analyzed. A number of other performance metrics are also introduced and analyzed in the same chapter.

11.7. SUMMARY

In this chapter, we have navigated through a number of concepts and system configurations related to the issues of multiprocessing. In particular, we have provided the general concepts and terminology used in the context of multiprocessors. A number of taxonomies for multiprocessors have been introduced and analyzed. Two memory organization schemes have been introduced. These are the shared-memory and message-passing systems. In addition, we have introduced the different topologies used for interconnecting multiple processors. In Chapter 2 of our book on Advanced Computer Architecture and Parallel Processing (see reference list) more will be said about interconnection networks and their performance metrics. Shared-memory and message-passing architectures are explained in Chapters 4 and 5, respectively, of the same reference mentioned above.

EXERCISES

1. Consider the five classifications of computer architectures discussed in this chapter. You are required to provide a list showing the advantages and disadvantages of each classification in view of the degree to which each classification satisfies the purpose for which a classification is needed.

2. You are required to derive, out of the five provided classifications, a new classification that outperforms each of the five classifications. Provide, in a tabular form, the additional advantages and eliminated shortcomings of the proposed classification.

3. Provide a list of the main advantages and disadvantages of SIMD and MIMD machines.

4. Provide a list of the main advantages and disadvantages of shared-memory and message-passing paradigms.

5. List three engineering applications, with which you are familiar, for which SIMD is most efficient to use, and another three for which MIMD is most efficient to use.

6. Consider the case of connecting N processors and N memory modules using each of the interconnection networks shown in Figure 11.1. Assume that T is the time required for a processor to access an item in a memory module and that all processors make a request to access distinct memory module. Compute the worst-case possible delay expected in each of the four interconnection networks.

7. It was mentioned that a given SIMD machine could be characterized using a five-tuple (N, C, I, M, F). You are required to select three different recent SIMD machines and provide in a tabular form each of the five-tuples that characterizes them.

8. Assume that a simple addition of two elements requires a unit time. You are required to compute the execution time needed to perform the addition of a 40×40 element array using each of the following arrangements:

   (a) An SIMD system having 64 processing elements connected in nearest-neighbor fashion. Consider that each processor has only its local memory.

   (b) An SIMD system having 64 processing elements connected to a shared memory through an interconnection network. Ignore the communication time.

    (c) An MIMD computer system having 64 independent elements accessing a shared memory through an interconnection network. Ignore the communication time.

    (d) Repeat (b) and (c) above if the communication time takes two time units.

9. Provide a concise discussion on the suitability of each of the four attributes of interconnection networks (mode of operation, control strategy, switching mechanism, and topology) for each of the four different interconnection networks shown in Figure 11.1. Make sure that you justify the suitability of a given attribute to a given interconnection network.

10. Consider the case of a multiprocessor system consisting of N processors. Assume that the time needed for each processor to execute a given critical section is t and that f represents the fraction of operations that can be parallelized. Assume also that a single processor will need a time T to execute the same task. Show that the total execution time using N processors is given by

$$T_N = (1 - f) \times T + \frac{f \times T}{N} + t.$$

What is the number of processors, N, needed in order to minimize the total execution time T_N.

REFERENCES AND FURTHER READING

S. Abraham and K. Padmanabhan, Performance of the direct binary n-cube network for multiprocessors, *IEEE Trans. Comput.*, 38(7), 1000–1011 (1989).

P. Agrawal, V. Janakiram and G. Pathak, Evaluating the performance of multicomputer configurations, *IEEE Trans. Comput.*, 19(5), 23–27 (1986).

G. Almasi and A. Gottlieb, *Highly Parallel Computing*, Benjamin Cummings, Redwood City, CA, USA, 1989.

K. Al-Tawil, M. Abd-El-Barr and F. Ashraf, A survey and comparison of wormhole routing techniques in mesh networks, *IEEE Network*, 11(2), 38–45 (1997).

L. Bhuyan, Q. Yang and D. Agrawal, Performance of multiprocessor interconnection networks, *IEEE Comput.*, 22(2), 25–37 (1989).

W.-T. Chen and J.-P. Sheu, Performance analysis of multiple bus interconnection networks with hierarchical requesting model, *IEEE Trans. Comput.*, 40(7), 834–842 (1991).

S. Dasgupta, *Computer Architecture: A Modern Synthesis*, Vol. 2: Advanced Topics, John Wiley, New York, 1989.

A. Decegama, *The Technology of Parallel Processing: Parallel Processing Architectures and VLSI Hardware Volume 1*, Prentice-Hall, NJ, 1989.

J. Dongarra, *Experimental Parallel Computing Architectures*, North-Holland, Amsterdam, 1987.

A. Goyal and T. Agerwala, Performance analysis of future shared storage systems, *IBM J. Res. Devel.*, 28(1), 95–107 (1984).

J.-Y. Juang and B. Wah, A contention-based bus-control scheme for multiprocessor systems, *IEEE Trans. Comput.*, 40(9), 1046–1053 (1991).

T. Lewis and H. El-Rewini, Introduction to Parallel Computing, Prentice-Hall, Englewood Cliffs, NJ, 1992.

D. Linder and J. Harden, An adaptive and fault tolerant wormhole routing strategy for *k*-ary *n*-cubes, *IEEE Trans. Comput.*, 40(1), 2–12 (1991).

L. Ni and P. McKinely, A survey of wormhole routing techniques in direct networks, *IEEE Comput.*, 26(2), 62–76 (1993).

J. Patel, Performance of processor–memory interconnections for multiprocessor computer systems, *IEEE Trans.*, 28(9), 296–304 (1981).

D. Reed and R. Fujimoto, *Multicomputer Networks: Message-Based Parallel Processing*, MIT Press, MA, USA, 1987.

H. El-Rewini and T. Lewis, Distributed and Parallel Computing, Manning & Prentice Hall, 1998.

H. El-Rewini and M. Abd-El-Barr, Advanced Computer Architecture and Parallel Processing, John Wiley, Hoboken, NJ, USA, 2005.

E. Sima, T. Fountain and P. Kacsuk, *Advanced Computer Architectures: A Design Space Approach*, Addison Wesley, MA, USA, 1996.

H. Stone, *High Performance Computer Architecture*, 3rd ed., Addison Wesley, MA, USA, 1993.

B. Wilkinson, *Computer Architecture: Design and Performance*, 2nd ed., Prentice-Hall, Hertfordshire, UK, 1996.

Q. Yang and S. Zaky, Communication performance in multiple-bus systems, *IEEE Trans. Comput.*, 37(7), 848–853 (1988).

H. Youn and C. Chen, A comprehensive performance evaluation of crossbar networks, *IEEE Trans. Parallel Distribute Syst.*, 4(5), 481–489 (1993).

M. Zargham, *Computer Architecture: Single and Parallel Systems*, Prentice-Hall, NJ, USA, 1996.

INDEX

Fundamentals of Computer Organization and Architecture, by M. Abd-El-Barr and H. El-Rewini
ISBN 0-471-46741-3   Copyright © 2005 John Wiley & Sons, Inc.